Study Tasks in English

ENGLISH FOR ACADEMIC PURPOSES titles from Cambridge

Study Skills in English *by Michael J. Wallace*

Study Listening – Understanding lectures and talks in English *by Tony Lynch*

Study Writing – A course in written English for academic and professional purposes *by Liz Hamp-Lyons and Ben Heasley*

Study Speaking – A course in spoken English for academic purposes *by Tony Lynch and Kenneth Anderson*

Study Reading – A course in reading skills for academic purposes *by Eric H. Glendinning and Beverly Holmström*

Study Tasks in English *by Mary Waters and Alan Waters*

Study Tasks in English

Student's Book

Mary Waters
Alan Waters

CAMBRIDGE
UNIVERSITY PRESS

CAMBRIDGE UNIVERSITY PRESS
Cambridge, New York, Melbourne, Madrid, Cape Town, Singapore, São Paulo, Delhi

Cambridge University Press
The Edinburgh Building, Cambridge CB2 8RU, UK

www.cambridge.org
Information on this title: www.cambridge.org/9780521426145

First published 1995
13th printing 2009

Printed in the United Kingdom at the University Press, Cambridge

A catalogue record for this publication is available from the British Library

ISBN 978-0-521-42614-5 Student's Book
ISBN 978-0-521-46908-1 Teacher's Book
ISBN 978-0-521-46907-4 cassette

Contents

Thanks

We would like to thank gratefully all those who have helped in the preparation of this book, especially Katharine Mendelsohn, for her persevering and painstaking work with the Pilot and final versions, the many teachers and students around the world who provided feedback on the Pilot Edition, the reviewers of the Pilot Edition and earlier drafts, and the course participants at the Institute for English Language Education, Lancaster University, who took part in the recording of the cassette for the Pilot Edition.

To the student

Welcome to *Study Tasks in English*!

This book is for students who want to learn how to study effectively in English.

    Study Tasks in English is based on the idea that there is no single best way to study successfully. We believe it is important for you to have the chance to find out for yourself which study techniques suit you best. This book therefore consists of a series of tasks. These are problems about studying for you to solve. We will help you to draw conclusions from the tasks about the kind of skills that will help you to study as successfully as possible in English. However, it is important to remember that you will also need to apply the skills in situations outside those you meet here in order to master them.

    The tasks in this book involve discussing problems, taking notes of answers, presenting ideas clearly and logically, keeping records of your progress and so on. We strongly recommend you use English for these activities, as this will increase your ability to study in English. It is likely that your knowledge of English in general will improve as well. As you work through the activities you will therefore have lots of chances to use English while you learn how to study. However, please note that this book is not directly intended to teach you grammar, vocabulary and so on. For this purpose we advise you to use a normal book for learning English along with this one.

    Finally, we hope you enjoy using *Study Tasks in English*, and we wish you every success in your studies!

Mary Waters
Alan Waters

Note Two symbols are used throughout the text.

indicates an activity to be performed or a task to be carried out.

indicates that you should listen to the cassette.

This part will help you to become more aware of the basic learning, thinking and questioning skills you need for successful study in English. Without these skills, it is difficult to study effectively. With them, skills such as note-taking, essay writing, and so on become much easier.

UNIT **1 How do I learn?**

The first step in learning to study successfully is to know as much as possible about yourself as a learner. This involves asking and answering questions about what resources you need for learning, how you learn best, how you can organise your learning, what you have already learned and what you still need to learn, and so on. This unit will introduce you to some of these questions.

1 GETTING TO KNOW *STUDY TASKS IN ENGLISH*

First of all, let us introduce you to working with this book.

Task 1.1

It is important to become familiar with any book you use for study.

With two or three other students, answer these questions about *Study Tasks in English*.
1 Look at the title page at the front of this book. What is the title of the book? Who are the authors? When was it published?
2 Turn to the Contents on pages v–vii. What information does the table of contents provide? How many units are there in the book?
3 Look at Unit 2. How many tasks are there? In which ones are you expected to discuss in English? How many require you to take notes?
4 The index is at the back of the book. What does the index list? Which pages in this book tell you about libraries? Study preparation?
5 Look at the last section in each unit. What is it called? Look at the tasks. What do you think 'assessment' means?
6 Where are the appendices[*1] in a book? What information is given in the appendices of this book?

Task 1.2

Two basic tools that are very useful for successful study in English are a notebook and a wordbook[*].

You need a *notebook* for each subject you study. It should contain all your notes and assignments for the subject.

1 Words which have an asterisk (*) after them are explained in the *Glossary of study terms* in Part D.

2

We recommend that you arrange your notebook for this book by unit, and date each day's work, as in these examples:

A *wordbook* will help you to improve your English. It is like a personal dictionary. You can keep a record of new vocabulary and spelling words in this book. You may wish to include notes about grammar as well. It is a good idea also to record how or where the new words were used.

We therefore suggest that your wordbook for this book is also arranged by listing the new words by unit. Here is an example:

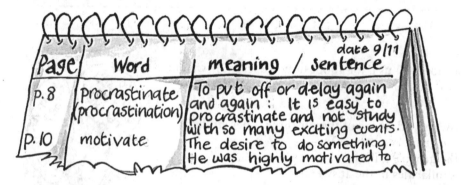

Now prepare both books so that you are ready to use them as required. If you use a ring binder*, you may wish to put the notebook in the front and the wordbook at the back.

2 HOW DO *YOU* LEARN BEST?

A very important step in effective learning is to understand how you learn best. Not everyone learns in the same way; it is important to know what helps you to succeed and what makes learning difficult for you. This will help you know how to study more successfully.

Task 2.1

Everyone is successful at some activities and less successful at others. Sometimes students do well in a subject one year but are less successful the next year. Other students may always do well in one subject but be very weak in another.

Think about any two things you have learnt successfully, and any two things you feel you have not learnt as successfully as you would have liked. Copy the table that follows into your notebook and complete it.

What did you learn successfully?	How did you learn it?	How did you know you were successful?	Why were you successful?	How did it make you feel?
1.	1.	1.	1.	1.
2.	2.	2.	2.	2.
What did you not learn successfully?	How did you try to learn it?	How did you know you failed?	Why did you fail?	How did it make you feel?
1.	1.	1.	1.	1.
2.	2.	2.	2.	2.

Task 2.2

The answers to these questions tell us a lot about how we learn. If we put all the answers together, we can form a picture of what usually leads to successful learning.

Compare your answers with those of two or three other students.
1 What contributed to the group's successes?
2 What contributed to the group's failures?
3 What are the general similarities in the answers?
4 Are there any major differences?

Task 2.3

We can use our knowledge about how we learn to write a 'recipe' for successful studying. Here is one student's example.

With two or three other students, write a recipe for successful learning of your own. What are its essential ingredients?

Task 2.4

Students often feel that they cannot succeed because they have little or no control over their own learning, like the student in this diagram:

It is important that you feel you are in control of your learning, that you feel confident enough to make decisions, and you understand what factors lead to your success.

With two or three other students, list some of the steps students can take to help themselves be more successful.

Task 2.5

A very important part of knowing how to learn successfully is to be clear about why you are learning.

a) Choose a course you are already taking or hope to take in the future, preferably taught in English. Write down why you are taking the course in as much detail as possible. Here are some general reasons you may wish to include and expand.
- to get a qualification
- to get a better job
- to learn new information
- to improve my skills in specific areas
- to get a new perspective on how to do things
- to become a learner again
- for a challenge

b) With a partner, discuss in as much detail as possible why you are taking the course and what you hope to learn or gain. In what ways can this knowledge help you to learn more successfully?

3 PREPARATION AND PACING

Successful study involves careful planning. But to prepare an effective study plan, you obviously need first of all to think about how you organise your life in general – your 'life-style'. Part of successful study is a healthy life-style.

JOG FOR SUCCESS — AVOID CUL-DE-SACS.

Task 3.1

A healthy life-style varies from person to person. It is important to understand what a healthy life-style is *for you* before you begin designing your study plan.

a) With two or three other students, discuss the following:

1 What do you tend to eat? Do you feel it is healthy?
2 How much sleep do you need? Is it enough? How do you know?
3 How much exercise do you get? Is it sufficient?
4 Do you work best in the morning or at night?
5 How do you relax when you feel tense?
6 How do emotional problems affect your study? What can you do about them?

b) Note down the points that most affect your learning and any changes or suggestions about your life-style that you would like to remember.

Task 3.2

We all need to study in a place where we can concentrate*, feel relaxed, and study efficiently. Where can you concentrate best and study most efficiently?

a) Look at the list which follows. Copy it into your notebook and write a plus next to those items which are essential for you to study efficiently. Write a zero next to those which do not influence your learning. Write a minus next to those which slow down your concentration and learning.

.... peace and quiet
.... bright lights
.... regular timetable
.... comfortable, soft chair
.... reference books
.... a word processor*
.... warm/cool room
.... background music

.... own desk
.... friends around
.... peaceful atmosphere
.... files or shelves
.... a typewriter
.... proper stationery
.... clean surroundings
.... space

b) Do you think you need to change your surroundings to study more effectively? Discuss with a partner.

Task 3.3

Students often find their work takes them too long and they do not have enough time to get it all done. It may be that the student needs to learn to manage time more effectively.

PROCRASTINATION: AN EASY WAY TO WHILE AWAY THE HOURS.

AN ADVISOR WILL HELP YOU GET YOUR PRIORITIES RIGHT.

KEEP A CLOSE WATCH ON TIME.

a) How did you spend the last 24 hours? In your notebook, write down how much time you spent on each of the activities below. (Feel free to add any other activities not included in the list.)

.... sleeping	.... quiet study
.... eating meals	.... eating snacks
.... attending classes	.... shopping
.... housework	.... exercise
.... reading for pleasure	.... personal hygiene (washing etc.)
.... watching television	.... listening to the radio
.... chatting with friends	.... discussing homework

b) Do you feel that this was a typical day? Make a note of where any differences occur – and be realistic. You will only be fooling yourself if you note you study all the time and never sleep!

Task 3.4

Of course, not every day or week is the same. Usually we have a weekly routine which means we do some things every Monday, different things on Tuesday, and so on.

a) What classes and activities do you have planned for different days? List those which occur regularly.

b) Compare your routines with those of two or three other students.
1 Where are they similar?
2 Where do they differ?
3 Are there any areas where you could make better use of your time?
4 Do you find that you waste a lot of time deciding what to do or trying to get yourself organised? Discuss.

c) Often, friends come to visit you, teachers give you new assignments, or your favourite actor appears at the local cinema! What 'unexpected' activities tend to interrupt your studies? Can you control any of them?

Task 3.5

How to use time is an important decision for all students to make – and it is not an easy decision. Some students work best for short periods interrupted by other activities; others need to concentrate for long periods of time. Some students need to take a lot of time reading; others find they need more time on writing activities. Some students work best at night; others find the morning best. There is no single best timetable for study.

 Which factors to do with how you use time do you consider to be the most important? The least important? Compare your answers with those of two or three other students.

Task 3.6

It is often helpful to draw up a weekly study plan at the weekend.

a) Draw up a study plan for yourself for next week. You may wish to use the framework below as a model. Keep in mind the points you felt were important in Task 3.5.

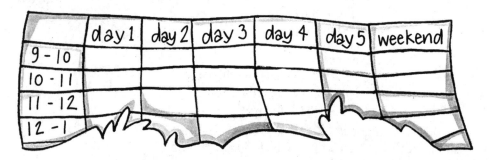

	day 1	day 2	day 3	day 4	day 5	weekend
9 - 10						
10 - 11						
11 - 12						
12 - 1						

b) Do you think you can actually follow a daily or weekly timetable? Discuss the advantages and difficulties with the rest of the class.

4 STUDY SKILLS

LISTENING   SPEAKING   READING   WRITING

'Study skills' are the techniques you need for studying successfully. They are the ways of thinking and behaving that you need in order to learn any academic subject effectively.

Task 4.1

Whatever you are studying, your knowledge of the subject or of English is not enough to guarantee success. What additional skills might you need?

a) With two or three other students, write a list of the skills you need to study successfully.

b) Which skills apply only to reading? Speaking? Listening? Writing? Which skills are needed in several areas of study?

Task 4.2

Here is a list of some of the study skills presented in *Study Tasks in English*.

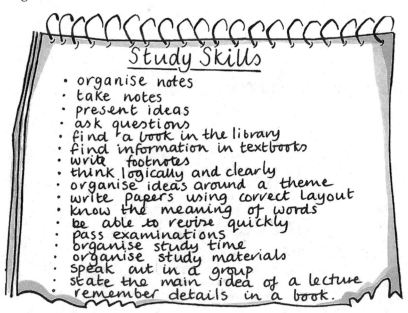

a) Compare this list with the list you wrote in Task 4.1.
1 Which skills do you feel are the most important for your own study?
2 Which do you feel are the least important?

b) With two or three other students, choose what you feel are the ten most essential skills for successful learning. Feel free to add to our list, as we may have omitted items that you feel are essential!

Task 4.3

Self-assessment is an essential element of successful study. This knowledge enables you to make sound decisions about how to approach your studies. It is therefore vital to develop the habit of thinking about what you can do successfully and what you need to practise more.

a) Think honestly and critically about your own learning skills.
1 Which skills do you feel you have mastered?
2 Which skills do you think need a lot more practice?

b) Copy the table below and complete it. Write the ten most essential skills from Task 4.2 in the first column and then tick (✓) the response which accurately indicates what you can do.

SKILL	I can do this well.	OK, but I need more practice.	I can't do this.	I don't need this skill.
1				
2				
3				
4				
5				
6				
7				

A complete guide is at the end of this book.

5 UNIT ASSESSMENT AND APPLICATION

An important part of studying is the ability to:
- summarise the ideas presented in what you study
- assess how well you have mastered these ideas
- use and apply the material more generally.

Task 5.1

You will find it a good idea to get into the habit of looking back over a unit and your notes in order to assess what were the most important parts for you.

With two or three students, discuss:
1 what you feel was the aim of this unit;
2 what were the most important points for you to remember;
3 in what ways you feel more prepared for your future studies in English.

Task 5.2

When you study with books written in English, you may find they involve vocabulary, grammar, and so on that you cannot understand. It is therefore useful to get into the habit of noting these down for future reference.

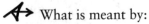 What is meant by:
1 title page;
2 (table of) contents;
3 index;
4 appendix?

Task 5.3

These are Maria and Ahmed's study targets.

Note Maria and Ahmed will need to look at these targets frequently, and set new ones as these are reached.

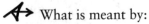 Think about what are the most important skills for you to master. Consider your interests, the requirements of the classes you are taking or will take, and your own strengths and weaknesses. Write a statement of your attainment target(s) for this course – what do you realistically hope to be able to do?
Hint Remember to look at your targets as your studies progress. Your needs or priorities may change as you become more skilled at studying in English.

UNIT 2 Thinking it through

Studying effectively requires you to ask questions, consider alternatives, and recognise different points of view – in other words, to think things through. This is the case whatever the studying involves – whether it is listening, reading, project work* or examinations.

1 HOW WELL DO YOU THINK THINGS THROUGH?

Probably the best way to learn more about this aspect of studying is to find out how you tend to analyse a study topic at present. How good are you at thinking things through?

Task 1.1

You have been given the information in the table that follows in a geography class as part of your study of the worldwide distribution of wealth.

Country	Average earnings	Male life expectancy	Population density	Climate
Japan	6052	74 years	326 p/km^2	temperate
Kenya	197	54 years	36 p/km^2	tropical
Guinea	180	42 years	24 p/km^2	tropical
Puerto Rico	2422	71 years	375 p/km^2	tropical
UK	4689	71 years	359 p/km^2	temperate
UAE**	14,375	61 years	17 p/km^2	hot and dry
Canada	6381	73 years	3 p/km^2	continental

**United Arab Emirates

With two or three other students, discuss the information in the table and decide what conclusions can be drawn from it.

Task 1.2

Now look back at the process your group used to arrive at its conclusions. The process can be divided into the questions you asked:
1 when you first looked at the data;
2 the questions you asked when you began to form different conclusions; and
3 the questions asked when a conclusion was reached.

a) In your groups, list the questions that were asked at the beginning, i.e. when you first looked at the data.

b) Are there any questions you feel you should have asked when you began that you did not ask? Discuss.

Task 1.3

Your group probably continued to ask questions as it attempted to arrive at a conclusion about the distribution of wealth.

a) Say what further questions your group asked after it began analysing the data, i.e. as you began trying to draw conclusions.

b) When your group finally arrived at its conclusion, had all your questions been answered? Do you feel it is possible to arrive at a final, unquestionable conclusion? Did you have to qualify* your answer? Discuss this in your group.

Task 1.4

Do you think your group did a good job of thinking Task 1.1 through? Why or why not? What do you feel are the most important points to keep in mind when trying to think a study topic through?

2 . . . ALL THOSE WH-QUESTIONS!

No matter what you are studying, the habit of thinking things through is vital. This means forcing yourself to ask questions before you begin, while you are studying and when you have finished. The main questions are the 'wh' ones: *what, why, when, how, where* and *who*. Using these questions in this way will help you to remember what you study and understand and use what you learn effectively. It should also save time in the long run.

LOOK BEFORE YOU LEAP

ONLY A FOOL JUMPS RIGHT IN.

Task 2.1

You are studying architecture. You have been asked to design a new play area for a primary school (i.e. for school children aged 5–11).

a) Write at least ten questions you would need to ask before you begin your design. Try to use each question word at least once.

➤ b) With two or three other students, compare the questions you listed. How might these questions affect the design? Which questions do you feel are the most important? Why?

Task 2.2

Stephen and Alison are in your architecture class. The questions they wrote are on page 205.

➤ With two or three other students, discuss where Stephen and Alison could get answers to their questions.

Task 2.3

The answers to Stephen and Alison's questions formed the basis for the decisions they made about their initial design.

➤ a) Listen to them discussing the answers they got. The plan of the school as it is at present is on page 206. What are the most important factors for their design?

➤ b) Make a sketch of a play area that meets the criteria* requested by the teachers and head teacher.

   Compare your design with those of other people in your class. Are they the same? If not, how do they differ, and why?

Task 2.4

The questions you asked did not stop when you began to sketch your design. Questions should continue throughout the design process.

➤ With two or three other students, discuss which questions you asked while you sketched the play area and which questions you asked after you finished your sketch. Why did you ask these questions? How did they help you improve your design? When do you think the process of asking questions concerned with an assignment or problem should end?

3   WHAT DO THE WORDS MEAN?

Task 3.1

> ' "When I use a word," Humpty Dumpty said,... " it means just what I choose it to mean. " ' Lewis Carroll:
> Alice Through the Looking Glass.

Words are symbols representing ideas and experiences – but the ideas and experiences of the people using words often differ. As a result, the same word can mean different things to different people.

➤ Write the meaning of the following words, or groups of words, and what you associate* with them. Then, with two or three other students, compare your answers. Were there any differences. Why?

1 study skills
2 peace
3 typical house
4 good English
5 democracy
6 marriage
7 freedom
8 discipline
9 fluent in English
10 endangered
11 conservative
12 happiness
13 successful students
14 scientist
15 a good party

Task 3.2

Communication, which is essential for study, involves at least two people – the speaker and the listener or the writer and the reader. If the words used are not precisely defined, misunderstanding can easily result.

➤ Read these extracts from conversations. With two or three other students, discuss what the problem is in each example.

1 ANDREA: The government said it would fully support measures to improve the health service.
  ABBASS: I'm relieved. I never thought they would agree to provide better funding.

2 SINY: What makes human beings different from all the other animals is language.
  ESRA: But most animals make sounds – surely it's just that we don't understand what they're saying, because their language is different from ours.

3 HANS: I sometimes think the world would be a better place if there was no more development going on, especially in the Third World.
  GLORIA: That remark is just typical of those in the West who want to hold back progress in the rest of the world!

4 HIROKO: One day computers will be able to think.
  SORIN: I don't think so, because they can only do what you tell them to do.

5 NOEMI: The way that scientists think is quite different from the rest of us.
  ALI: I don't agree at all – I think very logically and I'm studying literature.

Task 3.3

It is often helpful to define words by stating what is included and excluded in the meaning of the word. For example, suppose you read that boys are better than girls at football. You might want to ask which boys and girls are being referred to. Is it:
- boys and girls in a secondary school where girls are not taught football;
- boys and girls in nursery school;
- boys and girls who play football regularly;
- boys and girls attending private, single-sex schools;
- all children between the ages of five and sixteen years?

a) In each of the following statements, the word in italics is not specific and can therefore have more than one meaning. On your own, define the word in italics so that its meaning is precise. It must be clear both what is included and excluded by the word.
1 *Tall* buildings are safer in earthquakes.
2 Few *working-class* children go on to higher education.
3 *Large* classes are difficult to teach.
4 *Thin* people live longer.
5 *Old* houses are more expensive than modern ones.

b) With two or three other students, compare your answers. What can you conclude?

4 DON'T LET BIAS RULE!

Task 4.1

What is said ... and what is not? A speaker or writer cannot include everything known about a topic – some concepts and facts must be omitted. What is included and excluded will depend on space, clarity, lack of information, carelessness, purpose, prejudice*, bias*... . It is a good habit to try to decide what has been left out and why. Does the omission result in a misrepresentation* of the information or does it clarify or simplify the information without misrepresentation?

   Remember to consider whether the speaker or writer has an axe to grind*.

a) What is being said ... and what is being omitted? Read the information by noted authorities* (the originals) and then compare how it has been used in the essays.

b) With two or three other students, discuss:
1 What information has been omitted in the essays that was in the originals?
2 Do the writers of the essays misrepresent or clarify the information? Justify your answers.
3 For the inaccurate paraphrases*, how should the information have been summarised?

Original

1 The causes of the Second World War were varied. Although the one most commonly identified in the public mind, namely the Hitler factor, was certainly among the major reasons for the conflict, there were clearly several other causes as well.

(Wells, F. *Causes of Wars*. Hill, Beveridge & Lock. 1978)

2 There is no such thing as 'the' scientific method. Scientists use a great variety of ways of discovering knowledge, and although scientists have a certain way of going about things that is more likely to bring success than the methods used by the non-scientists, they use no set, logical procedure for discovering knowledge. According to Popper's methodology, every identification of truth is preceded by an idea in the imagination of the scientist of what the truth might be – by hypotheses such as William Whewell first called 'happy guesses'.

Most of the day-to-day business of science consists of making observations or experiments designed to find out whether this imagined world of our hypotheses corresponds to the real one. An act of imagination is therefore the foundation of every improvement in our knowledge of the world.

(Medawar, Sir P. *The Limits of Science*. OUP. 1985 – slightly adapted)

3 It would be wrong to assume that a skilled language-user is a skilled thinker. It would be wrong to assume that a person poor in verbal expression is therefore poor in thinking. We need language in order to let other people know what we are thinking, but grammatical coherence is not of itself the same as thinking. It is difficult, even impossible, to assess the thinking of a person who is unable to express it in language, but that does not mean that he has no thinking skill. In thinking lessons a pupil whose language ability was low enough for him to be regarded as backward has often blossomed as a thinker.

(de Bono, E. *Teaching Thinking*. Penguin. 1976)

Essay

1 As Wells says, Hitler was one of the causes of the Second World War. He also points out that it is Hitler that most people think of as being the chief cause of the Second World War. Therefore, in discussing the origins of the Second World War, it makes sense to concentrate on Hitler.

2 Medawar (1985) argues that the so-called scientific method does not exist. He says that scientific discovery is very much a matter of informed guess-work. Experiments and so on are the means of confirming whether the guesses are right or not, according to Medawar, but they are not the methods of discovery themselves.

3 As de Bono says, 'It would be wrong to assume that a person poor in verbal expression is therefore poor in thinking' (de Bono, 76:36). Thus, it is probably the quieter and less verbal members of society who are the deeper thinkers – 'Still waters run deep', as the saying goes.

Task 4.2 From whose point of view?

It is important to get in the habit of looking at an issue from a variety of angles. The conclusions you draw may be quite different depending on which point of view you adopt.

For example, take what appears to be a simple problem: Anita got a sweater for her birthday which she did not like and wants to return. From Anita's point of view, it seems reasonable to return the sweater to the shop and get one that she likes and would wear.

However, from the shop's point of view this may not be reasonable. They may not find another buyer, they may be involved in additional record-keeping and expense, and they may be suspicious about Anita's reasons for returning the item.

Eric, who gave it to Anita, may feel rejected, resentful or angry, as he took a long time selecting a sweater that he felt suited Anita perfectly; after all, he would have given her the money if the gift itself wasn't important.

Even if Anita considers these different points of view, she may still decide to return the sweater. However, she will be better prepared to cope with the consequences of this decision.

With two or three other students, discuss the situations below. Whose perspective* should be considered? How might they view each situation?

1 The Ministry of Trade and Industry in your country has announced that inflation has increased by 2% and unemployment has decreased by 3%. Consider the points of view of the political party in power, the opposition, the banks, the various members of the public, ...

2 A method of genetic engineering has been recently developed that will prevent genetically-inherited blindness. Consider the points of view for research, religion, parents of blind children, parents of mentally handicapped children, ...

3 There is a shortage of inexpensive homes in your neighbourhood. The city decides to allow 200 new houses to be developed on the children's playing field near your house. What various points of view should be considered?

4 The parents of an eight-year-old child receive a letter from school saying that their child, Emma, has hit a classmate, Mark. How will this be viewed by the various people involved?

5 Some evidence has recently been uncovered that people from Somalia in Africa sailed to America 200 years before Christopher Columbus. How will this evidence be viewed by different groups of people?

Task 4.3

Often a statement is made as if it were an absolute truth. For example, you may hear or read:

'... it is a fact, like it or not ...'

'... research has shown that this is true ...'

In other words, the statement is considered always true. However, the truth of a statement often depends on your point of view.

a) Which of these statements, if any, do you think are absolute truths?

1   A free press is essential for democracy.
2   No country should interfere in the affairs of any other one.
3   Inflation must be controlled for an economy to be sound.
4   Murder is a crime and must be punished.
5   Water boils at 100° C.

b) With two or three other students, compare your answers. Discuss whether you think there are any absolute truths. If so, give examples.

Task 4.4

Considering different points of view can be helpful in discussions and written assignments – this skill is essential for higher education. However, you also have to form your own point of view.

a) Consider the following statement:

Capital punishment should be made illegal wherever it is practised.

1   Do you agree or disagree?
2   Now, take the opposite stance: if you agree, disagree, and if you disagree, agree. List all the arguments and facts that you can think of to support your new position.
3   Now, think how each of your arguments could be rejected or disproved.
4   Write a short article supporting your *original* position. Use your knowledge of the other point of view.

b) Discuss with two or three other students how the skill of considering different points of view can be helpful in discussions and written assignments. Give examples from your own studies.

5 UNIT ASSESSMENT AND APPLICATION

Successful students do not just ask questions to find out facts about an assignment*. They have formed the habit of also asking questions in order to help think ideas through, understand the issues behind the facts, and guide the development, organisation, and content of their work.

Task 5.1

Michael is writing an essay on 'How to reduce heart disease'. Here is an excerpt* from his essay:

How to reduce heart disease

It is becoming increasingly clear that there is a direct link between eating habits and health. Heart disease claims 180,000 lives in Britain every year. At least two million British people are believed to have heart problems. The purpose of this essay is to show what can be done about this.

Let us begin by looking first at nutrient needs:

Age (years)	Boy 5–11	Girl 5–11	Male 12+	Female 12+
Fat (g)	65–85	60–75	75	70
Fibre (g)	20–25	20–25	25–30	25–30
Calcium (mg)	700+	700+	500+	500+
Iron (mg)	12	12	10	12
Energy (calories)	1700–2200	1600–2000	1800+	2000+

This table shows that there is not much difference between the nutrient and energy needs of adults and children over the age of five. Even though children are much smaller, they need large amounts of all nutrients because they are growing. In fact, they need more calcium and Vitamin D than adults, to ensure that their bones and teeth are strong.

British eating habits are changing. There is a much greater variety of foods to choose from nowadays. Also, the population is becoming much more aware of how choice of food can affect health. As a result, people are eating less fat, sugar and salt and more fibre-rich starchy foods. This is undoubtedly doing a lot to lessen heart disease. For example, research in 1983 by the U.K. Department of Health and Social Security into children's eating habits showed that:

- 30% ate too much fat;
- many diets were too heavily dependent on chips, cakes and biscuits;
- there was no evidence that any of the children were suffering because of these apparent deficiencies;
- children who were out of school at lunchtimes at cafés, fast food outlets, etc. had lower intakes of many nutrients than other children. In particular girls were short of iron.

To lessen the risk of heart disease, there are two major changes that are needed in the way people in Britain eat:

1 the amount of fat eaten, especially saturated fat, must be reduced;
2 the amount of foods rich in starch and fibre must be increased.
   If this is done, then the British people will be much healthier. At the . . .

 **a)** Copy the evaluation form below into your notebook, and then use it to assess Michael's paper. You are only to evaluate his ability to think things through. You are not concerned with whether you agree with him or not, nor are you concerned with his general English ability. Mark each skill on a scale of 5 to 1: if you feel Michael was excellent at a particular skill, give the skill a rating of 5; if you feel he was particularly weak, give it a rating of 1.

SKILL	Rating	Comments
1 had a clear purpose 2 defined his terms 3 answered essential questions 4 included relevant information 5 excluded bias and unsupported opinion 6 considered all viewpoints		

 **b)** With two or three other students, compare the results of your evaluations. Try to arrive at a final evaluation of Michael's ability to think things through.

Task 5.2

How well have you mastered the art of thinking things through?

 With two or three other students, look back through this unit, then discuss the questions which follow.
1 What skills are the most difficult to master?
2 What skills do you feel you have already mastered?
3 What skills do you feel you still need to work on?
4 How can the ideas presented in this unit help you in your future study?

UNIT 3 Asking critical questions

The thinking skills presented in Unit 2 can help you to uncover the facts and get a clearer picture of what is being studied. However, it is often also necessary to look *behind* the facts – to infer* causes, forecast* consequences*, discuss implications*, put forward alternatives*, and look at where and how 'facts' were obtained. This unit looks at the critical questions that will help you analyse* and evaluate* information you are given.

1 WHY DID IT HAPPEN?

When two events are related, one *may* be the cause of the other. For example, let's look at this fact: the dog barks when the postman delivers letters. In this statement, the postman appears to be the cause of the dog barking, and the dog's bark is one effect of the postman's delivery. If so, this statement can be rewritten like this: if the postman delivers letters, the dog will bark.

Task 1.1

There are four important points that need to be considered when two events are presumed to be related.

1 *Causal* relationships have direction. In a causal relationship the first event is seen as causing the second. In the example just given, this means that the postman will cause the dog to bark, but the dog barking will not cause the postman to come. **The order of the two**

parts of such statements cannot be reversed. The same one always comes before the other.

2 *Not all relationships have causal links*. Not all relationships are cause and effect. The relationship may be only a coincidence[*]. Unfortunately, relationships are often assumed to be cause/effect ones when they are not. For example, the dog may bark every morning because it wants to be fed, and this may be at the same time as the postman is delivering letters. The postman therefore does not cause the dog to bark.

It is therefore very important to examine causal statements carefully to make sure they are not really just two independent actions which, by chance, happen to occur at the same time.

3 *A cause may have more than one effect*. When the postman comes, the dog barking may be one effect; the letters you receive are obviously another. Often, research emphasises one effect of some action while ignoring other effects of the same action. If you fail to look at all the effects, there is always a chance that the conclusions you reach will be distorted[*].

4   *Events don't happen in a vacuum**. Related events always occur within a wider context. This wider context is often ignored for the sake of clarity. However, we need to be sure that important extra factors in the context are taken into account. In the case of the postman and the dog, it may be that the dog barks when people carrying bags come to the door (but we have only observed the postman carrying a bag); it may be that the letter box squeaks and this irritates the dog (the fact that this occurs when the postman comes is coincidental); or it may be that the dog barks when it sees a stamp (unlikely as this may be!). **In other words, the problem is that a cause is often identified simply because it is the obvious one, though other factors may in fact influence the relationship.**

With two or three other students, look at the statements that follow.

1   What appears to be the cause in each, and what is the effect? Indicate the likely direction by rewriting each statement in terms of 'If …, then …'
2   Where possible, discuss how the statement may simply be a matter of chance (i.e. no causal links).
3   Where possible, discuss other possible results stemming from the cause.
4   Where possible, discuss what conditions might affect the relationship.
   a) Water, heated to 100°C, boils.
   b) Your motorbike stops and the fuel gauge points to empty.
   c) You studied hard last week and got a good result in your exams.
   d) Some mosquitoes carry malaria; John has malaria.
   e) A new supermarket is built and three small grocery shops close.
   f) Car drivers are required by law to wear seat belts and the number of deaths due to drunk driving increases.
   g) Inflation is high and wage demands are high as well.

Task 1.2

Often we are presented with an effect and asked to infer its cause or causes – we know something has happened or is happening, but the question is why? Returning to our previous example, if we are told that the dog is barking and asked to determine* why, we cannot answer with certainty that it is because the postman has come – obviously there are other possible reasons for the dog barking that need to be considered.

Look at the following effects and discuss with two or three other students all the possible causes for each effect. Try to decide which ones are the most likely, and discuss why.

1 You are studying late at night and your light suddenly goes out.
2 You can't start your car.
3 Most good secretaries are women.
4 Your bank balance is lower than expected.
5 Your application for study in Britain is refused.
6 Your girl/boyfriend doesn't keep a date.
7 You get the bottom mark in mathematics.
8 A friend gets a higher mark than you in English.

Task 1.3

As we have seen, searching for the cause behind an event can become absurd if taken to extremes. Nevertheless, the good student tries to uncover indirect causation.

a) Listen to this group of students, who are discussing the causes of the First World War for an essay they are writing for their History course. Make a diagram of the string of events that they describe.

b) With two or three other students, compare your diagram with those of other students. Discuss what problems you think the students may have in writing their essays.

Task 1.4

When you begin with an event and are asked to determine its cause, you can never determine it with absolute certainty. You can only describe the likely possibilities.

With two or three other students, discuss whether you agree or disagree with this opinion. Give examples to illustrate your decision.

2 WHAT WILL HAPPEN?

When you are asked to consider the consequences of different actions, it may be helpful to look at not only the immediate effects but the long-term consequences as well.

Task 2.1

Often people concentrate so much on the immediate problem at hand that they fail to take into consideration long-term consequences that are foreseeable if past events, current trends, and general knowledge are taken into account.

a) Read this account of the introduction of the rabbit into Australia.

The rabbit plague

Rabbits were first introduced into Australia by British settlers in the middle of the 19th century. The reason for their introduction may have been in order to provide a source of food, or for sport, or simply as pets. Whatever the reason, they eventually caused a devastating ecological disaster.

They soon escaped from captivity and began to multiply very rapidly, especially because they had few natural enemies in the Australian environment. At the time, sheep-farming was the mainstay of the Australian economy. But the rabbits ate up huge areas of the vegetation needed by the sheep. As a result, sheep-farming and thus the Australian economy as a whole began to suffer enormously.

The damage done by the rabbits was more than to simply deprive the sheep of their source of food.

They also turned thousands of square kilometres into dustbowls, and caused some native species of mice and other browsing animals to become extinct.

It was only by 1950 that the rabbits were controlled, with the introduction of the disease myxomatosis, which killed them off rapidly in large numbers. Even then, the complex unforeseen chain of events surrounding them did not end. The spectacular success of myxomatosis as a means of cutting down on rabbits led to its introduction into England in 1954. Here also the rabbits died out in great numbers as expected, but the weeds previously eaten by the rabbits started to spread rapidly. In addition, the mice and beetle populations dropped sharply because foxes began to eat more of them in the absence of rabbits. And so on, all the way down the food chain.

---

b) Complete the flow chart that follows, showing the short, medium and long-term consequences of introducing the rabbit into Australia.

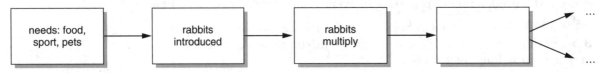

c) Discuss with two or three other students:
1 why the rabbit was introduced;
2 why the long-term consequences may not have been foreseen;
3 if the consequences had been foreseen, why they might have been ignored.

d) Can you think of any similar instances in which some action or policy had unexpected long-term consequences? Discuss how it happened.

Task 2.2

As can be seen in the problem in Task 2.1, it is necessary to consider a variety of short-term and long-term consequences. It may be that an immediate solution has a long-term effect that is worse than the original problem.

a) Look at the situations that follow. With two or three other students discuss the possible consequences of the actions proposed. Remember to consider all possible consequences, immediate and long-term, direct and indirect.

1 All football teams must have at least two women players.
2 All paper products must be recycled.
3 Police are required to patrol on bicycles in your country.
4 All students at your school or college have to do three hours volunteer work each week.
5 All adults in your country are required to have a yearly health check.
6 The government must pay wages to those individuals who raise children in the home rather than taking outside employment.
7 All international debts to the IMF** are cancelled.
8 Flies are eliminated from the face of the earth.

b) With two or three other students, determine which consequences are the most likely to occur.

Task 2.3

Often the chance of two events occurring at the same time is expressed as a correlation coefficient. The symbol for the correlation coefficient is *r*.
- If r = 1.00, it means that every time one event happens, the second event will also happen. This is a certainty.
- If r = 0.00, it means that the two events occur randomly and any perceived relationship is merely chance.
- If r = –1.00, it means that every time one event happens, the second event will not happen (this is also a certainty).

Outside science, most relationships are not certainties, and must be expressed as a probability concerning the likelihood of something happening.

Look at the statements that follow. With two or three other students, discuss how likely it is that the event will occur. In some instances an r value has been given; in other instances, guess the likely value of r.

1 A person has smoked for 20 years and has lung cancer. (r = 0.50).
2 A person has a high IQ and is successful in school. (r = 0.25).
3 A person has a low IQ and earns a good income. (r = –0.15).
4 A person earns below the poverty line and has a large family.
5 Someone gets caught stealing a car and goes to jail.
6 A very tall sunflower is grown in the shade.
7 A person watches violent television shows and behaves violently in real life.

Me, superstitious, never!

But I found the correlation between ladders and bad luck is 0.89!

** IMF = International Monetary Fund

27

3 WHAT HAPPENS IF ...?

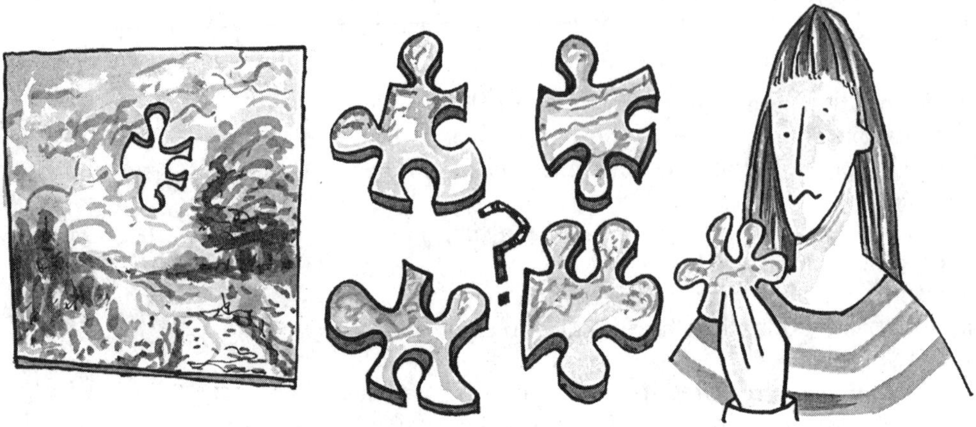

As a student, you are likely to be given a problem to investigate. If this happens, you may need to look at a variety of solutions, evaluate the consequences of each, and determine which is the 'best' solution.

Task 3.1

If you are in a position where you must determine a variety of possible solutions to a problem, it is often helpful to ask the question, 'What if ...?'

Look at the following problems. With two or three other students, select one (or two) problems to work on. Then suggest a variety of solutions to your problem. Consider the short- and long-term consequences of each solution. Which solution would your group recommend? Why?

1 House prices have doubled in the last two years. This is causing a lot of trouble for young families and people needing to move home, and has led to high inflation.
2 Young people (16–18 years old) are increasingly becoming involved in the taking of illegal drugs. This has led to an increase in crime and violence.
3 Very heavy traffic jams have brought traffic to a standstill in the capital. This has led to problems for the police, the fire service, and for ambulances, as well as creating problems for the environment. Workers and tourists suffer alike.
4 Periodic famine disasters occur throughout North Africa. Many people suffer each time this happens.
5 The percentage of people leaving school unable to read and write in their own language has increased to 20% of the population. This is causing a wide variety of problems, both for the individual and society.
6 The world population will double to over 10 billion in the next 60 years if something isn't done immediately. Should anything be done, or isn't this a problem? If it is a problem, what can be done, if anything?

Task 3.2

You may have found that thinking of alternative solutions is easier than selecting which is the best solution. This is because the 'best' solution must meet specific criteria. This will often involve a set of value judgements.

A→ A small town decided that it needed to modify the town centre and asked two development companies to submit plans. The town councillors could not agree about which to accept. With two or three other students, decide which plan was supported by each councillor. Which plan do you think the three councillors should agree on? What did you base your decisions on?

PLAN 1
– clear the buildings from the town centre
– build a large covered shopping mall
– facilities for large and small shops
– areas for 2 new cinemas and a bingo hall
– indoor sports hall with pub within shopping mall
– multi-level parking
– a variety of food outlets
– 3 large chain stores are supporting this plan as they want to expand here

PLAN 2
– upgrade the existing shops
– restrict traffic by creating a pedestrian zone
– add trees and plenty of benches and picnic tables
– parking on the outskirts of town
– free park-and-ride to town centre
– create a youth centre with bowling, a disco, and table tennis
– create a museum of local crafts
– maintain existing facilities including bingo, the cinema and pubs

Councillor Jones:
– believes saving money is of primary importance
– likes modern, covered shopping areas
– feels good car parking is essential
– believes large superstores bring in shoppers
– sees the town centre as primarily a shopping centre
– is supported by the local business community

Councillor Roberts:
– believes people will be willing to pay for good facilities
– likes small shops that encourage variety and competition
– feels cars are best kept out of town centres
– feels the town centre should be the centre of the community's social life
– is worried about the local youth as well as the pensioners

Councillor Allison:
– wants to retain the small shops of the past
– feels cars are the only possible transport in this farming locality
– feels that it is important to have a developed centre primarily for shopping as this is necessary to encourage jobs
– wants to encourage tourism
– is largely supported by the middle-class

Task 3.3

Unfortunately, sets of criteria for making a decision are not always given. When this happens it is necessary to try to determine a basis for the decisions that have been made.

 Look at the statements below and discuss the underlying basis for the action that was taken.

1 Private citizens are forbidden to own guns.
2 Abortions are free on demand to any woman over sixteen.
3 All passengers in cars must wear seat belts.
4 Attendance is compulsory in all classes at your school or college.
5 Public transport is free to all users.
6 People should pay for medical treatment if they have the money to do so.

Task 3.4

Sometimes there is a conflict in the criterion being used for decision making. For example, someone may believe it is wrong to steal but could be placed in a position in which a life depended on stealing food, and would therefore steal because life has a greater importance to that person.

In other words, some values have a greater importance than others, and the hierarchy of importance varies from person to person, according to the situation they are in or how they see the world. Sometimes it is helpful to prioritise the criteria used to make a decision.

 a) Listen to Joan and James discuss the problem of testing drugs on animals for a biochemistry class. Which of the statements below correspond to Joan's or James' views? Which views are associated with both? With two or three other students, compare your answers, and justify your decision where necessary.

1 Experiments involving animals are justified.
2 Experiments involving animals are not justified.
3 It is worth killing animals if we discover more about the effects of medicines as a result.
4 The lives of all animals are of equal value.
5 The lives of human beings are more important than the lives of other animals.
6 The choice is not whether or not to kill animals but what will cause less loss of life in the long run.
7 Progress always has its price.

 b) Prioritise* the statements in terms of your own feelings. Then discuss your views with two or three other students, and try to agree on a common list of priorities.

 c) Were you able to agree about your priorities? Why or why not?

4 DOES IT FOLLOW?

Logical thinking is an important skill when dealing with facts.

Task 4.1

Misha and Daniel have been conducting a wide-ranging survey into perceptions of differences between married, working men and women in the UK, as part of a Sociology assignment. Here are some of the results they obtained:

	Men			Women		
Question	Yes	No	No opinion	Yes	No	No opinion
1 Do you help with the housework?	24%	71%	5%	93%	2%	5%
2 Have you ever been discriminated against in your job because of your sex?	5%	87%	8%	56%	20%	24%
3 Are women better than men at looking after children?	82%	12%	6%	78%	7%	15%
4 Are men better than women at studying scientific subjects?	85%	11%	4%	65%	27%	8%
5 Are men better than women at studying non-scientific subjects (languages etc.)?	67%	17%	16%	56%	41%	3%
6 To what extent have you fulfilled your life's ambitions?	65%	31%	4%	19%	73%	8%
7 Is your wage lower than that paid to a member of the opposite sex doing the same job?	2%	88%	10%	85%	13%	2%

a) Do these statements follow *logically* from the statistics* above? Please note that you are not required to question the validity or reliability of the statistics. Rather, your task is to assess whether the conclusions drawn from the statistics are sound or not.
1 More men should help with housework.
2 Better legislation is needed against sexual discrimination at work.
3 Women are generally better than men at looking after children.
4 Women lack self-confidence in their ability to study.
5 Women have far fewer satisfying career opportunities than men.
6 Women should be paid higher wages.

b) With two or three students, discuss your answers. Did you find this task easy or difficult? Discuss.

Task 4.2

It is possible to look at a series of events and arrive at a conclusion that is not justified. This is called an over-generalisation. For example, I may notice it has rained every Monday for the last four weeks. To conclude that it rains every Monday is unjustified – it is likely to have been just chance that it rained four Mondays in a row. However, had it rained every Monday for the last three years, I would be much more justified in concluding that it is likely to rain next Monday, though of course there is no guarantee that it will do so.

Fernando has been studying in England for two months. He is writing to a friend thinking about coming to England. Do you feel his conclusions are justified? Explain.

Oxbridge University,
England.
5th December.

Dear Juan,
   Thanks very much for yours. Glad to hear you and the family are all well. I've decided to write to you in English — it's good practice for both of us!
   You asked for my advice about coming to England yourself. Well, let me give you my impressions so far. One thing comes immediately to mind — be prepared for bad weather. It's always cold, windy and wet. The food is a bit of a shock as well — nobody seems to eat rice, just chips with everything!
   I'm living on campus in a single study-bedroom. The university is about 3 miles from the town, so I haven't been out much. There's very little need — the campus has its own shops, a supermarket, a bank, a post office and so on. Most of the other students live on campus as well. British universities certainly have everything conveniently located!
   As for studying, well, I must say, a lot of it comes as quite a surprise. We seem to have so much to read — never-ending. On the other hand, there don't seem to be any exams — at least, nobody's mentioned them yet. What we do have are essays — lots and lots of them. I've got three all due in next week. So be prepared for lots of writing if you come over here! Then there are the seminars — that's when a group of about 10 of us meet with one of the lecturers for about an hour to discuss something we've read. I really find the way the others speak very difficult to understand. They go so fast, and they don't have the same sort of accent as our English teachers. They don't always seem to be able to understand me either. So I don't think these seminars are much use for people like us — if you come over here, I would advise you to concentrate on the reading and writing.
   Well, that's about it for now. I'm getting on OK, despite the weather and the food. Looking forward to hearing from you soon and knowing whether you might come here as well — hope so!
All the best,

Fernando

Task 4.3

Sometimes it is helpful to draw a special kind of diagram (known as a 'Venn' diagram) for a series of statements in order to determine whether the conclusion is true or not. For example, imagine that you are told that tall people have big feet and that, since Jack is a tall man, he must have big feet. You want to know if the conclusion is justified. In this example, there are two premises*: tall people have big feet and Jack is a tall man. The conclusion is, therefore, Jack has big feet.

Diagram 1 shows that, logically, the conclusion is a true statement. Each circle represents one variable*. In this case, the variables are height and foot size. People in the dotted circle are tall and those in the hatched circle have big feet. As Jack is in both circles, the conclusion that Jack must have big feet is logical.

Note Short people may also have big feet.

However, if we change the premises, the conclusion is not necessarily logical. For example, if we change the statement to read 'Most tall people have big feet', then it is possible that Jack does not have big feet. This can be seen in Diagram 2, where Jack could be in either the dotted circle (tall) or the area where the circles overlap (tall and big feet).

Unless a statement includes words such as *some* or *most*, it implies that it refers to all members of the group.

a) Look at the list of statements below. Tick the ones that you feel follow logically. It may be that, in some instances, you know the conclusion is false but is nevertheless logical.

1 English is a mandatory subject in higher education. John is entering technical college (i.e. an institution for higher education). Therefore, he will have to study English.
2 Green apples are sweet and sweet apples often have worms. The apple I'm eating has a worm in it so I know it is green.
3 I like tall teachers and Mrs Smith is a good teacher so Mrs Smith must be tall.
4 All murderers should be hanged. Mr Smith has been convicted of murder. Therefore he should be hanged.
5 Most clever people write books. Eliza Jackson must be clever because she recently wrote a book.
6 Pupils should be forbidden to wear scarves in school since they are dangerous in some lessons.

b) With two or three other students, compare your answers. Discuss any statements where your answers disagree. Try to uncover where the problem lies. It may be helpful to draw a diagram of the statement (though this is not always necessary).

c) Write the logical conclusion for each set of premises where the conclusion was illogical.

Task 4.4

Drawing logical conclusions is often difficult. The conclusions may seem to go against what we know or believe to be true. In this case, it may be that the premises are not true and need to be investigated.

For example, if you know that Jack does not have big feet, then the premise that tall people have big feet is incorrect – and needs to be investigated further. It may be that what the research actually indicates is that tall people tend to have big feet, that 'tall' refers to people over 170 cm (and Jack is only 162 so the premise does not apply) or it could be that the research was not valid or reliable, and should be challenged.

Look at the following statements. What are the premises and conclusions in each case? Which do you feel are logical? Discuss the factors that affect the truth of each set of statements. The first one has been done for you.

1 As young babies should only eat nutritious food, they should be fed minced beef which is a good source of protein.

> *Premise a:* All nutritious food is good for babies.
> *Premise b:* Beef is nutritious.
> *Conclusion:* Beef is good for babies.
>
> If *premises a* and *b* are correct, then the *conclusion* is logical. However, it is likely that *premise a* is incorrect, and should read:
>
> Only certain nutritious food should be fed to babies.
>
> This premise implies that some, not all, nutritious food is good for babies, and the conclusion based on the original premises is therefore illogical.

2 Jack will make a good pilot because he has fast reflexes. After all, all pilots have fast reflexes.
3 People who study a lot are good students. We know Maria studies hard because she is a good student.
4 'Spare the rod and spoil the child.' James, a very naughty boy, has never been spanked.
5 Some vegetables which are grown with chemicals can be dangerous to humans. Therefore, organically-grown vegetables are healthier than other vegetables.
6 More television channels means more choice in what people can view on television.
7 Leela wants to be a good student. Therefore, she should go to bed early since most good students go to bed early.

8 A well-known expert said that the world climate was changing, so it must be true.

5 UNIT ASSESSMENT AND APPLICATION

This unit examined some of the critical thinking involved in assessing research, determining various causes underlying events, assessing various alternatives, and logically questioning statements and opinions. It is easy to confuse cause with effect, to emphasise one cause to the extent that other possible causes are ignored, and to assume a relationship exists with no proof. Keep your eyes (and mind!) open for causal errors in thinking – you may find them in readings, discussions, and lectures – as students are not the only ones that sometimes do not think critically!

Task 5.1

Thinking things through involves asking questions and looking at the facts in a variety of ways. You need to avoid jumping to conclusions or accepting the so-called obvious.

a) 'The world is becoming a global village.' If you agree with this view, individually outline what you believe might be the cause(s) for this. If you do not agree, outline why you think the world has not become a global village.

b) With two or three other students who have the same view as you about the statement, list all your reasons for the position you have taken.

c) How sound do you feel each of your group's reasons are? What questions do you think you need to ask to evaluate them? You may wish to ask questions such as:
  1 What evidence is the reason based on?
  2 What assumptions are being made?
  3 What is meant by 'global village'?
  4 How subjective is the reasoning?

d) Now, number the reasons which your group feels are valid, in order of importance, and select the most important three to present to another group.

e) How valid do you feel the other group's reasons are? Discuss.

Task 5.2

How well have you mastered the art of critical thinking?

With two or three other students, look back through this unit, then discuss the questions that follow.
1 What parts are the most difficult to master?
2 What skills have you already mastered?
3 What parts do you feel you still need to work on?
4 How can the ideas presented in this unit help you in your future study?

PART B   Specific Skills

In Part A of *Study Tasks in English*, the focus was on acquiring the kind of thinking and learning skills which are important for any area of study. In this part, the focus is on helping you to combine the skills you studied in Part A with the further skills you need for particular aspects of study. The topics focused on in this part thus include aspects of studying such as using a library, note-taking, reading books and articles, discussing seminar* topics, listening to lectures, writing essays, doing research projects, preparing for examinations, and so on.

UNIT **4 Finding information**

An important feature of further and higher education is that you are expected to find much of the information you need *by yourself*. This means you need to be able to use study resources such as libraries and books as independently as possible.

1 FINDING YOUR WAY AROUND THE LIBRARY

The first step in making good use of a library is to find out what it contains. In most cases there is a great deal more than just textbooks. All of these other items are also vital aids for successful study.

Task 1.1

Libraries vary widely in the number of books they have and the variety of services they offer. The library you use at the moment may be smaller than the one you will use in your future studies.

With two or three other students, discuss the libraries you have used in the past. Which of the following sources of information were available? What is each used for? Were there other sources of information available as well? Which sources did you use?

1 science books (biology, chemistry, physics, …)
2 social science books (psychology, sociology, …)
3 literature books
4 recent journals
5 general references such as dictionaries, encyclopaedias and atlases
6 back issues of journals (often bound together yearly)
7 reference books on specialist topics

8 recent newspapers
9 pamphlets[*]
10 government publications
11 subject-specific references such as bibliographic indexes and abstracts
12 dissertations

Task 1.2

Many large libraries offer a wide range of services that help you find the
books or information you need. Some of these are described by Mano, an
Italian student attending a university in the north of England. He met
Ahmed while on holiday in Egypt. Ahmed is considering studying in
England next year. He has written to Mano for information about the
university. In this part of the letter Mano is describing the library.

17 Walnut Street
Peterstown
10 November.

Dear Ahmed,

   I was so pleased to hear from you so soon, and I do hope you will be able to
come and study in England next year. It would be very good to see you again.
Life here is interesting and the studying keeps you busy. You wanted to know
about this university. I'll begin with the library, as I spend much of my time
there.

   It's a large, two-storey building with a good stock of books and journals as
well as videos, tapes and newspapers from around the world. They even have *The
Times* on microfiche, going back 25 years — but I find reading it difficult!
The computer reference service tells you all the books available on any topic
(or almost any topic!) as well as letting you know if the book you want is
out. It even tells you what books you have out and when they are due back. If
you want a book, you can put in a request and the book will be recalled. If
the library doesn't have the material you need, you can put in an inter-
library request (there's a small fee for this). It takes about 4 weeks to get
the book or journal. The library also has a special short-loan section for
popular books. You can only take these books for 4 hours. Most other books can
be taken out for a term!

   I spend lots of time in the library. I enjoy wandering up and down the
aisles looking at books that catch my eye. It has a lot of study areas —
including some with sofas and armchairs. It also has 40 word processors for
students to use to write their essays on. I'm actually writing this on a word
processor in the library right now, as I'm getting quite good at two-finger
typing!

   The library has a special room devoted to the works of Wordsworth — his life
and times as well as a collection of everything he wrote. They also have a
special room devoted to hill-walking with lots of local maps and information
about the weather, footwear, climbing equipment, and so on.

➔ a) Which of the following services does Mano describe? Are these available in your library?

1   reserved books for special classes (short loan)
2   records/music scores
3   book binding
4   slides/videos
5   microfiche of newspapers
6   card catalogues
7   computer catalogues
8   word processors/student computers
9   tapes, recorders, and language laboratory
10 inter-library book or magazine requests/loans
11 photocopying facilities
12 laminating and enlarging of pictures, posters, maps, ...
13 subject specialist librarians to help students find information
14 photocopying
15 study areas
16 computers and typewriters for student use
17 special collections about the work of a famous person, group or activity
18 rare books
19 exhibitions
20 ——————————

➔ b) With two or three other students, discuss what kinds of services you have found in different libraries you have used or visited. What kinds of services do you find to be the most valuable?

Task 1.3

Whenever you begin studying in a new place, one of your first tasks should be to visit its library and find out what sources of information are available and where.

➔ Explore a library. It can be your local library, the library at the school or college you attend or a university library. With two or three other students, discuss these questions:
1 How is the library organised?
2 Are there any leaflets or booklets available to help you know what information is available and how to find it?
3 Were you able to find any other kinds of books that might be useful for studying? List them.

FINDING YOUR WAY AROUND THE LIBRARY.

Task 1.4

Most English-speaking libraries use one of two systems for arranging items in the library:
– a *decimal* system in which items on a specific topic have the same number. For example, all the items on bees would be located together. Items are filed on the shelves numerically.

– an *alphabetical* (or mixed letter and number) system in which items are arranged alphabetically, with items on a related subject area located together. Under this system, a book on the biology of the bee would not be located with a book on bee-keeping, as one is a biology book and the other is an agricultural one. Larger libraries tend to use variations of this approach.

With two or three other students, discuss how the books are arranged in your library or in ones that you have used. Have you usually been able to find the book you need? Have you been able to locate related books by looking at those nearby? What kinds of problems have you had, if any?

Task 1.5

The *card catalogue* tells where all the books in the library are located. In many libraries there are at least three cards for each book – a *title* card, an *author* card, and a *subject* card. Title cards are alphabetised by the title, author cards by the author, and subject cards by the subject. In many libraries these cards are mixed together and then alphabetised. For example, *The Hobbit* by J.R.R. Tolkien may be located in the card catalogue under Hobbit (The), Tolkien, or Fairy Tales.

TWO ESSENTIAL TOOLS FOR FINDING YOUR SOURCES.

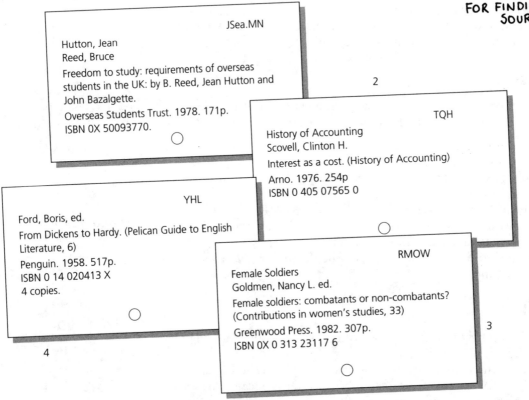

1

JSea.MN

Hutton, Jean
Reed, Bruce
Freedom to study: requirements of overseas students in the UK: by B. Reed, Jean Hutton and John Bazalgette.
Overseas Students Trust. 1978. 171p.
ISBN 0X 50093770.

2

TQH

History of Accounting
Scovell, Clinton H.
Interest as a cost. (History of Accounting)
Arno. 1976. 254p
ISBN 0 405 07565 0

YHL

Ford, Boris, ed.
From Dickens to Hardy. (Pelican Guide to English Literature, 6)
Penguin. 1958. 517p.
ISBN 0 14 020413 X
4 copies.

RMOW

Female Soldiers
Goldmen, Nancy L. ed.
Female soldiers: combatants or non-combatants? (Contributions in women's studies, 33)
Greenwood Press. 1982. 307p.
ISBN 0X 0 313 23117 6

4

3

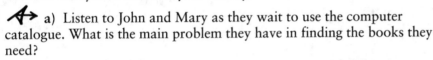 Use the sample cards opposite to answer these questions.

1 Card 1 is an author card. How many authors does the book have? Who are they? What is the name of the book? Where is it located in the library?

2 Card 2 is a subject card. What is the subject of the book? What is the title of the book? Who wrote the book? Where is it located?

3 Card 3 is a title card. What is the title? Is the author given? Why not? Who published this book? Where is it located in the library?

4 Look at Card 4. Who edited *From Dickens to Hardy*? What is its ISBN*? What series of books is it part of? When was it published?

Task 1.6

In many libraries, the card catalogue has been replaced by a computer catalogue. The information given by the computer is similar to that found on cards, i.e. it is possible to request information by author, title, or subject.

In many libraries, the computer can also tell you if a book is on loan. This saves you time looking for the book as well as allowing you to check what books you have out, to request books and so on. You need to find out how the system works in your library.

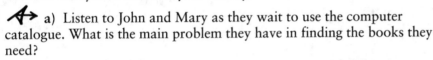 a) Listen to John and Mary as they wait to use the computer catalogue. What is the main problem they have in finding the books they need?

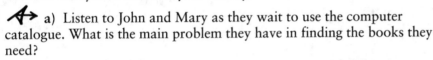 b) What subjects could you try if you needed to find information about the following topics?

1 the use of television advertising to raise money for charities
2 the causes of death of world leaders in the twentieth century
3 the long-term consequences of introducing the rabbit into Australia
4 the use of art treasures as an economic investment
5 the influence of soap operas on children's reading patterns
6 the success of economic projects sponsored by the World Bank in the Third World

2 FINDING YOUR WAY AROUND A TEXTBOOK

For Tasks 2.1–2.5, it will be helpful if you have a variety of academic books to refer to, preferably in English. If these books are not available, you may use *Study Tasks in English* and books in any other suitable language.

Task 2.1

Most academic books have certain features in common. You need to know what these are and how to use them. It can save you a lot of time and worry.

a) Look at several academic books and use them to make a table like the one below. In the appropriate space, write where each part is found. If it is not in the book, leave the space blank.

Name of Book						
title page bibliography or references date of publication publisher index preface table of contents appendices comments on back cover – – – – – – – – – – – – – – – –						

b) With two or three other students, discuss what most of the books have in common. Where is each part of a book usually located?

Task 2.2   The title page

Peter E. Murphy

Tourism

A community approach

METHUEN
New York and London

First published in 1985 by Methuen Inc.
29 West 35th Street, New York, NY 10001

Published in Great Britain by Methuen & Co Ltd
11 New Fetter Lane, London EC4P 4EE

© 1985 Peter E. Murphy

Typeset by Keyset Composition
Printed in Great Britain at the
University Press, Cambridge

Library of Congress Cataloging in Publication Data
Murphy, Peter E.
    Tourism: a community approach
    Bibliography p
    Includes index
    I. Tourist trade   1 Title
    G155 M86   1985   380. 1'459104   85–13884
    ISBN 0 416 39790 5
        0 416 35930 2 (pbk)

British Library Cataloguing in Publication Data
Murphy, Peter E.
    Tourism: a community approach
    I Tourist trade
    I Title
    338 4.4 791   G155.A1
    ISBN 0 416 39790 5
        0 416 35930 2 Pbk

➤ Look at the title page opposite and locate these parts of the book.
a) title of book
b) subtitle of book
c) author
d) publisher
e) place of publication
f) ISBN

Task 2.3   The table of contents

The table of contents can help you decide whether a book has the information you need and, if it does, where it is likely to be found.

➤ a) You are writing a project on tourism and need to locate information on the topics which follow. You saw *Tourism* by Peter Murphy in the library and thought it might be useful. Use its table of contents to determine whether the following information is likely to be in the book, and, if it is, where.

1 planning tourism
2 local places of interest for tourists in Scotland
3 economic benefits of tourism
4 tourism in the 1960s
5 social changes resulting from tourism
6 local decision making
7 long-term financial loss
8 political influences of tourism
9 what makes a good holiday
10 influence on marine life of large-scale seaside hotels

Contents

➤ b) With two or three other students, compare your answers. Are there any differences? Justify your answer.

➤ c) Discuss when and how you usually use the table of contents.

Task 2.4   The index

The index is useful if you are looking for specific details or information.
The information is always listed alphabetically at the back of the book.

In your essay on tourism, you need specific information on the
following questions:

1 What are the effects of population growth on tourism?
2 Are safari parks an effective use of land resources?
3 What is REKA?
4 What examples are there of parks improving the tourist industry?
5 How does train travel affect tourism?
6 What is the difference between recreation and play?
7 How can different occupations influence the tourist trade?
8 How can outdoor recreation be educational?
9 How do package tours affect the over 60s?
10 How have the Olympic Games affected tourism?

From: Murphy, P. E. *Tourism: A Community Approach.* Methuen, 1985.

From: Cheek, N. H. and Burch, W. R. *The Social Organisation of Leisure in Human Society*. Harper and Son, 1976.

Nonagressive acts, 202
Nonwork, 6, 192, 194
Norbeck, Edward, 7
Normative system, 183–185
Norms, classification, 184, 187
North-Hatt scale, 51
Nuer society, 83
Number, in social groups,
 96–97

Occupations, 192, 193
 and extra time, 65
 and life-style, 54–71
 and outdoor activities,
 58–59
Ogburn, W.F., 97
O'Leary, J.T., 118
Olympic games, 212
Opposition, 55, 57, *See also*
 Compensatory
 hypothesis
Orzack, L., 57
Outdoor activities, 19–21,
 69–70, 112–113. *See also*
 Parks; Wilderness areas
 and education, 51, 52–53
 location, 31
 and occupation, 56,
 58–59
 participation, 44–48,
 114–115
Outdoor Recreation
 Research Review
 Committee, 14

Parks, 157, 177, 230
 activities, 160
 behavior at, 160–161
 crime, 166
 freedom in, 166
 group size, 162–163
 group structures, 161–162
 intragroup bonding,
 162–165
 participation, 116
 sexual composition of
 groups, 162
 socialization characteristics,
 159–160
Parsons, Talcott, 95, 101–102,
 130, 181, 188
Passive entertainment, 61
Persona, 191–192
Piaget, J., 99, 204–205, 206
Play, 105–107, 196–197, 216,
 230
 defined, 7–8
 free, 197
 and games, 200–207
 governed by rules, 198
 make-believe, 198
 separate, 198
 uncertain, 198
 unproductive, 198
Playgrounds, 230
Polanyi, K., 87–88

Reading, 81, 89, 110
Recreation, 222–223, 241,
 242–243
 defined, 7
 and enterprise, 229–232
 as industry, 232–235
 movement, 229
 public funding, 234
 in United States, 225–229
Recreation areas, 116–117,
 154–157
 bonding, 156
 class of visitors, 50–51
 custodial, 156
 exchange, 156
 fantasy, 156
 integration, 156
 population stability,
 174–176
 solidarity, 156
 transitional, 155
Reissman, L., 46
Religious values, 172
Research answering the
 Nation's Needs, 15
Response, validity of, 36–37
Retirement groups, 244
Richards, A.I., 78
Riesman, D., 64
Ritualization, in play, 106
Rituals, 94–95
Roberts, J.M., 105, 198–199,
 200

a) Often the hardest part of using an index is thinking of the word to look up in the index. What words could you look up in an index in order to find the answers you need to the questions above?

b) With two or three other students, compare the lists of word headings you made. Are there any differences?

c) Now, use the excerpts, opposite and above, from indexes from two books on tourism to locate where the answers might be found. Compare your answers. Which pages are the most likely?

d) Discuss when you usually use an index, how you tend to use it and any problems you may have had.

Task 2.5   Getting the most out of a book

One problem for foreign students studying in English is how to cope with the vast amount of reading material. You will need to learn how to determine quickly whether or not a book has the information you need and where it is located. Otherwise, you may find yourself reading a whole chapter or book, whereas you may have needed to read only a few pages. In your own language, this may have been interesting, and you may have had the time. This is unlikely to be the case in English.

a) Match the part of the book with the kind of information it contains. Some may have more than one answer. You may wish to refer to one of the textbooks you used in Task 2.1.

1 the preface
2 title page
3 back of the title page
4 table of contents
5 index
6 appendices
7 introduction
8 back cover 'blurb'

a when the book was published
b the publisher
c what the book is generally about
d data that supports the information in the book
e whether or not a specific topic is in the book
f the point of view of the author
g the general topics covered in the book
h title and author
i where the book was published

b) With two or three other students, make sure you know what is the full range of information that there can be in each part. The list above is not comprehensive*.

3 USING JOURNALS AND OTHER PRINTED SOURCES OF INFORMATION

Task 3.1

In addition to textbooks, *journals* are widely used in further and higher education as a further source of essential information. Journals are academic and professional magazines on specific subjects. They may also be referred to as *serials* or *periodicals* in some libraries.

↗ Think about the journals you have read or seen in libraries and elsewhere. Then look at the statements below. Which statements apply primarily to textbooks; to journals; to both? With two or three other students, compare your answers.

 1 an up-to-date source[*] of material
 2 detailed reports on research
 3 reviews of published material
 4 an on-going debate of a specific issue
 5 a brief explanation or summary of a topic or idea
 6 a bibliography of related information
 7 extensive, developed argument or idea drawing on a variety of resources
 8 a variety of opinions on a topic
 9 a detailed analysis of a topic
10 a review of the research and thinking on a topic

Task 3.2

Finding out what articles have been written on your topic is often even more of a problem than finding books on your topic. You need to think of yourself as a detective, as much of your library time may be spent in tracking down the information you need. The most common ways of knowing which journal has an article on the topic you are interested in are:

1 a bibliography supplied by your tutor
2 a reference in an article in a journal
3 a bibliography in a textbook
4 an abstract or index of articles in journals (abstracts and indexes are usually on specific topics and do not cover all the journals in print)
5 browsing through the journals stocked in your library that relate to your topic of interest

↗ You are looking for *up-to-date* information on tourism trends in Britain. Show how you would find the relevant information by putting these statements in the correct order. Alternatively, you may describe how you would go about finding the information in your own words.

a) find the list of journals in stock
b) request an inter-library loan to obtain a copy of the article
c) look up the topic in abstracts and indexes of articles on sociology and social trends of study

d) ask the librarian for assistance
e) look tourism up in the computer or card catalogue to find out what
   journals and pamphlets deal with tourism
f) look up the topic in the index of specific journals

Task 3.3

The reference section of a library contains a variety of books that cannot usually be taken from the library. These books contain a wide range of facts and statistical data[*], bibliographies, maps, and similar information. In addition, in larger libraries, reference material on specific subjects is located throughout the library. It is a good idea to look at what reference material is available in the library you use. It can save you a lot of searching at a later date.

✦ a) What kinds of information are in the following references[*]? Be specific. Remember that many references provide a wide variety of information. It would be helpful to visit the library for this task.
  1 atlas
  2 dictionary
  3 encyclopaedia
  4 Books in Print
  5 Thesaurus

✦ b) What other references are in your library? List four or five you feel might be useful to you in your studies.

Task 3.4   Writing source cards

Once you have found the information you need, it is helpful to keep an accurate record of *where* you found it. It is not uncommon to find students frantically trying to find the reference for the information they used in some assignment or essay (*all* the books and articles used must be accurately listed in the bibliography at the end of the work).

One way to keep a record of your sources is to put them on small filing cards (approximately 8 cm by 12 cm). This makes it easy to select and alphabetise the references you have actually used – and without having to sort through your notes, teacher handouts and other bits of paper, or having to go back to the library to search for the actual reference.

Source cards such as these are quite different from notes, as source cards only contain bibliographic information, whereas notes contain the information obtained from the source.

• Source cards are similar to card catalogue cards: you may wish to annotate the source card with a brief description of what the source is about and how useful it may be.

• Notes contain the detailed information found in the source and may take the form of notes written on cards, photocopies, extended notes on lined paper, and so on. You will need to write out the source on each set of notes unless you develop a card code that serves the same

purpose. Remember that each set of notes should also have the page
number that the information was taken from.

a) Look at the two sample source cards. With two or three other
students, discuss:

1 What information is given (or omitted) on each card, and why?
2 What system do you use at the moment? Have you had any problems
   with it?
3 Do you think you would find using cards for source references
   helpful? Why or why not?

b) Write a source card for the book used in Task 2.2.

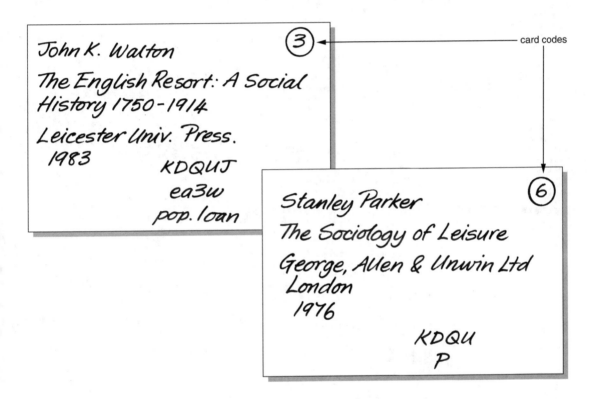

card codes

4 READING BIBLIOGRAPHIC REFERENCES AND NOTES

The bibliography is a list of all the references* the author used in writing
the book or article. Sometimes this information is located in a section
headed 'notes' or 'references'. This information can be helpful in
indicating additional sources of information that you may wish to refer
to. For example, a book may briefly refer to someone's work that you
would like to know more about. The bibliography will give the original
source and perhaps other relevant sources on the topic.

   Tasks 4.1–4.6 refer to the following excerpt from a bibliography.

Brownrigg, M. and Greig, M.A. (1976) *Tourism and Regional Development*. Fraser of Allander Institute Speculative Papers, 5. Glasgow, Fraser of Allander Institute.

Bryan, A. (1973) *Much Is Taken, Much Remains*. North Scituate, Mass., Duxbury Press.

Bryan, W.R. (1981) 'Improved mileage, discretionary income, and travel for pleasure.' *Journal of Travel Research*, 20, 28–9.

Bryden, J.M. (1973) *Tourism and Development*. Cambridge, Cambridge University Press.

Buck, R.C. (1977) 'Making good business better: a second look at staged tourist attractions.' *Journal of Travel Research*, 13, 3, 30–2.

Buck, R.C. and Alleman, T. (1979) 'Tourist enterprise concentration and old order Amish survival: explorations in productive coexistence.' *Journal of Travel Research*, 13, 1, 15–20.

Budowski, G. (1977) 'Tourism and conservation: conflict, coexistence and symbiosis,' *Parks*. 1, 3–6.

Burde, J.H. and Lenzini, J. (1980) 'Timber harvest and aesthetic quality: can they coexist?,' in Hawkins, D.E., Shafer, E.L., and Rovelstad, J.M. (eds) *Tourism Planning and Development Issues*. Washington, DC, George Washington University Press, 121–32.

Burkart, A.J. and Medlik, S. (1974) *Tourism: Past, Present and Future*. London. Heinemann.

Burt, J. and MacKinnon, W.C. (1977) 'Convention centres – their development and outlook.' *Tourism Development: Approaches for the Future*. Proceedings of The Travel Research Association, Canadian Chapter, Ottawa, 137–55.

Chadwick, G. (1971) *A Systems View of Planning*, London, Pergamon.

Chadwick, R.A. (1981) 'Some notes on the geography of tourism: a comment.' *Canadian Geographer*, 25, 191–7.

Chapin, F.S. (1965) *Urban Land Use Planning*, 2nd edn. Urbana, Ill., University of Illinois Press.

Chasis, S. (1980) 'The coastal zone management act.' *Journal of American Planning Association*, 46, 145–53.

Chau, P. (1973) 'The economics of travel by Canadians in Canada.' *Research for Changing Travel Patterns: Interpretations and Utilizations*, Fourth Annual Conference Proceedings of The Travel Research Association, Sun Valley, Idaho, 79–90.

Chau, P. (1977) 'Unification of tourism measurement criteria.' paper presented at World Tourism Organization Seminar on Tourism Statistics, Caracas, Venezuela.

Cheng, J.R. (1980) University of New England.

Coppock, J.T. (1977a) 'Second homes in perspective.' in Coppock, J.T. (ed) *Second Homes: Curse or Blessing?*. Oxford, Pergamon, 1–15.

Coppock, J.T. (1977b) 'Issues and conflicts.' in Coppock, J.T. (ed) *Second Homes: Curse or Blessing?*. Oxford, Pergamon, 195–215.

Coppock, J.T. and Rogers, A.W. (1975) 'Too many Americans out in the wilderness.' *Geographical Magazine*. 47. 8. 508–13.

Coppock, J.T. and Sewell, W.R.D. (eds) (1977) *Citizen Participation in Planning*. Chichester, Sussex, John Wiley.

Corsi, T.M. and Harvey, M.E. (1979) 'Changes in vacation travel in response to motor fuel shortages and higher prices.' *Journal of Travel Research*, 17, 4. 7–11.

Cosgrove, I. and Jackson, R. (1972) *The Geography of Recreation and Leisure*. London, Hutchinson.

Countryside Commission (1972) *The Goyt Valley Traffic Experiment*. London, Countryside Commission.

Countryside Commission (1974) *Farm Recreation and Tourism*. London, HMSO.

Countryside Commission (1976) *The Lake District Upland Management Experiment*. London, HMSO.

Cowan, G. (1977) 'Cultural impact of tourism with particular reference to the Cook Islands.' Finney, B.R. and Watson, K.A. (eds) *A New Kind of Sugar*. Santa Cruz, Calif., Center for South Pacific Studies, University of Santa Cruz, 79–85.

Cox, D.F. (1964) 'Clues for advertising strategies.' in Dexter, L.A. and White, D.M. (eds) *People Society*.

Cybriwsky, R.A. (1970) 'Patterns of mother tongue retention among several selected ethnic groups in western Canada.' *Papers in Geography 5*. University Park, Penn., Department of Geography, Pennsylvania State University.

D'Amore, L. (1983) 'Guidelines to planning harmony with the host community.' in Murphy, P.E. (ed.) *Tourism in Canada: Selected Issues and Options*. Victoria, BC. University of Victoria, Western Geographical Series 21, 135–59.

Dann, G. (1976) 'The holiday was simply fantastic.' *Tourist Review*, 31, 3, 19–23.

Darlington, J.W. (1981) 'Railroads and the evolution of the Catskill Mountain resort area, 1870–1920.' *The Impact of Transport Technology on Tourism Landscapes* (Hugill, P.J., organizer), papers presented at the Annual Meeting of the Association of American Geographers. Los Angeles, 7–12.

Dartington Amenity Research Trust (1974) *Farm Recreation and Tourism in England and Wales*. Countryside Commission Paper 83. London, HMSO.

Dasmann, R.F. (1973) *Classification and Use of Protected Natural and Cultural Areas*, IUCN Occasional Paper 4.

Davidson, A.T. (1979) 'Public participation in national park planning: reply.' *Canadian Geographer*, 23, 176–9.

Davis, W.A. (1981) 'The slipways are loaded with a new wave of ships.' *Vancouver Sun*. October 24.

Dearden, P. (1983) 'Tourism and the resource base,' in Murphy, P.E. (ed.) *Tourism in Canada: Selected Issues and Options*. Victoria BC, University of Victoria, Western Geographical Series 21, 75–93.

Task 4.1   Books

a) Answer the following questions which refer to several books listed in the bibliography extracts above.

1 What is the name of the book A. Bryan wrote?
2 When was *Much is Taken, Much Remains* written?
3 What is the name of the publisher of *Much is Taken, Much Remains*?
4 Where was *Much is Taken, Much Remains* published?
5 What book did J. M. Bryden write?
6 What edition of the book by F. S. Chapin was used?
7 Where was the book by Burkart and Medlik published?
8 When was the book edited by Coppock and Sewell published?

b) With two or three other students decide how the following information is indicated, e.g. location, variety of type, punctuation.
  1 the name of the author(s)
  2 publisher
  3 date of publication
  4 place of publication
  5 two authors
  6 if the book is an edited collection of articles

Task 4.2 Articles in journals

Look at the article by R. C. Buck. It was printed in the *Journal of Travel Research*, Volume 13, Number 3, pages 30 to 32. The words *volume, issue,* and *pages* have been omitted.

a) Answer the following questions about the journals in the bibliography extracts opposite.
  1 When did S. Chasis write the article about coastal zone management?
  2 What volume of the *Journal of American Planning Association* did Chasis' article appear in? On what pages?
  3 What is the name of the article by Coppock and Rogers?
  4 Where can you find the article by Coppock and Rogers?
  5 In what issue of the *Tourist Review* did G. Dann write an article about good holidays?

b) With two or three other students, decide how the following information was indicated.
  1 the name of the article
  2 the name of the journal
  3 the year the article was published
  4 the volume of the journal it appears in
  5 the page numbers it is printed on

Task 4.3 Referring to other sources of information

Sources often include books of collected articles, pamphlets and papers published by universities or the government, and notes from conferences.

a) What kind of publication is being referred to in each of the references to these authors?
  1 J.T. Coppock (1977a)
  2 Countryside Commission (1974)
  3 R. A. Cybriwsky (1970)
  4 P. Chau (1973)
  5 W. A. Davis (1981)
  6 G. Cowan (1977)

b) With two or three other students, discuss how you decided what kind of source was being referred to. How can you tell whether a book, journal, collection of articles, or some other publication is being referred to?

Task 4.4   Varieties of bibliographies

Not all bibliographies are written in the same way. Different authors and publishers present the information in bibliographies in different formats[*]. You will need to be able to find information in a variety of formats. Most bibliographies are arranged alphabetically, by author.

Study the bibliographic excerpts below and compare the format to the one at the beginning of section 4. With two or three other students, list what the bibliographies have in common and how they are different.

Monkin, D., 'Work and Leisure in a Zero-Growth Society', paper presented at 81st Annual Convention, *American Psychological Association*, Montreal, 1973.

Morrell, J. G., *Business Forecasting for Finance and Industry* (London, Gower Press, 1969)

Obermeyer, C., 'Final Observations', in M. Kaplan and P. Bosserman, eds, *Technology, Human Values and Leisure* (Nashville, Abingdon Press, 1971), p. 222.

Clarke, J. and Critcher, C. (1985) *The Devil Makes Work: Leisure in Capitalist Britain*, London, Macmillan.
Yeo, E. and Yeo, S. (1981) 'Ways of Seeing: Control and Leisure versus Class and Struggle' in Yeo, E. and Yeo S. (eds) *Popular Culture and Class Conflict 1590–1914: Explorations in History of Labour and Leisure* Brighton, Harvester Press.

Collins, L. R. (1978) "Review of hosts and quests: an anthropology of tourism," *Annals of Tourism Research, 5: 278-80.*
Rojek, Chris (1985) *Capitalism and Leisure Theory* Tavistock
Wrong, D. (1977) *Skeptical Sociology* Heinemann

Task 4.5   Organising a bibliography

All the sources referred to in an essay or project must be listed in the bibliography. In addition, you need to include those books which you have read and used ideas from in your writing. You do not need to include all the books on the topic you are writing about.

Use the bibliographic excerpt at the beginning of section 4 to answer these questions.
1 How are the sources generally arranged?
2 If an author writes two articles in the same year, how are they noted?
3 If an author writes two articles in different years, which comes first?
4 If a book has two authors, which generally comes first?
5 If there is no author (e.g. it is written by a commission or some other body), where is it listed?

Task 4.6   Writing a bibliography or reference at the end of an essay

There is no one right way to write a bibliography. Generally, use the method your tutor or department recommends. Otherwise, use one that is found in a leading journal in your field[*].

↗ Decide on the format that you prefer. Then write a bibliography including the following information. Remember, you will need to organise it alphabetically.

a) the books in the card catalogue, Task 1.5
b) the book on tourism, Task 2.2
c) the two source cards, Task 3.4
d) your study skills book
e) an article by J. Beard and M. Adams entitled 'Holidays at Home' in
   The Journal of Travel Agents, Volume 10, on pages 12 to 15

5 UNIT ASSESSMENT AND APPLICATION

This unit has been concerned with finding information in books, journals, and libraries. If you are studying in a second language and in an unfamiliar study situation, it is often difficult to know where to find what you are looking for.

Task 5.1

↗ a) Use the skills developed in this unit to state where and how you would find this information:

1 What unit deals primarily with listening skills?
2 List four different methods of assessment.
3 Will Unit 5.2 help students write better notes? Give a reason.
4 Where will students find out how to improve their memory?
5 What is the symbol for the correlation coefficient?
6 How can you improve your listening skills in a seminar?
7 What is a Venn diagram?
8 What does ibid. mean?

↗ b) Answer the questions above. This task should not take more than fifteen minutes. All the answers are in *Study Tasks in English*.

Task 5.2

↗ a) How well do you feel you answered the questions in Task 5.1? With two or three other students, discuss the problems you have had in finding information for essays or research you have had to write in your own language. Do you think you will have the same problems when you study in English?

↗ b) Look back over this unit. What skills had you already mastered? Which skills were unfamiliar? What skills do you feel still need practice?

UNIT 5 Taking and making notes

Taking and making notes is a part of every student's life. This does not mean that students are like secretaries, writing down every word they hear or read. Note-taking involves actively deciding what to note, how it should be noted, and later, how the notes are to be used.

1 WHAT MAKES GOOD NOTES?

Good notes help you study more effectively by cutting down the amount of information in English you need to handle. They also help you to think actively about what you are reading or listening to.

Task 1.1

 What are notes for? With two or three other students, discuss what you think the uses of note-taking are. How can notes help your studying while you are taking them? What can they be used for after you have taken them?

Task 1.2   What should good notes be like?

a) With two or three other students, think about when you have taken effective notes (e.g. when you didn't have to borrow someone else's later on!). What were the features that made them effective?

b) Compare your results with the list of characteristics of good notes on page 207. Were your ideas similar? Are there any differences?

c) Which aspects of good notes have you already mastered? Which aspects do you need to improve?

Task 1.3

Good notes need to be organised appropriately. There are two main methods for this:
1 *linear* notes: the topic is outlined one point after another, using numbers and letters to organise information in order of importance, sequence, ... Important features may include indentation*, spacing, numbering and/or lettering, and so on.
2 *pattern* notes: the shape of the notes shows how the main ideas are related and reflects the organisation of the information. Notes of this kind take the form of flow charts, diagrams, spider-like drawings and so on. They include circles, arrows, lines, boxes, ...

54

✦→ Copy the table that follows and complete it using the examples of
notes which follow. What kind of information is being noted in each?
What are the important features of each?

example	kind of note	information being recorded	main features
a)	linear and pattern	3 main ideas about how languages originated	• indentations • tree diagrams • symbols • abbreviations • headings

a) *Origin of language*
      ~~Was there ever an original language?~~

   - *3 main views*

- *Monogenesis:* ~~ie there was once one~~ only one original *language → migration etc. → many languages, i.e.:*

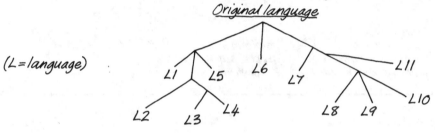

(L = language)

- *polygenesis:* ~~ie~~ *several different original langs qt c. same time*

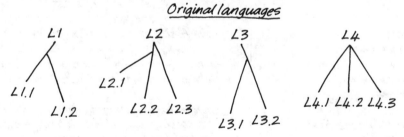

- *third possibility:* ~~only one~~ several *original languages, but only one main family extant*
(*i.e. others now extinct*)

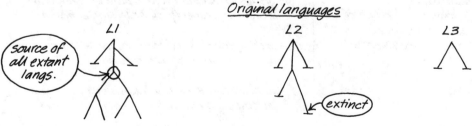

b)   *Electromagnetic spectrum*

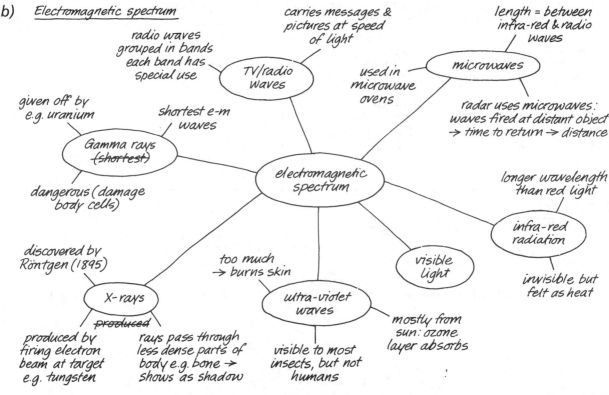

---

c)   *Pros & cons of whaling*

- Norway & Japan want annual quota so can kill <u>minke</u> whales (smallest kind)

For	Against
- numbers are increasing → low quota would not endanger species	- overfishing is main reason for lower quantities of fish
	make money
- some whales eat fish → threaten income of fishermen	- whales more ~~useful~~ alive → increasing income from whale watching by tourists
too many	
- small whales ~~are~~ reduce the food needed by larger whales	- whales live longer than humans, live in families, are specialised and intelligent animals; emotional part of brain well-developed
- whales are no more intelligent than other animals which can be killed	- methods of killing are cruel (can take 30 mins. to die)
traditional	
- whaling part of national way of life of ~~some~~ countries such as Norway & Japan → ~~resent~~ foreign interference unjustified	- groups of whales migrate around the world; are ∴ not property of any single nation
	- lack of scientific evidence about whether numbers of whales are really increasing
	- just because there is a tradition of whaling in a country does not justify it = ~~fighting cocks~~

d)   <u>Maslow's Hierarchy of Needs</u>
 - Maslow identified number of basic human needs
 - seen as being in a ~~hierach~~ hierarchy i.e. lower ones must be satisfied before individual motivated by higher ones, <u>viz</u>:

   - ~~aesthetic needs: desire to appreciate beauty etc~~.

   - desire to know and understand

   - ~~need for self-actualisation~~

<u>Type of need</u>   <u>example</u>

Self-realisation	- Achievement - Psychological growth
Ego	- Station - Respect - Prestige
Social	- Friendship, group acceptance - Love
Security	- Freedom from danger - Freedom from want
Physiological	- Food, drink, shelter, sex, warmth, physical

e)   <u>Causes of the collapse of communism in E. Europe & S. Union</u>
   - complicated set of reasons why comm. collapsed in E.E. & S.U.

<u>1. Political</u>   in S.U.
   - Gorbachev (1985 →) encouraged public criticism (~~glasnost~~) → ~~emerge~~ rise of political opposition & independence movements in e.g. Baltics.
   - effect also felt in E.E.

<u>2. Economic</u>
   - perhaps largest single factor
   - communist parties ~~f~~ had failed in main aim i.e. improve living standards of whole pop.
   S.U.
   - ↓centralised economy → prices set by govt.
     → in 20s & 30s (Stalin) state ownership of most companies, "collectivisation" of farms
       → ~~sate~~ produced industrialisation, full employment etc. but no long-term development,
       ∴ lack of incentives to ~~the~~ innovate
 - low agric.
 productivity ⎫   - diff. industries concentrated in diff. areas (e.g. Ukraine - iron, steel, coal etc.) → high costs
 & high   ⎬   of transporting ~~was~~ raw mats ~~slow~~
 transport ⎭
 costs   ⎭ → - ~~for much of economy also used for~~ focus on military production → fewer resources for
                    other areas
   - in 1980s, communist countries began to spend more on imports than earned from exports; also, ban by West on trade in new technology
   - prices of food and consumer goods rose faster than wages
   - from 1987, Gorbachev opened up economy to international & private trade

Task 1.4

There is no single, best layout for notes – it depends on what suits you best, the purpose of the notes, and the topic you are taking notes on. The point is that notes need to show the connection between ideas, i.e. the way the information is organised. This should be reflected in the way your notes are laid out.

↗ Think about the notes you have taken for various classes. You may wish to refer to some of these notes if they are available.

1 What method(s) of note-taking do you tend to use?
2 Do you sometimes use one method and at other times another? If so, when do you tend to use them?
3 Have you ever simply copied word-for-word, in sentences, from the text? Why? Is it an efficient method? Discuss.
4 Look at the list of main features in Task 1.3. Which of these features do you use? Are there any additional features that you feel should be added? What are they?

Task 1.5

It is important to make notes with an active frame of mind about the value of the information. One way of doing this is to make two kinds of notes as you go along: firstly, notes about the points in the reading or talk, *and, secondly, notes about what the points bring to your mind* (e.g. about any questions you have about the information, any connections it brings to mind with other information you know or are studying, and so on).

↗ a) When you have taken notes in the past, have you made any personal comments or notes? If so, what kind of comments did you make? If not, why not?

↗ b) With two or three other students, discuss the importance of making these kinds of notes, using examples from various notes you have made in the past.

Task 1.6

Notes must be significantly shorter than the original. Thus, abbreviations and symbols should be used whenever possible.

a) Look at the abbreviations used in the notes in Task 1.3. What do they stand for?

b) Make abbreviations or symbols for the following:

1 equal to	11 therefore
2 approximately	12 that is to say
3 does not equal	13 this is important
4 especially	14 greater than
5 for example	15 degrees
6 compare	16 as a result
7 century	17 less than
8 because	18 reference
9 number	19 similar to
10 equivalent to	20 and

c) What other abbreviations and symbols do you know? What do they mean?

Task 1.7

A final note on note-taking! We advise you always to write down where your notes have been taken from. It will save you hours of searching for some detail you need for your work or bibliography. In lecture notes, make sure you note the name of anyone quoted and where the quote has been taken from. You can then find it if you wish to make more detailed use of the information. (See pages 48–9, about source cards.)

Look at the notes that follow. Which have adequately noted where the information can be found? List the items you think are essential to a good reference note.

1 'Black Holes' – *Journal of Physical Sciences*, 3/6
2 Hoggart on D. H. Lawrence (BBC), audio tape 53
3 Kennedy re Macroeconomics (1985)
4 Moore Greenhouse Effect, (2nd edition) p35–38

2 TAKING NOTES WHEN READING

An important part of effective reading for study purposes is the ability to take concise, precise notes. This means asking yourself why you are taking the notes (for an essay, exam, background information, ...), what is the best method to use for the information (outline, flow chart, spidergraph, linear notes, ...) and what method is most convenient for yourself.

Task 2.1

Albert has been making notes on the article on 'Global Warming' (opposite) for his Environmental Sciences course.

➤ a) Evaluate Albert's notes in terms of the criteria from Task 1.2. Discuss your findings with two or three other students.

Greenhouse effect
great threat – need solution: first causes and effects
1. CO_2 from burning forests and oil and coal; chlorofluorocarbons 23%?
24 bill. tons carbon di. every year
$\times 2 = 1740$
$20\,C$
temperature $> 1/20$
*   oceans $> 10\,cms$*
kettle boils 30 years Present g.w. thus from 60s
$2030 = +1.3$ $2070 = +3$
effects: flooding in Egypt and on islands (my country)
b) less rain $>$ smaller harvests (20%)
c) Britain warmer
CO_2 in ice and sea $>$ escape $>$ more warming (positive feedback!)

➤ b) With two or three other students, make any improvements in Albert's notes that you feel are necessary.

Task 2.2

It is easy for notes to become more detailed than they need to be. One technique for coping with this problem is to highlight[*] (or underline) the most important information or ideas in your notes. This technique can also be used with your own books and photocopies, and this helps to cut down on note-taking as well.

➤ a) Take notes on the passage in Unit 11, Task 5.1, 'Is the planet Earth cracking up?' Use whatever method of note-taking you feel is the most suitable and comfortable for you.

➤ b) With two or three other students, compare the content of your notes. Which parts do you have in common? Do you feel these are the most important parts? See if you can agree on what is the most important information, and then highlight or underline it.

Global Warming – The Greenhouse Effect

It is generally agreed that the greatest threat facing the world today is the warming up of the earth's atmosphere, commonly called global warming or the greenhouse effect. It is the world's biggest problem because it is truly a world-wide problem. It involves everything in the world, from the North to the South Poles, from the bottom of the oceans to the edge of the atmosphere. We therefore obviously need to find a solution to it. But first of all, we need to be clear about what it is that causes the greenhouse effect, and what the likely future consequences of global warming will be, if it is allowed to go on happening unchecked. This should help us to see more clearly why we need to do something about it, and what we might do.

First, then, the causes. Basically, we have been producing too many of the gases which, when they are released into the earth's atmosphere, trap heat, and thus raise its temperature. There are several gases involved, but the main ones are carbon dioxide and chlorofluorocarbons – often called CFCs. The carbon dioxide comes from burning forests and from burning fossil fuels such as oil and coal. The CFCs are given off by refrigerators and air-conditioning systems. Carbon dioxide is to blame for 56% of the greenhouse effect, and CFCs for 23%.

We now dump 24 billion tonnes of carbon dioxide into the atmosphere every year. If this figure were to double, the average global temperature could go up between 1 to 4 degrees C. That may not sound like much, but a two degree rise would make the world hotter than it has ever been in human history. Unfortunately, to make matters worse, the warming effect may not make itself apparent until it is too late. The temperature of the world has risen by more than half a degree this century, and the oceans have risen by at least 10 cms. But just as it takes time for a kettle of water to boil, so it may have taken 30 years or so for the oceans to swell. This means that the global warming we are experiencing now is only a result of the carbon dioxide and other gases we have dumped into the atmosphere up to the 1960s. Since then, our use of fossil fuels has increased rapidly. In other words, the damage may have already been done. Temperatures are expected to increase by at least 1.3°C by 2030, and 3°C by the year 2070.

What will such rises in global temperature mean for the peoples of the world? A warmer climate will increase sea levels. In Western Europe, the Dutch and the people in some eastern parts of England will have to build more effective sea defences. But the effects will be much greater for the developing countries. Egypt will lose land in the Nile Delta, a food producing area. Millions of people could lose their homes in the Ganges Delta of India and Bangladesh. The same is likely to happen to the dwellers on the hundreds of low-lying islands in the Pacific and Indian oceans.

Another effect will be to threaten food supplies. There have been reports which show that if the world becomes warmer and drier, crop harvests in parts of Europe, North America, North Africa and the southern CIS will be cut. The famine problem in northern Africa will also worsen, since rainfall in the Sahara and beyond will fall by 20%.

But rising seas and falling harvests will only be the start. The world will not necessarily become warmer at the same rate everywhere. The tropics could still experience the same temperatures, but the poles could heat up by an extra 10 or 12 degrees. This could cause changes in the routes of the ocean currents, such as the Gulf Stream, which warms Britain. This could have a drastic effect on the climate of the countries affected.

Also, the land between the temperate zones and the North Pole area contains a lot of carbon dioxide, which, at present, cannot escape because it is frozen. If this region warms up, however, the gas will escape into the atmosphere, warming it still further. Another similar effect may take place as the seas become warmer. Cold seas dissolve carbon; warm seas release it. At present, more carbon is stored by the seas than released. But suppose warmer seas started giving off more carbon than they absorb? This is called positive feedback – each change further increases the rate of change. In other words, the greater the warming of the atmosphere, the greater the chance that other changes will occur which will also warm the atmosphere further, and so on. This is the ultimate nightmare: that the greenhouse effect may reach a critical mass, as in a nuclear chain reaction, where it is no longer possible to control.

Task 2.3

It is helpful to be able to take notes using a variety of techniques in order to choose the one most suitable for a particular reading.

 a) Read this passage and write linear and pattern notes on it.

Sick Work Places

It is being increasingly recognised that the way many modern buildings are constructed and maintained is leading to poorer health among the people who work in them.

5 The main problem is the way that air is handled. In the past, it was possible to open a window for relief from the smoker at the next desk. Nowadays, however, many buildings are sealed because air-conditioning and

10 ventilation are supposed to eliminate problems. But, as the frequent black streaks on the ceiling near air vents show, much of the dirt in the air is merely being recirculated and therefore constantly breathed by the

15 inhabitants of the building.

Most office blocks have air ducts and vents running right through them. These can become full of dust and pollutants such as fumes from cigarettes and photocopiers and

20 chemicals like formaldehyde leaking from carpets or adhesives from materials used to construct the building, and so on. These substances can stay in the air for years.

Unfortunately, energy conservation can

25 make the problem worse. Switching off air-conditioning and heating at night causes condensation. This creates the damp conditions that help bacteria and fungi to grow. When the system comes on again in the

30 morning, they are sprayed into the building. One third of buildings operate on perpetually recycled air.

One study has claimed that 80% of air-conditioned office blocks are 'sick' – in other

35 words, staff complain of headaches, allergies, rashes, nausea and lethargy. However, other studies have shown that workers in normally ventilated offices sometimes have the same symptoms. Thus, there must be factors other

40 than air-conditioning which are also to blame.

Some researchers feel that stress may be important in understanding the causes of sick building syndrome. For example, it may be that with the change from typewriters to word

45 processors in many offices, workers are 'chained' to their desks and driven at the speed of their machines. These working conditions cause stress, and people under stress are much more aware of physical

50 discomfort and are much more likely to suffer from backache, eyestrain, sore throats and other symptoms of sick building syndrome.

Some scientists have found that another possible cause of the problem is sensitivity to

55 everyday materials such as carpet fibres and furniture adhesives. An international conference on health and buildings in Stockholm last year was told that 40% of people in Sweden had some form of common

60 allergy to such materials. When many people are put in a building full of such materials, it is therefore natural that some of them will react negatively.

Finally, another view is that the problem

65 stems not from air-conditioning but air changing. According to this explanation, managers of buildings are so incompetent or ignorant about them that they do not ensure workers have enough clean air. Normal

70 maintenance, such as cleaning ducts regularly, is neglected, and air is constantly recycled instead of being exchanged.

---

 b) In groups, compare the different notes you took. Did everyone include the same details? Did the different methods of taking notes lead to different information being recorded? Is the relationship between ideas the same in both sets of notes? Which method did you feel made you more actively involved in the text? Which method do you feel is best suited to this passage? To you?

3 TAKING NOTES WHEN LISTENING

Task 3.1

When you are trying to take notes from someone speaking, it is important to realise how spoken communication differs from writing. When listening to a lecturer, you need to consider the following:
– the way of speaking (e.g. speeding up or going slower; using less or more emphasis; repeating a point, etc.);
– use of aids (blackboard, OHP*, etc.);
– use of set expressions (e.g. 'Right', etc.)
Hint If you are inexperienced in listening to lectures in English, think of examples from your own language – the points will be similar.

communication goes beyond words.

a) Think about what lecturers you are familiar with normally do.
1 Do they change their speed of speaking? When? Why?
2 Do they repeat or rephrase ideas? When? Why?
3 Do they use gestures or change position? When? Why?
4 Do they use any pictures or aids? What kind? Why?
5 Do they use any set expressions? Which ones? Why?
6 What other non-verbal clues* do they use? Which ones? Why?

b) With two or three other students, discuss your ideas.

LISTEN TO THE WAY THE WHOLE BODY TALKS.

Task 3.2

It is important when listening to the speaker to anticipate what will be said, and what method of note-taking will be needed.

a) Listen to these extracts from different lectures and decide which note style would be most appropriate. Choose from the following styles, and be prepared to give your reasons.
Note More than one style may be possible for each extract.
1 spidergraph
2 flow chart
3 table
4 linear
5 diagram
6 other (explain)

CHOOSE THE RIGHT NOTE STYLE!

b) Now take notes on each extract using the appropriate note style. Compare your notes with two or three other students.

Task 3.3

Taking notes while listening requires listeners to make decisions about organisation and the importance and relationship of ideas as they listen. The listener rarely gets a second chance to hear something that was missed.

a) Take notes on this lecture about what can be done to reduce the dangers of global warming.

b) With another student, compare and evaluate your notes using the criteria discussed earlier in this unit. What made you decide to take the notes in the style you chose?

c) How well do you feel you did? Discuss any problems you had and how these might be overcome.

d) You may wish to listen to the cassette again in order to improve your notes, or to try an alternative method of recording the same information.

4 MAKING NOTES FOR WRITING OR SPEAKING

Writing and speaking for study purposes require you to put your ideas into note form – to make notes, often drawing from different sets of notes you have previously taken when reading and listening. You will need to use this skill in the units on discussions and writing later in this book.

Task 4.1

One of the more difficult parts of note-taking is organising notes so that they can be retrieved when needed. You may need to locate notes that you took months or even years ago and then be able to make sense of them. Many notes may never be looked at again after they have been taken, but it is often difficult to know which notes you may need.

   Different students organise their notes in different ways: some put them according to class/date or class/topic, and store them in ring binders. Others store them according to importance and likely use, highlighting key words so that topics can be readily located. Some students organise by topic, mixing notes and photocopies of related materials together; some keep each separate. There does not seem to be any one best way.

a) With two or three other students, discuss what use you make of your notes: for exams, for essays, for seminars and discussions, ... Are there some notes you make no further use of?

b) How do you organise your notes at the moment? How do you think your system could be improved, or is it just right now? How do you think you may need to organise notes for future studies?

Task 4.2

One way to organise specific notes that are likely to be used in future note-making is by using *note cards*. These can be filed according to topic, and then be shuffled or rearranged when making notes. Note cards usually contain important quotes, points, summaries of main ideas or statistics – *one quote/topic* to a note card. This is important: if a note card contains three or four different topics or quotes, it becomes like a piece of paper and difficult to rearrange ideas as needed. The *topic* of the card should be at the top of each note card so that you can store similar cards together and know roughly what is on the card without reading it in detail. If you do decide it is helpful to put your notes on cards, remember to record the source and page on each card. (See pages 48–9 for details on how to make source cards.)

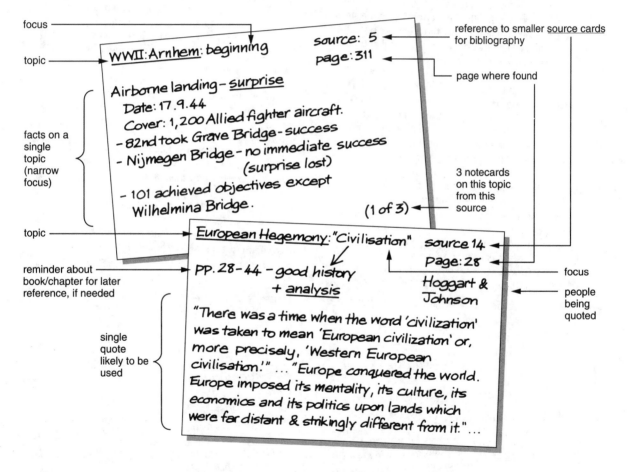

focus

topic

facts on a single topic (narrow focus)

topic

reminder about book/chapter for later reference, if needed

single quote likely to be used

reference to smaller <u>source cards</u> for bibliography

page where found

3 notecards on this topic from this source

focus

people being quoted

WWII: Arnhem: beginning   source: 5   page: 311

Airborne landing – <u>surprise</u>
   Date: 17.9.44
   Cover: 1,200 Allied fighter aircraft.
   – 82nd took Grave Bridge – success
   – Nijmegen Bridge – no immediate success
                              (surprise lost)
   – 101 achieved objectives except
      Wilhelmina Bridge.   (1 of 3)

European Hegemony: "Civilisation"   source 14   Page: 28

PP. 28-44 – good history
          + <u>analysis</u>   Hoggart &
                                            Johnson

"There was a time when the word 'civilization'
was taken to mean 'European civilization' or,
more precisely, 'Western European
civilisation!' ... "Europe conquered the world.
Europe imposed its mentality, its culture, its
economics and its politics upon lands which
were far distant & strikingly different from it." ...

a) Use the two note cards above as models for making your own note cards, one on global warming and one on the characteristics of the world's main religions. You will need to use your original notes for reference.

b) Do you feel that making note cards could be useful in your studies? Discuss.

Task 4.3

Often different sources present conflicting information on a topic. As a student you will be required to acknowledge both sets of information.

a) You are studying International Politics. Read and take notes on the main points in the passages below, which are concerned with the peace-keeping role of the United Nations. Use whatever note-taking method seems most suitable. Your purpose is to gather background information for an essay on the topic.

The peace-keeping powers of the UN

The United Nations Charter states that one of its main aims is 'to save succeeding generations from the scourge of war'. But how effective are the steps the UN can take if a country threatens the peace?

5   First, the Security Council – a 15-member body – can ask the warring countries to settle their differences peacefully. The International Court of Justice may be asked to decide who is right and who is wrong. The Security Council may also ask
10   UN members to stop trading with one or more of the countries (i.e. impose 'sanctions'), and so on. But, if moves such as these fail, the UN may use military force to stop the countries fighting.

The Security Council may decide to send a
15   'peace-keeping force' to prevent new outbreaks of fighting, supervise the withdrawal of troops, maintain a buffer zone between two hostile nations or groups, and patrol areas where a ceasefire has been agreed. It may also send an 'observer'
20   mission, which is unarmed, to monitor troop withdrawals or a ceasefire. The UN Charter also allows military 'enforcement' action to be taken

when sanctions and peaceful methods of resolving the conflict have failed.
25   However, in practice, the provisions laid down in Chapter VII of the Charter for such military action have not been followed. What happened in Korea (1950) and in Kuwait (1991) was that member states sent their own troops to enforce specific UN
30   resolutions. This was authorised by the Security Council. As the term 'peace-keeping' does not appear in the UN Charter and has never been formally defined, the technique has evolved according to events.
35   The first peace-keeping force was used in 1948, and others have been involved regularly in conflicts around the globe since then. But the role of these forces is limited. Under present regulations, such forces are only lightly armed for self-defence. They
40   work under strict limits: they must be impartial; they can fire only in self-defence; the countries involved must consent to their presence; and they are not supposed to be sent in until ceasefires take effect.

Strengthening the UN's peace-keeping role

It is increasingly recognised that the current peace-keeping resources and powers of the UN are too limited to enable it to intervene effectively in many conflicts. One solution would be to create 'peace
5   enforcement units', to be made available in clearly-defined circumstances. These would be more heavily armed than peace-keeping forces. They would be on call to do jobs the peace-keepers do not expect to do, such as restore and maintain a ceasefire.
10   Another proposal is the creation of a strong,

permanent UN force – made up from members of ten to twenty UN member states – which could be sent to a trouble zone at 24 hours notice. This well-equipped force would be used to deter potential
15   aggressors, to halt conflict between warring sides in a civil war (such as in former Yugoslavia) and, if necessary, to fight as well as police. Article 43 of the Charter allows for this, but until now the international climate has not made it possible.
20   Another idea is to strengthen the powers of

the UN to intervene in conflicts taking place within the borders of a single country, as opposed to between two or more countries. Historically, the UN has tended to limit its role to the latter, as the
25 sovereignty of individual nation states has been regarded as the more important factor. However, as critics of this policy point out, it is often the case that internal conflicts threaten the peace as much or even more than international conflicts.
30 Therefore, to play a meaningful role in global peace-keeping, it is argued that the UN's powers to intervene in internal conflicts should be strengthened.

Finally, in order to get around the problem that
35 the UN already has of getting its members to pay their subscriptions, on which its peace-keeping efforts depend, it has also been proposed that there should be a new tax on arms sales, which would help to pay for current and future UN
40 peace-keeping activities.

Problems

The end of the Cold War in 1989–90 saw a dramatic change at the UN. Western and communist countries no longer blocked each other's plans automatically. This was shown most clearly in the Gulf conflict.
5 The US, Britain, France and the Soviet Union worked closely together, even though the Soviet Union and France did not always agree with the US proposals and made independent proposals of their own. China was the least co-operative, but did not use its
10 veto (the power to reject a resolution) in the Security Council. In other countries where hostility between East and West had been one reason for lack of action, such as in Cambodia and Angola, it was now possible for the UN to send forces.
15 But there are many controversies over the expansion of the UN's peace activities. First, the 1990–91 Gulf conflict created an expectation that there would be more military enforcement rather than peace-keeping operations. But many small and
20 middle-sized countries are worried that a precedent might be set, justifying intervention in their affairs by more powerful nations.

Secondly, some conflicts have been dealt with mainly by the US, which has received approval for its
25 actions. But critics say this is not the same as a proper UN operation. They fear that, in practice, such a policy will enable the US to use the UN for its own interests, rather than create a stronger peace-keeping role for the UN. They point out that, already,
30 the US has tended to decide on action and then seek UN approval afterwards. Also, where it has been ready to send in its own troops, it has kept them under US command, as in both the Gulf and Somalia.
35 Thirdly, critics say that sending troops to a zone of conflict such as Somalia can mean the real difficulties of a country are neglected. Instead of trying to solve the political and economic problems of such countries, in other words, the military option
40 might be used more and more as 'the be-all and end-all'.

Fourthly, there are doubts about the value of both old and new UN peace-keeping operations. They have been criticised, for example, for only limiting
45 the danger of war, rather than bringing about a genuine settlement. Thus, Canada withdrew its UN troops from Cyprus, because it felt it could no longer justify their presence after 28 years of failure to achieve a settlement. Similarly, both sides in the
50 Bosnian conflict have reacted negatively to UN intervention.

b) Now, make notes for an essay on 'Should the peace-keeping capabilities of the UN be strengthened?', using the information from your notes.

c) Were your notes satisfactory, or did you have to go back to the original passages? Compare your notes with those of two or three other students. How did they differ? How could the notes have been improved?

Task 4.4

Sometimes you will be given material to study which illustrates different perspectives on the same topic. As a student, you need to be able to take into account both perspectives.

a) You are doing a course on Teaching and Learning in Higher Education. Listen and take notes on the two lectures about 'Training in learning how to learn'.

b) Prepare your own point of view on the topic, for a discussion about 'The value of training in learning how to learn'. Make notes on what you wish to say, using your notes from both lectures.

c) Compare your notes with those of two or three other students. What kind of notes did you use? How did you combine the sets of notes? Did you make use of all the information in both sets of notes that you took?

5 UNIT ASSESSMENT AND APPLICATION

Much of a student's life seems to revolve around notes – either taking or making them.

Task 5.1

Notes can serve a variety of purposes. It is important for students to realise what these are in order to take notes effectively and efficiently.

Which of the following reasons for note-taking are the most important; the least important? Discuss.
1 to record facts and processes accurately
2 to remember precisely what was said or spoken
3 to help the note-taker think things through
4 to make a short record of long, involved ideas
5 to jog the memory at a later time
6 to keep a record of different points of view
7 to organise ideas for note-making
8 to focus the reader's/listener's attention

Task 5.2

Note-taking and making require lots and lots of practice to master. It is not enough to be told how, and then to try several examples. It must become an integral part of your study.

With two or three other students, discuss what parts of note-taking and note-making you find most difficult. How much extra practice do you feel you need? Which of the following do you find most difficult: taking notes about facts; about processes; about opinions; combining notes to make a set of your own ideas; or what?

UNIT 6 Coping with extended English

When you study in higher education in English, you have to be able to extract and make use of information from large quantities of written and spoken English in a short amount of time. This unit focuses on strategies* for handling this aspect of your studies.

1 READING AND LISTENING FOR STUDY PURPOSES

Some strategies for dealing with large amounts of reading and listening in English are more successful than others. Which ones do you use at the moment?

Task 1.1

How do you usually read a chapter in a textbook or an article in a journal?

THE JUMP INTO HIGHER EDUCATION.

a) Look at the statements which follow. Write down the numbers and put a tick (✔) if the statement corresponds to what you normally do, put a cross (✗) if it doesn't, and put a question mark (?) if you are not sure.
1 I skim-read (look quickly through) to get a general idea of what it is about before I begin.
2 I start to read at the beginning and read right through.
3 As I read, I ask myself what I already know about the topic.
4 As I read, I ask myself what I will be tested on.
5 I ask myself how the different parts relate to each other.
6 Whenever I come across an unknown word, I look it up in the dictionary.
7 I try to use diagrams and visuals to help me understand.
8 I read every word carefully.
9 I highlight the main ideas.
10 My approach is basically the same, whatever book or article I am reading.

b) With two or three other students, discuss why you use the strategies you ticked, and why you do not use the other ones.

c) With two or three other students, discuss which statements you think indicate good reading habits. Give reasons for your views.

Task 1.2

Extended listening is different from extended reading in certain aspects, and therefore some additional strategies are required. How do you usually listen to a lecture?

a) Listen to Marion and Alistair discuss their experiences in listening to lectures. Make a list of their problems.

b) With two or three other students, discuss how Marion and Alistair's problems with listening to lectures compare with any problems you have had. Are there any similarities? Are there any additional problems you have experienced?

c) With two or three other students, make a list of statements you would associate with a good approach to extended listening. Your statements should be similar to the statements for good reading habits in Task 1.1.

Task 1.3   How good is your current approach?

How satisfactory is your current approach to reading and listening for study purposes? What are the main differences and similarities between your approach and the good reading and listening strategies you have identified? What areas do you need to concentrate on improving?

2 READING AND LISTENING ACTIVELY

Effective reading and listening for information is an *active* process. In order to understand and remember new information, it has to be linked as closely as possible to what you know already. This means actively using the knowledge you already have.

Task 2.1

Students who adopt an active approach constantly ask themselves questions as they read or listen.

a) Marion and Alistair made a list of some of the basic questions they ask themselves when they are reading and listening. Here are the three they thought were the most important ones:

1 Why am I reading or listening?
2 Where does the reading or talk fit into what I am studying?
3 What do I know about the topic already?

What do you think of their questions? Are there any others you would add?

↬ b) With two or three other students, compare and discuss your ideas. Reach a consensus* about a list of all the most important questions.

Task 2.2

Whenever you listen or read you need to understand what your goals are.

↬ a) Why are you reading *Study Tasks in English*? List your reasons, then compare them with those of two or three other students. How have the reasons affected the way you have read *Study Tasks in English*? Have you all read all the book with equal interest and concentration? Do some parts seem more interesting or relevant?

↬ b) Discuss whether you usually have clear reasons for reading or listening in your studies. Give three examples. How do your reasons affect the way you read or listen?

Task 2.3

Another important part of reading or listening actively is predicting. This means using your existing knowledge about the information you are reading or listening to so that you can make intelligent guesses about what is going to come next. This helps your mind to be more prepared, and therefore to understand better.

↬ a) Look at the following excerpts from the beginnings of readings or discussions. What predictions can you make about what will follow? What main points will probably be covered? What key words are likely to be used?

1 War Crimes Trials

'War is hell,' said General Sherman, a commander in the American Civil war. This statement accurately describes the bloody campaign that he waged. Yet it was this war which marked the beginning of the modern laws of warfare. At the end of the Civil War in 1865 Henry Wirz, a former confederate officer, was tried and convicted for ill-treating and murdering prisoners.

There had been rules before, but this war saw the introduction of a formal and comprehensive code to guide troops in the field. These ideas have been progressively refined, first in the Hague Conventions of 1899 and 1907, and then in the Geneva Conventions of 1949 and 1977 . . .

2 Censorship

Views about censorship are of two main kinds. Supporters of censorship take the view that the loss of freedom that censorship involves is a necessary evil, because there is likely to be a far greater loss of freedom without censorship than with it. Opponents of censorship argue that censorship itself is a far greater threat to freedom than any of the dangers it supposedly guards against . . .

> ### 3 From a Sociology seminar on poverty:
>
> RICHARD: In my view, poverty is the major cause of crime. If we got rid of economic problems, most crime would disappear.
>
> ALAN: I agree that poverty is one of the major causes of crime, but is your argument that if we got rid of poverty, we would get rid of crime?
>
> LINDA: Just a minute, can I just get clear what you two are saying? First of all, is your point that crime is caused by poverty?

b) Now look at the whole of each of the texts on pages 79, 82–3, and 86–7. Compare your predictions with the actual contents.

c) Do you feel you did a good job of predicting? What helped you make successful predictions? Were there any 'clues' you overlooked? Were any of your conclusions illogical? Discuss your ideas with two or three other students.

Task 2.4

Another part of adopting an active approach to dealing with extended English is to look for the way ideas are connected together. Study information is always organised into some kind of pattern or framework. Actively looking for this pattern helps you to understand the information better, because you can see how the parts fit together.

IT'S ALL A MATTER OF HOW THE PIECES FIT TOGETHER

a) Match the following types of information with the ways you would expect them to be organised. More than one type of organisation may be used with the same information.

Information	*Organisation*
1 how a general election takes place	a) comparison/contrast
2 studying in the UK vs. US	b) cause > effect
3 experiment with different materials	c) list of points
4 how AIDS is spread	d) series of steps
5 reasons for developing a town centre	e) points for and against
6 evaluation of alternative methods of transport	f) less > more important
7 description of an aspect of language	g) general > particular
8 survey of opinion about the United Nations	h) hypothesis* > procedure > result > conclusion
9 discussion of different concepts of history	i) chronological * order
10 causes of global warming	j) set of examples
11 explanation of a computer program	k) categories
12 ideas for overcoming inflation	l) hierarchy*
13 study of the influence of a novelist	
14 how the US is governed	
15 wildlife in a nature reserve	
16 study of child development	

b) What are the patterns of organisation in the texts on pages 61 and 82–3?

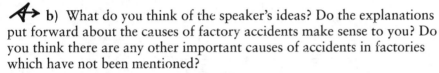 c) Look at an article in a journal or a chapter in a book for another class if one is available. With two or three other students, discuss how the information in it is organised. What clues help you decide?

Task 2.5

Getting the main ideas from what you read or listen to is obviously vital. However, another important part of active reading and listening is to *think about* the information in the reading or lecture as much as possible.

In other words, as you read or listen, it is important not only to ask the question:

What is the reading or talk about?
but also:

What do I think of the ideas?

How can I use the ideas?

This will help you to remember and understand the information more deeply.

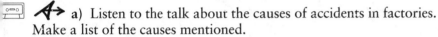 a) Listen to the talk about the causes of accidents in factories. Make a list of the causes mentioned.

b) What do you think of the speaker's ideas? Do the explanations put forward about the causes of factory accidents make sense to you? Do you think there are any other important causes of accidents in factories which have not been mentioned?

c) Use the information in the talk and your own ideas to make a set of recommendations for preventing accidents in factories.

d) Think about a recent reading or talk in your studies. With two or three other students, discuss these questions:

1 What was it about?
2 What did you think of the ideas put forward?
3 How did (or could) you put them into practice?

Task 2.6

Not all readings or lectures are equally useful. You must always actively assess your purpose for reading or listening and then structure your reading and listening techniques accordingly. This is the *active* approach to extended reading and listening.

How successful and efficient are you at using the active approach? Which aspects of it do you feel you have mastered? What do you feel you need more practice in?

3 READING AND LISTENING EFFICIENTLY

In addition to reading and listening actively, it is just as important to read and listen *efficiently*, i.e. to do what is necessary to obtain the information you want as straightforwardly as possible. This means, for example, varying your techniques of reading or listening to suit your purpose, developing strategies for dealing with unfamiliar grammar and vocabulary, making effective use of study aids, and so on.

Task 3.1

How efficient is your reading and listening? How relevant and accurate is the information you collect?

a) Make a table like the one below and list three articles or books and two lectures you have read or attended recently. How efficient was your reading or listening, i.e. did you obtain the information you wanted?

Book/lecture	Your approach: how efficient?		
	I obtained the information I wanted	I had difficulty obtaining some of the information I wanted	I was unable to obtain most of the information I wanted

b) Why do you think your reading or listening was efficient or inefficient in these cases? Compare your reasons in groups.

Task 3.2

When you are reading or listening for information, you need to locate the information you want as quickly as possible. The techniques for doing this are similar whether the source is a textbook, a short article in a journal, or a lecture, and largely depend on the type of information being sought.

If the information concerns the main ideas – the gist[*] – you will need the techniques involved in *skimming*[*].

If it concerns specific details, you will need the techniques involved in *scanning*[*].

It is important to identify the kind of information being sought in order to select the appropriate technique to find the information.

Say which reading strategy (i.e. skimming or scanning) you would use to locate each of the following by deciding whether the information is concerned with the *gist* or with *specific details*:

1 kinds of hydraulic systems used in cars
2 why, in economics, 'Small is beautiful'
3 the year the U.N. was founded
4 types of light waves
5 how the laser works
6 teachers' attitudes towards large classes

7 number of children bitten by dogs
8 procedures for preventing dogs attacking children

Task 3.3

The techniques used in skimming and scanning are largely based on using cues* within the text.
Note There are some differences between written and spoken texts in this respect, but the principles are similar.

Look at the following list of parts of texts. What kind of information is contained in each part – main ideas or specific details?
1 title of whole text or section
2 introduction
3 information after '*for example*'
4 information after '*in other words*'
5 first sentence in a paragraph
6 body of a paragraph
7 footnotes
8 conclusion
9 parts with special emphasis, bold print, slower, clearer speaking
10 information after '*to illustrate this*'
11 key words related to the specific questions you formed beforehand
12 layout of a piece of writing

Task 3.4

Skimming is often used in order to summarise the main ideas in what you are reading or listening to, or to determine whether it is necessary to read an article in greater detail.

a) What is the gist of each of the paragraphs in the article in Unit 5, Task 2.1?

b) Listen to the talk by Mrs Peters on the British educational system. What is the gist of her talk? What are the five main aspects she covers?

➤ c) With two or three other students, compare your answers. What parts of the reading and talk did you use to find your answers? Did you need to read/listen to all of it equally closely?

➤ d) With two or three other students, write down at least three techniques that can help you to get the gist of a reading or a talk.

Task 3.5

Often extended reading or listening involves looking for specific details. In this case, your reason for reading is not to determine the main ideas, or even to know how the ideas are organised. You are searching for specific facts, often hidden in a dense forest of words, i.e. scanning the information. If this is your reason for reading or listening, you need to let your eye or brain 'float' over the words, until key words are encountered which focus your attention. The points you are looking for can usually be stated as questions.

➤ a) Scan the text on Global Warming on page 61 to answer the questions that follow.
1 What are the two main gases involved in the 'greenhouse' effect?
2 How much has the world's temperature risen this century?
3 How much are temperatures likely to rise to by 2070?
4 How much will rainfall in the Sahara area fall by?
5 How much could the temperature rise by at the poles?

➤ b) Listen again to Mrs Peters' talk, this time scanning it in order to answer the following questions.
1 What is the age for compulsory schooling in Britain?
2 How many universities are there?
3 What are the two main secondary-level examinations called?
4 What is the teacher:pupil ratio at the primary and secondary levels?
5 What is the highest point on the basic salary scale for primary and secondary school teachers?

➤ c) With two or three other students, compare your answers. What were the key words in each question? (The key words in the first question have already been underlined.) Discuss how you located the answers. Where were the answers normally located?

➤ d) With two or three other students, write down at least three techniques that can help you to locate specific information.

4 COPING WITH WORDS

When dealing efficiently with extended English, it is helpful to know as much grammar and vocabulary as possible. But it is unlikely that you will ever know as much as you would like. There will probably always be unfamiliar words or structures that you come across.

Task 4.1

Unknown words, just because they are unknown, are not necessarily worth trying to understand. Also, the meaning of unknown words which are important to understand can often be worked out using knowledge you already have, i.e. without going to the dictionary. On the other hand, there will be times when using the dictionary or grammar book is the best course of action. The key is to adopt a flexible approach, using the most appropriate strategy for each problem.

a) Go through the following text quickly (i.e. without trying to understand it) and underline all the words you do not know.

Global warming

Global warming, caused by 'greenhouse' gases such as carbon dioxide, could radically alter the lives of millions of people. Many scientists believe that the world's climate is already growing warmer, and that
5   industrial nations must take urgent action.
    The rising concentration of carbon dioxide in the atmosphere over the past two centuries has been a direct result of industrialisation. Although there is still disagreement about the amount by which
10 governments need to limit such emissions, there is a growing consensus that new controls are needed urgently. However, some countries, including Britain, the United States and some Arab oil producers, believe that tough new laws to limit pollution will be
15 politically unpopular and economically difficult and expensive to implement.

---

b) The text is the beginning of an article you want to use in your Economics class for an essay on 'Economics and the environment'. Now read it again carefully.

1 Which of the words you underlined is it essential to understand?
2 Of these words, which of them can you work out the meaning of?
3 Which of the words do you feel you need to look up in the dictionary?

c) Compare your ideas with two or three other students. Were your words in each of the categories similar or different? Discuss your reasons for the way you grouped the words. What strategies did you use to deal with the words you worked out the meaning of? How did you work out the meanings? Did you use any of the following strategies?

1 checking to see if the word is defined in the text
2 looking for similarities with words in your own language
3 working out the meaning from the other words in the text
4 looking for how the words fit into the organisation of the ideas in the text
5 consulting your own vocabulary/grammar notebook

Did you use any other strategies? How effective were they?

Task 4.2

Coping with unfamiliar words when listening often requires different skills than when reading.

a) Listen to the talk by Professor Henkut on 'Stress at work'. As you listen, decide on what the main point of the lecture is, and answer the following questions.

1 What is the normal explanation for stress at work?
2 Why is this explanation unsatisfactory?
3 Why is it important to study 'self-conversations'?
4 Why are techniques such as 'time management' of limited use in dealing with stress?
5 What are the main additional causes of stress in work?
6 What three main strategies can companies use in order to reduce stress?

b) With two or three other students, compare your answers for **a**.

c) Listen to the lecture again. Which of the words and phrases on page 207 did you need to know in order to answer the questions? Which were defined in the lecture? Which would you note down to look up later?

d) In groups, make a list of strategies for understanding new and unfamiliar words you hear.

Task 4.3

Listening to extended English is often more difficult than reading: in reading, you have plenty of time; in listening, the words move on – you cannot go back. One way to make lectures easier to understand is to prepare: do the pre-reading, decide what words are associated with the topic and learn them, list the questions that may be answered, and sit near the speaker where you can easily see and hear him or her.

a) The pre-reading for tomorrow's International Law lecture includes the passage below. With two or three other students, decide:

1 What is the main idea?
2 What do you expect the lecture to be about?
3 What questions might be answered in the lecture?
4 What words is it important to understand before the lecture?

War Crimes Trials

'War is hell,' said General Sherman, a commander in the American Civil War. This statement accurately describes the bloody campaign that he waged. Yet it was this war which marked the
5 beginning of the modern laws of warfare. At the end of the Civil War in 1865 Henry Wirz, a former confederate officer, was tried and convicted for ill-treating and murdering prisoners.

There had been rules before, but this war saw
10 the introduction of a formal and comprehensive code to guide troops in the field. These ideas have been progressively refined, first in the Hague Conventions of 1899 and 1907, and then in the Geneva Conventions of 1949 and 1977.
15 Armies have often adopted procedures for the punishment of war criminals. Initially, they were designed to discipline soldiers and were mostly conducted by the authorities of the state to which the offenders belonged. However, towards the
20 end of the Second World War (1939–45), it became clear that the outrages committed by the Nazi regime in Germany – such as the Holocaust, in which an estimated six million Jews were killed – and by the Japanese were so great that those
25 responsible should, in a sense, be tried by all mankind. Thus, in October 1943, two years before the end of the Second World War, representatives of the Allied nations, led by Britain and the United States, met in London and established a

30 commission to investigate such outrages.
Three categories of offence were established, which, loosely, came to be defined as 'war crimes'. They were: crimes against peace, such as the plotting of war against non-aggressive
35 countries; violations of the customs and laws of war, such as the murder of prisoners, hostages and civilians; and crimes against humanity, which included extermination, enslavement and other inhumane acts committed against any civilian
40 population.
With the Germans defeated, the Allied leaders decided to try Nazi leaders for a series of war crimes. The first session of the hearing took place in Berlin in October 1945. Charges were lodged
45 against 24 former Nazi leaders. They were charged with crimes against peace, war crimes, genocide, and the wanton destruction of towns and cities.
In November 1945 the hearings were moved to the German town of Nuremberg. Three of the
50 defendants were acquitted; twelve were sentenced to death; three were sentenced to life imprisonment; and four were sentenced to imprisonment for between ten and twenty years. The decision of the tribunal was unanimous. A
55 similar trial was also held of Japanese war leaders and 25 of them were convicted for crimes committed in Asia.

b) Listen to Ms Robertson's lecture the next day. In groups, decide:

1 What is the main idea? (Did you predict correctly?)
2 Which of your questions were answered? (See if you can answer them.)
3 What other important questions were answered? (Do you think these could have been predicted? If not, were you able to cope anyway?)
4 Did you understand most of the words? (If not, could you understand the lecture anyway?)
5 How could you have been better prepared? (Discuss strategies to improve your listening.)

Task 4.4

Although it is a good idea to see if you can manage without looking up unfamiliar language in a reference book, there will also always be times when you need the guidance of dictionaries and grammar books.

 a) With two or three other students, compare the kinds of dictionaries you use. (If possible, bring them to the class for the others to look at.)

- Why did you choose the types you have?
- How do you use them?
- What information do they contain?
- Do you know the meaning of the abbreviations and symbols that they use?
- What aspects of them do you find most useful?
- What sorts of words do you tend to look up in them?
- What problems do you have using dictionaries?
- How well do you feel you use dictionaries?

 b) Review your grammar books and how you use them in a similar way.

 c) Review your own vocabulary/grammar notebook. How useful do you find it? Discuss what you think is the best way to organise it to help you in your studies.

5 UNIT ASSESSMENT AND APPLICATION

This unit has been concerned with learning to cope with the language demands of extended study in English.

Task 5.1

 a) Listen to Jane and Jill talking about the differences between the reading and listening they did at school and what they now have to cope with at university.

 b) Make notes about the problems they mention.

 c) What advice would you give to them, to help them solve their problems?

Task 5.2

 How would you assess your own ability to cope with extended English? What skills do you feel need more attention? How do you intend to master them?

Note Active reading and listening skills need to be part of you – they have to feel and be automatic and natural. *This will only happen if you practise them as frequently as possible.*

UNIT 7 Taking part in discussions

Discussion is a very important part of study. Good discussions expose you to a variety of different views, and force you to clarify and defend – or modify – your views. However, taking part in discussions is not always a successful or enjoyable experience. A number of things can go wrong. The purpose of this unit is to help you to avoid the pitfalls and get the most out of discussion-based study.

1 BEING PREPARED

Getting the best out of a discussion depends a lot on how you prepare for it.

Task 1.1

Alastair has been asking the other students on his course how they prepare for classes involving discussions.

a) On your own, first make a list of the ways you normally prepare for a discussion session such as a seminar (be honest!), or, if you lack experience of discussion work, how you think you should prepare.

b) Now listen and make notes of the main points in Alastair's report. Which of the statements are similar to your own approach to preparing for discussions?

c) With two or three other students, discuss whether you think the ideas in the statements are helpful or not in preparing for discussions. Give reasons for your views.

d) Make a list of the most important points you feel you personally need to bear in mind when preparing for discussions.

Task 1.2

Discussions usually involve making up your mind about an issue. To do so, you need to prepare your argument thoroughly. In most study situations where English is used, this means looking at both sides of the matter. This is because, in such situations, you are usually expected to arrive at a conclusion only after trying to take into account as many aspects as possible of an issue. (You may wish to refer to Unit 2, Task 4.2 for revision/further practice of this skill.)

a) You are preparing for a discussion about 'Censorship' as part of your Politics course. Decide which of the following views is closest to your own:

1 Censorship is never justified.
2 Censorship is justified in times of national emergencies, e.g. wars, etc.
3 Censorship in some aspects of national life is always necessary, in order to protect government secrets, etc.
4 Censorship is an essential way of protecting citizens from harmful lies, obscenities, etc. It therefore prevents dictatorship and unrest.

b) List the reasons for your point of view.

c) Now prepare arguments *against* your view, i.e. the opposite side of the case.

Task 1.3

When preparing your views on a discussion topic, you will usually have to take the ideas in readings into account as well as your own arguments.

a) Make notes on the points about censorship in the passage that follows. Remember to take your notes *actively* (see Units 5 and 6)!

Censorship

Views about censorship are of two main kinds. Proponents of censorship take the view that the loss of freedom that censorship involves is a necessary evil because there is likely to be a far greater loss of freedom
5 without censorship than with it. Opponents of censorship argue that censorship itself is a far greater threat to freedom than any of the dangers it supposedly guards against.
   Those who favour censorship base their arguments on
10 the view that, if left to their own devices, human beings do not always act in the best interests of their fellow men and women. They need to be protected from themselves by governments in much the same way that parents need to protect their children from the
15 consequences of some of their natural instincts. To

believe otherwise is seen as at best naive, at worst plain foolish.
   Thus, without censorship, supporters of this view argue, it would be impossible for governments to
20 prevent military secrets from reaching a country's enemies. Likewise, unless the government has some control over the media, irresponsible journalists or broadcasters would be free to create unrest by spreading false information. By the same token, it is argued that it
25 is necessary to have laws against matters such as pornography in order to protect the rights of vulnerable groups within society, such as women.
   Supporters of this general view believe that the threat to human rights would be much greater without the
30 protection of censorship. The means are seen as

justifying the end: it is better to sacrifice a small amount of freedom in the interests of ultimately creating much greater overall freedom. According to this view, there is really no such thing as freedom, merely uncontrolled
35 opportunities for the more powerful and unscrupulous to exploit the weaker and law-abiding.

Opponents of censorship accept that human beings do not always act in the best interests of their fellow citizens. They differ from supporters of censorship,
40 however, in terms of what they see as the remedy. According to their view, the best guarantee of human rights is a society with as few restrictions as possible, much as the role of parents can be seen as not just to control their children but to help them to grow up to be
45 responsible adults. Thus the responsibility for regulating society is seen to belong primarily to the ordinary citizen rather than the government. This view acknowledges human weaknesses, but also recognises the potential of humanity for self-regulation.
50 Thus, from this point of view, it is up to the individual citizen to take whatever action the law permits regarding matters such as unfair or inaccurate newspaper, television or media reporting, pornography, and so on. As a first line of defence, citizens have the
55 choice of denying the offending material an audience, simply by switching off or refusing to buy. Beyond this, the argument runs, citizens can use the existing laws of the land against obscenity, libel, slander and so on,

without the need for an extra level of censorship-based
60 legislation. It is also argued by supporters of this view that a responsible citizenry is the best defence against irresponsible behaviour by those set on attempting to exploit their fellow citizens.

Thus, while allowing that there may be times of
65 national emergency, such as war, when censorship is justified, opponents of censorship would argue that it is in general unnecessary, and takes away from ordinary citizens a role that is rightfully theirs, and gives to government one that is inappropriate. Opponents of
70 censorship also point out that its supporters are naive in their assumption that governments are always more benign than the forces they oppose. It is only too easy for the censorship to be exploited as a weapon of oppression by a ruthless government.
75 In conclusion, censorship can perhaps best be regarded as a mixed blessing. It has the potential to protect society from harmful influences, but, equally, it may act as a harmful influence itself. It may be impossible to say whether censorship is ever totally
80 beneficial or not. Much will depend on the circumstances in which it operates. In a society which is relatively immature and insecure, it may provide much-needed stability and protection. In other societies, however, it may act as a brake on liberties, or, worst of
85 all, be used as an instrument of repression and terror.

↰ b) Use the points from the reading to modify your arguments as necessary.

Task 1.4 Discussion

↰ a) As a group, choose a topic that you would like to discuss. The topic should be of general interest and one where there is the possibility for a range of views and which you can read about in order to develop your thinking. The reading does not have to be in English, however.

↰ b) Develop your point of view on this topic on your own. Remember to take into account *both* sides of the case.

↰ c) Consult relevant readings and other resources if available in order to modify* your argument.

↰ d) As a group, discuss the topic.

Task 1.5 Review

Review the process you went through in Tasks 1.2, 1.3 and 1.4. Did you consider all the arguments you should have? Did you find you had to modify your views as a result of the ideas in the reading? How helpful was the basic procedure in preparing you for the discussion (i.e. decide point of view → prepare arguments for and against → do background reading → modify your arguments)?

2 GETTING YOUR MESSAGE ACROSS

Putting forward your own point of view effectively in a discussion means organising your ideas well. Also, it isn't just a matter of speaking into a vacuum – it's important to take into account and to build on what others have been saying, especially the last speaker.

TELL THEM WHAT YOU'RE GOING TO SAY, TELL THEM IT, THEN TELL THEM WHAT YOU SAID.

Task 2.1

How you present your arguments will affect how easy they are to understand.

a) Anne and Paul are taking part in an Economics seminar on the effect of robots on employment. Listen to and make notes on their views.

b) Whose arguments did you find it easier to understand? What are the factors that make one of the arguments easier to understand than the other? Listen to the cassette again in order to consider these aspects:
   – relevance of ideas
   – organisation of ideas (how logical they are)
   – illustration of ideas (use of examples)
   – 'signposts' (telling the listener the direction of the argument)
Note You are not asked to decide whether or not you agree with the speakers' views at this point.

c) Revise the weaker argument so that it is easier to understand. Build it up as follows:
   – note the main points you feel should be included
   – decide on the most appropriate order for the points
   – add concrete examples to make your points clearer where appropriate
   – make a short beginning and ending to say what your overall point is

Task 2.2

Making your argument persuasive involves building on what others have said. In this way, they will feel you have taken their views into account, and so be more willing to accept your views.

 a) As part of your Urban Planning course, you are going to take part in a discussion about whether or not robots could be used as drivers on underground trains in cities such as New York, London, Paris, etc. Prepare your argument using the techniques you practised in Task 2.1.

 b) Listen to the discussion so far, and take notes about the points that have been raised.

 c) Now listen to the discussion again. What expressions were used by the speakers to show that
   1 they agreed with the earlier points
   2 they disagreed with them, and
   3 they partly agreed and partly disagreed?
What other expressions with similar meanings could be used instead?

 d) Now it is your turn to join in the discussion. Modify the argument you prepared at the beginning to take into account the points that have been made so far.

 e) Discuss your views with two or three other students, using the expressions you have been studying.

3 UNDERSTANDING OTHERS' VIEWS

The success of a discussion depends a great deal on how well the members of the discussion group listen to each other. This means using the right language to show agreement, asking for clarification and so on, as well as skills such as paraphrasing, questioning and so on.

'I'M ALL EARS'

Task 3.1 Discussion language

 a) Isabel and Omar are Politics students. They have been taking part in the discussion about censorship. Listen to their discussion for the expressions they use to ask for clarification, and to express agreement or disagreement.

b) Listen to the discussion a second time, and list all the phrases that are used to express a) asking for (*Note* not giving) clarification, b) agreement, and c) disagreement. Compare your list with those of two or three other students. Add any phrases you missed to your list.

c) What other expressions do you know that can be used for the same purposes?

Task 3.2 What do you think?

a) Do you agree or disagree with Isabel and Omar? Prepare your arguments, then discuss your views with two or three other students, using the expressions you have been studying.

b) Review the discussion. Did you have any difficulties with using any of the expressions? Were there any other, similar ideas you wanted to express, but were not sure about the language for doing so?

Task 3.3

To participate effectively in discussions it is important to show you have understood properly what someone else has said.

a) Listen to part of a Sociology seminar on the topic of 'Poverty', and take notes on the main points the speaker, Joachim, makes.

b) Paraphrase Joachim's argument, using the following phrases. Compare your answers with a classmate.
1 'So what you're saying is that ...'
2 'Let me just make sure – your point is that ...'
3 'Have I got this right – your view is that ...'
4 'If I understand you correctly, your argument is that ...'

I REALISE THAT YOU UNDERSTAND THAT WHAT YOU THOUGHT I SAID IS NOT WHAT I MEANT, BUT I DON'T THINK YOU REALISE THAT I UNDERSTAND THAT WHAT YOU THOUGHT YOU SAID IS NOT WHAT YOU MEANT.

Task 3.4

Paraphrasing in a discussion often involves checking first of all whether one has correctly understood somebody else's basic point, and then paraphrasing the possible further implications of the basic point.

a) Look at the text which follows, which is a transcript of another part of the seminar discussion about 'Poverty'. Find the expressions which are used to introduce a paraphrase of one of the other speaker's or the speaker's own ideas (e.g. 'is your argument that ...').

RICHARD: In my view, poverty is the major cause of crime. If we got rid of economic problems, most crime would disappear.

ALAN: I agree that poverty is one of the major causes of crime, but is your argument that if we got rid of poverty, we would get rid of crime?

LINDA: Just a minute, can I just get clear what you two are saying? First of all, is your point that crime is caused by poverty?

RICHARD: Yes.

ALAN: Yes.

LINDA: In other words, because someone is poor, this inevitably means they will become involved in crime?

RICHARD: No, not exactly. My point is that those who become criminals in a society do so because they feel deprived of what they see others having in the same society. They feel they are not getting their fair share, so they do the only thing they can to deal with the problem – turn to crime.

LINDA: So let me see if I've got this straight – you feel that although not all poor people become criminals, those that do do so because they are poor?

RICHARD: Yes.

ALAN: I'd agree with that too.

LINDA: So just to take this a little further, if you don't mind. Would you go so far as to say, then, that everybody who has ever been a criminal became one because they were poor?

RICHARD: No, no, that's not what I'm saying at all.

ALAN: No, I wouldn't go along with that either.

LINDA: So could you tell me exactly what your point is then?

RICHARD: Well, I think you're taking the argument further than we intended. We didn't really mean to say that everyone who is poor becomes a criminal or that the cause of all crime is poverty.

LINDA: No, maybe not, but it certainly sounded that way.

ALAN: OK, OK, I accept that, but what we really meant to say was that if you're poor it makes it very difficult for you to avoid crime in one way or another.

RICHARD: Yes, so a poor person will not necessarily become a criminal, and, sure, obviously not all criminals are poor. But what we would argue is that a major cause of crime is poverty.

LINDA: Well, OK, I think I could go along with that. But I'm still rather worried about another aspect of your argument. What exactly do you mean by 'crime'? …

b) If you were a member of the Sociology class, what would be your position? Discuss this with two or three other students. Try to reach a consensus of opinion. Use the paraphrasing expressions you have been studying.

4 DISCUSSION STRATEGIES

So far, we have looked at discussions mainly from the point of view of taking part in them as an individual member of the discussion group. However, it is also helpful to look at discussions in overall terms, in order to identify what general discussion strategies seem to help a discussion go well, and which ones hinder this. How can each member of the group try to ensure that the discussion goes as well as possible?

Task 4.1

John and Zeinab are talking about a seminar in their Educational Studies course that they have just finished taking part in. Unfortunately, it didn't go very well.

a) Listen to their conversation and make notes about what they feel went wrong. Do you agree with their general conclusion? Who do you feel was responsible for the problems?

b) You are Zeinab or John. Your tutor has told you that he was also unhappy about the way the seminar went and has asked for your advice about how the next one could be improved. Use your ideas about what happened last time and your experience of other discussions to make a list of *dos* and *don'ts* for effective participation in discussions.

c) Discuss your ideas with two or three other students.

Task 4.2

In English-medium higher education, students are usually expected to share responsibility with the tutor for making a discussion go well.

a) Your next Educational Studies seminar is on the main purposes of higher education. Prepare your position, using the techniques practised in this unit.

b) With two or three other students, take part in a discussion about what you feel the main purpose of higher education is. Try to put into practice the *dos* and *don'ts* you discussed in 4.1.

c) How satisfactorily did you participate in the discussion? Rate your participation according to the criteria that follow.
1 I listened carefully to others' views.
2 Others understood me without much difficulty.
3 I took into account others' views when expressing my own.

4 I used terminology precisely.
5 I expressed disagreement politely.
6 I accepted disagreement with my views politely.
7 I avoided dominating the discussion.
8 I contributed sufficiently to the discussion.
9 I helped the discussion move forward.
10 I learned more about the topic.
11 I learned more about discussing.

d) Discuss your answers with the other members of the group. Account for any differences between your own views and those of the others.

e) Make a personal list of points to bear in mind in order to make your participation in discussions as effective as possible.

5 UNIT ASSESSMENT AND APPLICATION

Discussion is an important form of learning – or it should be. Having to debate your ideas face-to-face should help you to have a better idea about what you have already thought through clearly and what you need to reconsider. But this can only happen if you see discussion as a co-operative endeavour*. What you get out of it very much depends on how you prepare for it and how you take part in it.

Task 5.1

a) With two or three other students, prepare for and hold a discussion about what you think are the five most important subjects that all higher education students should take at least one course in as part of their programme of studies, regardless of their specialism. You must reach a consensus of views.

b) With another small group, discuss your ideas so that you can once again reach a consensus about what the five subjects should be.

c) As a class, continue your discussions until you reach a consensus as a whole.

Task 5.2

Review the discussions you took part in in the last task. What do you feel you have learned in this unit about preparing for and taking part in discussions? What techniques have helped you? What problems are you still experiencing? Look back through the unit to check on any helpful points you may have overlooked.

Business Studies?
Economics?
History?
ENGLISH?
Physical Education?
Science?
Study Skills?
Biology?

UNIT 8 Getting started on writing

It is natural to think of writing for study purposes in terms of the finished product, i.e. the actual words on the page. However, in reality, writing is first and foremost a *process*. The final result is only one of several stages. It is the 'invisible' steps which come before this which hold the keys to successful writing. We will look in turn at each of these main stages in this unit and the next one.

1 YOU AS A WRITER

'THE HARDEST PART IS GETTING STARTED.'

Writing is a complex process. However, probably the most important element is the *writer*, i.e. you! In other words, what you know about writing and what your attitude to writing is will have a strong effect on how well you write. Therefore, before looking in detail at how to construct a piece of writing, it makes sense first of all to find out as much as possible about yourself as a writer.

Task 1.1

Writing is made up of a large number of skills. Which ones have you already learned? Which ones do you need to develop further?

✦ a) Look at the list of 'academic writing skills' below. With two or three other students, discuss what you think each of them involves. Then check your ideas with your teacher.

ACADEMIC WRITING SKILLS		IMPORTANCE	LEVEL	SCORE
1	making an outline			
2	narrowing down the topic			
3	reading around the topic			
4	selecting relevant ideas			
5	ordering ideas logically			
6	making headings, sub-headings, etc.			
7	describing tables, charts and diagrams			
8	writing an introduction			
9	writing a conclusion			
10	constructing a bibliography			
11	including references			
12	proof-reading			
13	keeping the audience in mind			
14	getting the tone right			
15	being concise			
16	sticking to the point			
17	being clear			
18	quoting			
19	summarising			
20	paraphrasing			
21	spelling correctly			
22	using appropriate vocabulary			
23	using correct grammar			
24	punctuating correctly			

✦ b) Decide how important you feel each of the skills is for you in your studies. Give each of them a number out of 5. *5 = very important, 1 = not very important.*

✦ c) For all the skills you feel are the most important ones (those you rated 5 or 4), assess your present level out of 5. *5 = I have mastered this skill, 1 = I don't know how to do this.*

✦ d) For each skill, subtract the score for your level from the score for importance. Skills with a result of 4 or 3 are the ones you need to concentrate on most. You will need to find out more about them either by working through this and the next unit or by looking them up in the index.

Task 1.2

In addition to the academic skills involved, your *attitude* to writing can have an important effect on how well you write.

a) Think of the main kinds of writing (other than just brief notes) that you do at the moment – both in English and any other languages. Then make a table like the one which follows, and complete it. Be honest!

TYPE OF WRITING	LANGUAGE	ATTITUDE		
		enjoy	so-so	dislike

b) With two or three other students, compare your results. Discuss how you feel your attitudes affect the quality of your writing.

Task 1.3

In order to develop a positive attitude to writing, it is helpful to understand the reasons for your present attitudes.

a) Listen to and make notes of Fatu and Rosinda's discussion about their attitudes to writing and their reasons for them.

b) Are the reasons for your own attitudes similar? Are there any other reasons for your feelings about writing?

Task 1.4

Everyone is capable of developing their potential as a writer by improving their attitude to and widening their experience of writing.

a) Look at the suggestions that follow for improving writing ability. With two or three other students, discuss the reasoning behind each of them, i.e. what ideas are they based on? How effective do you think each of them would be for you? What other ideas do you have for improving your writing ability?

1 ask friends who write well what they feel helps them to succeed
2 get friends to give you feedback*
3 set yourself realistic goals – don't expect to create a masterpiece overnight

4 put *yourself* into the writing: don't let it just become a mechanical chore – if you like humour, then put some of it in your writing, etc.
5 do personally satisfying bits of writing, and lots of it, e.g. diary/journal writing
6 find out about the writing habits of successful writers
7 get clear what standards are really expected of you
8 don't try to write an entire essay all at once – break your writing down into chunks*

b) Make a list of five steps you intend to take to improve your own potential as a writer.

2 ESTABLISHING YOUR FOCUS

The first stage in writing for academic purposes is to decide on your *focus*. The general essay topic set by a teacher is intended to produce as many different responses as there are students in the class. *There is no single correct response. You therefore have to decide what your response should be, within the confines set.*

It is all too easy for students to give a mechanical response which lacks creativity, a personal point of view, and so on, and is therefore so general as really to say nothing.

The process you need to go through is similar to focusing a telescope. In order to see clearly, you have to adjust the lens until the image is clear to the viewer's eye – there is no single, set focus. Similarly, when planning a piece of academic writing, you have first of all to focus on the topic, i.e. decide exactly what it is about, what your general approach is going to be, and so on.

Task 2.1

One step in focusing on a writing topic is to make sure you understand what certain key words in the title or question imply about how you should approach the topic.

a) The following words are typically found in the titles of academic writing assignments. Match them with their meanings.

	Words		*Meanings*
1	account for	a)	consider all sides of an issue
2	analyse	b)	make a critical survey
3	argue	c)	bring out the meaning
4	compare	d)	explain the causes of
5	criticise	e)	show the path of development
6	define	f)	show the faults
7	discuss	g)	describe without details
8	evaluate	h)	give the main features and organisation
9	examine	i)	look at carefully
10	illustrate	j)	break into parts and look at the detail
11	interpret	k)	provide satisfactory reasons
12	justify	l)	look for similarities and differences
13	outline	m)	make clear with examples
14	review	n)	decide on the value of something
15	summarise	o)	present the case for or against
16	trace		

b) Are there any other words like this that you have come across? How would you define them?

Task 2.2

Another step in deciding on your focus is to ask questions about the questions!

a) Write a list of questions you should ask in order to begin to focus on the following writing topics:
1 Discuss the differences between the working classes in the CIS and the USA.
2 Evaluate the effects of deforestation on the economies of S.E. Asia.
3 Examine the view that nations get the governments they deserve.
4 Outline the role of women in the developing world.

b) Compare your questions with two or three other students. Decide whether there are any further questions you should add to your list.

Task 2.3

The process of questioning and doing related reading enables you to narrow down your topic and thus begin to decide on your focus. This usually involves deciding on a tentative* position and a preliminary* list of the main aspects of the topic which you propose to write about in order to support your position.

Remember, whole books may have been written on a topic you are expected to write about in 2,000 words; you must therefore make decisions about what to include and exclude. The basis for the decisions should be the criteria provided by your teacher and your own position concerning the topic.

a) For each of the topics in Task 2.2, say what position you could take and what main aspects you would cover. One possibility for the first paper has been provided.

Position: The biggest difference is economic, reflected in the standard of living.

Main points to be covered:

- describe working classes (who am I talking about)
  - describe other possible differences (showing not as significant)
  - describe economic differences
    - absolute terms
    - type of homes and furnishings
- holidays
- food and clothing
- savings and pensions
- cars and luxuries

---

b Compare your ideas with two or three other students. Were there a variety of positions? Did the main points support the positions?

Task 2.4

The key to focusing on your writing topic is to ask questions so that you get as clear a picture as possible about exactly what you are going to do. The questions will probably be to do with:
a) the criteria for the writing assignment
b) the focus, slant or position
c) the information you need to develop your focus

a) Classify the following questions according to each of the three main categories mentioned above.
 1 How long should it be?
 2 What does *analyse* mean?
 3 Who is the audience?

4   What is the main purpose of the assignment, i.e. what kind of knowledge am I expected to show?

5   How much detail will be appropriate?

6   Why am I writing on this topic?

7   What do I already know about the topic?

8   What aspects of the topic should I focus on?

9   In what depth or breadth should I treat the topic?

10 What do I think about the topic?

11 What books and/or articles could be helpful to read?

12 How does the assignment relate to the rest of the course?

13 Is there a set format for the work, i.e. are there certain aspects of the topic that must be covered?

14 Am I expected to present information and ideas only, or critically evaluate them as well?

15 How will the work be assessed?

16 What books must I read?

b) Were there other questions that you asked while doing Tasks 2.2 and 2.3? If so, what were they? You may wish to add them to the list of questions above.

c) With two or three other students, discuss where you can best find the answers to the list of questions.

3 PUTTING THE FOCUS UNDER THE MAGNIFYING GLASS

MAGNIFYING THE FOCUS

In section 2, we looked at how to 'zero in' on a writing topic – how to focus your work – by clarifying the writing in terms of the meaning of the topic, approach, basic content, and requirements. The next problem is to find something to say about the relatively narrow idea that has come into focus. The aim of this part is to help you learn how to do this effectively. Think of it as like looking at your initial writing focus through a magnifying glass. This means exploring the focus in detail – expanding it within the limits you have just established.

Of course, you may find that magnifying your focus in this way makes it necessary to adjust your original focus. It is important to remember that the focusing and magnifying stages are not really separate. We have divided them up in this book for the sake of clarity. In reality, however, it is normal to re-focus and re-magnify continually as you plan your writing.

Task 3.1

By now, you will be gathering more and more information from readings. To make this mass of information more manageable, it is important to develop an outline of your ideas which can be used to indicate how the bits of information are related – where they might fit into your writing.

✦ a) You are doing Educational Studies. You have been asked to examine some aspect of educational practice in the 1990s. You have narrowed down the topic of your paper to 'Rote learning: does it have a place in the 1990s?' (*Rote learning* is a teaching or learning method based on telling students information directly, which they then memorise and reproduce in the examination.)

   Listed below are some of the main ideas (or headings) you wish to include in your writing. Organise the statements into an outline of a paper by putting the main ideas into a logical sequence.
   1 define rote learning
   2 describe present thinking about how learners learn best
   3 define learning generally
   4 discuss why rote learning is unpopular among educationalists today
   5 describe past thinking about how learners learn best
   6 describe how rote learning could have a place in education today
   7 develop purpose of education to meet demands of society

✦ b) Compare your ideas with those of two or three other students. What order is easier for the reader to follow, and best conveys the message? Justify your answer.

Task 3.2

As you develop the shape of your paper in outline form, you need to fit in the notes you make as a result of your reading and thinking. As a result, you may need to modify your outline, especially if you feel you need to include information that just does not seem to fit. Your aim should be to end up with a piece of writing that presents your argument or point of view as a unified, consistent whole.

✦ a) Look at the notes that follow. Decide where they might fit into your outline on *Rote learning*. You may feel you need to alter your outline to make a more cohesive whole.
   1 Rote learning means memorising without necessarily understanding.
   2 People need to be able to recall information quickly.
   3 Children used to have to memorise long passages.
   4 Learning involves the whole person.
   5 Information needs to be understood to be useful.
   6 Education standards are declining, and children are able to recall fewer facts.
   7 The world is more complex, and people need to be flexible.
   8 Rote learning is easier to assess.
   9 The role of education is to provide the skills needed for tomorrow's world.
   10 Rote learning is boring.

b) You have just found this article on rote learning. What is the main idea of the article? Where and how could you use some of its ideas in your paper? Decide how you may need to alter your outline, if necessary.

Rote learning was a winner

**by Greg Hadfield
Education
Correspondent**

GENERATIONS of children who sat through endless lessons of "chalk and talk" in front of a bossy teacher can take some consolation. It helped them achieve better exam results.

Modern classroom techniques may make school days a good deal happier, but contentment was not the road to success at O-level, according to university researchers.

Their three-year study, monitoring the progress of 2,000 teenagers, tried to measure the influence of the "boredom factor" in 17 selected schools in the north of England. Surprisingly, the academics

discovered it may have been a blessing in disguise.

The Newcastle University team also found that the old-fashioned approach of teachers ordering pupils about is still alive and producing results.

Their conclusions were welcomed yesterday by educationists worried by the shift to less formal lessons.

The fifth-formers in the latest study were asked to award teachers marks to measure how frequently they followed or ignored today's fashion for "child-centred" education, the sort used on GCSE courses to develop problem-solving skills and teamwork.

A five-point scale was devised to spot the teachers who always told them what they should know and what to write down.

"It was significant and not

something you would get by chance or accident. Certainly, when you compare the pupils' interest and attitudes to school, there is a quite definite and highly significant difference," one of the researchers said.

But the rankings were turned upside down when the team of four researchers looked at how the children fared in O-levels and CSEs.

The sort of methods now frowned upon actually improved, if only marginally, the final grades.

"It is fair to say the improvement was only about the equivalent of a fifth of a grade, but that is after allowing for the different ability levels the children started from," the researcher said.

"There is nothing wrong with old-fashioned, didactic teaching in the right place, even if it isn't the flavour of the month at the moment."

However, he insisted the best teachers had always mixed the two techniques to match the needs of pupils, although O-levels forced some to concentrate more on dictation and learning by rote.

c) Write out your final outline (Task 3.1) and supporting points (Tasks 3.2a and 3.2b) under each of your main headings.

Task 3.3

As you magnify your writing focus, it is also important to keep your audience in mind. Your teachers will probably expect you to show not only that you understand the basic concepts related to your topic, *but also* that you are aware of any well-established additional or opposing points of view, data and so on. *And, in addition to this*, they will be looking for evidence of your own thinking, i.e. signs that you have thought independently about the topic as well. In other words, the ideas you collect should not just be an 'unthinking' telling back of the most obvious points. You need to ask yourself:
– what further information is likely to be expected?
– what ideas of my own will the teacher expect to see?

a) What is your own opinion about the role of rote learning today? Do you feel it is a good idea? If you were asked to write about teaching practices in your own country, what aspects would you want to focus on? What kind of information would you need to magnify this focus?

b) Draw up an outline of a paper on an educational practice in your country. Your outline should reflect your own thinking while taking into account other points of view.

Task 3.4

As your ideas multiply, it is vital to organise them so they are expressed as clearly as possible. Here are some examples.
1 If you are writing a description of a process (e.g. the events leading up to a war, the life-cycle of an animal or plant, etc.), then the main ideas in the essay should be in the same order as they occur in real life.
2 If you are comparing or contrasting ideas (e.g. arguments for and against a plan of action), then the ideas should be grouped in such a way that the similarities and differences you are highlighting are as clear as possible.
3 If you are writing about an experiment, then you will usually first of all describe the aims, then the general arrangements for the experiment, then what happened when you carried it out, and finally the results and the conclusions that can be drawn.

a) With two or three other students, choose a typical essay topic from your field of study and:
  1 develop a focus or position;
  2 make a list of headings for the main aspects of the topic that you think it would be important to cover;
  3 put them in the order you think would be best for the writing.
You may wish to use one of the topics that follow.
  1 Describe how the government is chosen in your country.
  2 Discuss changes in rural life in your country.
  3 Does religion have a place in government? Justify your answer.

b) Discuss the reasons for the choice and the order of your points with the other groups.

4 DRAFTING

Having filled out your focus and organised your points, the next stage is writing your first and subsequent drafts*. This stage is basically concerned with expressing your framework of ideas in a connected piece of writing. Getting down the right ideas in the right order should be the main concern here. Polishing up the details of expression is also important, of course, but comes later (see Unit 9).

Task 4.1

As part of his studies to become a Biology teacher, John is writing an essay on the pros and cons of zoos. He has collected the following ideas to use as the basis for his first draft.

 Put them in a suitable order.

a) Opponents of zoos argue that much of what people see in zoos is undesirable. Captive animals are often kept in poor and inhumane conditions, zoo opponents say. In the worst zoos, animals are still displayed for the entertainment of the public. Where animals are placed in impoverished and unsuitable surroundings they often behave in abnormal or neurotic ways.

It is common for polar bears constantly to pace up and down and twist their heads and circle over and over again. This behaviour is now recognised by scientists as a sign of stress and frustration. When people visit zoos where animals are acting in neurotic and abnormal ways, they are not being educated. Instead, opponents say, they are being given an inadequate picture of animal behaviour. A more precise and informative impression is available to the public through wildlife programmes on television. From this point of view, it could be argued that zoos actually have a negative effect on people's attitudes to wildlife.

b) Do zoos help or hinder the preservation of wildlife? There are a number of major arguments in both directions. In what follows, I shall first of all present each of them in turn. Then, in the light of these views, I will attempt to give my own answer to the question.

c) Do zoos help or hinder the preservation of wildlife? The answer would appear to be both 'Yes' and 'No'. Some would say that this is inevitable. All zoos are a compromise. No matter how hard they may try to take into account the needs of their animals, they must always balance these with the expectations of the visiting public. It would thus appear difficult for display and conservation to go hand in hand.

d) There appear to be strong arguments both in favour of and against zoos. It can be argued that zoos may have a positive effect in terms of education and conservation. However, it can also be argued that this is clearly not always the case, and zoo opponents point out that viable alternatives exist, such as television programmes and the protection of natural habitats.

e) Supporters of zoos argue that they have an important role in educating the public, millions of whom visit British zoos each year. Although television programmes about wildlife are available, there is no substitute for encountering real animals, they argue. The only way that most people can have first-hand experience of animals from around the world is by coming across them in zoos. Without this kind of contact, wildlife lacks reality for the ordinary person. It therefore becomes difficult or impossible to educate the public properly about wildlife: it is simply too remote from their experience. Such education is vital, however, if people are to become properly aware of their responsibilities for wildlife conservation. Thus, according to this view, zoos are seen to play an important indirect role in wildlife conservation, in terms of raising awareness about wildlife among the public in general.

f) Supporters of zoos point out that over the past twenty years zoos have developed programmes designed to help preserve endangered species. This involves breeding animals in captivity – in 'captive breeding programmes' – and then re-introducing them into their natural habitats to replenish the number living in the wild.

The Arabian oryx (a kind of deer found in the deserts of Saudi Arabia and Jordan) were hunted by shooting parties until there were only about 30 left. In 1962, three oryx were taken to Phoenix Zoo, Arizona. By 1972, Arabian oryx had become extinct in the wild but had bred successfully in Phoenix and other zoos. In 1982, oryx were released back into the wild in Jordan.

g) Opponents of zoos accept that some species have been saved from extinction by 'captive breeding programmes'. They also argue that this offers no solution to the worldwide conservation crisis. They say that the number of animals protected by zoos is tiny compared with the overall problem. It cost about £25 million to save the Arabian oryx from dying out; but could that amount be found for every species that is endangered? Zoo opponents say that zoos are not the answer because they are too costly. Habitat protection is the only solution.

Task 4.2

After looking at his draft, John's tutor suggested he should do some further reading. As a result, John produced the following additional points.

➔ Decide which of them would be useful to add to his first draft, and say where they should go.

h) The conditions in which zoo animals are kept have greatly improved over the last ten years. For example, Glasgow Zoo has pioneered new methods for caring for polar bears in an attempt to enrich their captive lives. One change has been to vary their diet with live crabs and frozen vegetables.

i) The value of zoo-breeding programmes is questioned on the grounds that some species, such as the African elephant, do not reproduce well in captivity. Some zoo opponents fear that the result of breeding programmes may be new species of 'zoo animals' which are adapted to living in captivity, not in the wild. They say that the money spent each year on zoos around the world (about £250 million) would be better spent on protecting animals' natural habitats, such as the Tsavo Rhino Sanctuary in Kenya, where the black rhino has been brought back from the brink of extinction through careful management in the wild.

j) Perhaps there is an alternative. The zoo environment and the natural habitat of wildlife have traditionally been thought of as opposites. But it might be more productive to think of developing zoos so that the conditions in which the animals are kept resembled their natural habitats far more than tends to be the case nowadays. This would help to develop the potential of zoos for education and conservation. In other words, rather than abolishing zoos, the answer may be to change their nature. This can only help to make zoos a beneficial factor in wildlife conservation.

k) Zoos co-operate with each other in order to ensure the success of their breeding programmes. Animals are passed from one zoo to another in order to prevent inbreeding – breeding from closely-related animals. If animals that are closely related to one another mate, there is a danger they will produce deformed offspring.

l) The dodo's claim to fame is that it was one of the first recorded species to have become extinct as a result of human actions. The birds, which could not fly, used to live in Mauritius, in the Indian Ocean. They were spotted by Portuguese sailors in about 1507. Human settlers on the island began hunting the birds, which rapidly declined in numbers. By 1681 dodos had become extinct.

m) Zoo opponents argue that the existence of zoos may actively contribute to endangering certain species, rather than conserving them. There is a thriving trade in orang-utans, which come from Indonesia. They are generally sold in Singapore and other cities in the Far East to pet shops and East European zoos. For every orang-utan that arrives in a zoo, five are thought to die during capture and transportation, which adds to the decline of the species.

n) There are thought to be only 28 monk seals left off the coast of Morocco, out of a total population of about 500 for the whole Mediterranean area. Recently, a French zoo attempted to capture five or six seals to set up a breeding colony. The Moroccan government refused permission to catch the seals after various conservation groups said such a move would threaten the remaining population.

5 UNIT ASSESSMENT AND APPLICATION

For your Study Skills class, you have been asked to develop a paper on how to write an academic essay. You are expected to give advice on the stages involved in academic writing prior to the editing stage, i.e. the parts of the process dealt with in this unit.

Task 5.1

What questions do you need answers to before you begin your planning? Your teacher will answer these.

Task 5.2

With two or three other students, outline your paper. Show the main stages in the process by making a flow chart. Begin like this:
    Establish your focus, i.e. decide on the approach.

Task 5.3

What does each of the main stages in academic writing involve? Are they connected together in a straightforward way, or is their relationship more complex? Compare your group's ideas with those of the other groups.

Task 5.4

Write a short paper on the stages of writing an academic essay. Remember to use linking words* to help the reader understand the process you are describing. (You do not need to edit the paper, i.e. do not worry about small mistakes in language at this point – instead, concentrate on getting the ideas down.)

Task 5.5

With two or three other students, discuss any problems you had in developing and writing your paper. Do you feel you still have problems drafting an essay? If so, discuss how these might be overcome.

WRITING FLOW CHART

SIT DOWN

RE-ARRANGE DESK

MAKE CUP OF TEA | COFFEE

WRITE TITLE

SHARPEN PENCIL

UNDERLINE TITLE

ANSWER TELEPHONE

ETC...

UNIT 9 Getting the writing right

Unit 8 was concerned with developing the ideas that go into a piece of writing. This unit focuses on how to express the ideas as effectively as possible. This involves looking at writing in terms of several different 'levels'.

1 The most basic level is that of the piece of writing as a whole, i.e. the order of the main parts (sections, paragraphs, etc.) and how they are linked together.
2 The second level is the question of the organisation within the section or paragraph, and how well individual sentences are connected together.
3 The third level involves the basic building blocks from which the other levels are constructed – the bricks and mortar of writing – i.e. vocabulary, grammar, spelling, punctuation, etc.
4 Finally, there is the level of the special conventions* that are found in academic writing – footnotes, references, bibliographies, etc.

We will look at each of these 'levels' separately, and one after the other. However, this does not mean that there is only one fixed order for following the levels as you develop your writing. Also, changes made in one level are likely to have a 'knock-on' effect, i.e. they will probably make it necessary to make further changes in the other levels, and may also affect the thinking and organisation developed in Unit 8. The most important point, therefore, is to pay attention to all the different parts of writing that go together to make the whole, and to make sure they all fit together properly.

WRITING
SHOP GUIDE

3RD FLOOR
  FOOTNOTES
  REFERENCES
  BIBLIOGRAPHY
2ND FLOOR
  VOCABULARY
  GRAMMAR
  SPELLING
  PUNCTUATION
1ST FLOOR
  SECTIONS
  PARAGRAPHS
GROUND FLOOR
  IDEAS
  OUTLINE

WRITING IS LIKE SHOPPING IN A DEPARTMENT STORE – MOVE AROUND TO MAKE SURE YOU GET EVERYTHING YOU NEED!

1 GETTING THE OVERALL STRUCTURE RIGHT

The overall organisation of your writing needs to be as clear as possible for the reader. This means making sure that the basic structure is logical

GUIDE TO MY IDEAS.
scenic route
warning: cul-de-sac
danger: wrong way

and that you provide the necessary 'signposts' to inform the reader about the structure, i.e. parts where you tell the reader where he/she is going, where he/she has reached so far, and where he/she has finally ended up. There are three parts of a piece of writing which have an important role to play in making the structure clear: the introduction, the body and the conclusion.

Task 1.1

The introduction should:
- say *what* your basic topic is, what main question(s) you are going to ask, what main view you have, etc.
- say *how* you are going to deal with the topic, question, etc., i.e. what the main sections will be

a) Marco, Silvana and Hiroko are writing essays for their Religious Studies class on whether or not euthanasia (i.e. bringing about the death of another person with that person's consent) should be legalised. Look at each of their introductions and decide which one you think is best.
Note You are *not* being asked to say which set of ideas you agree or disagree with.

b) With two or three other students, discuss and justify your views.

1 Marco's introduction
Euthanasia means helping someone else to die. There is no justification for euthanasia. Euthanasia involves killing, and as a pacifist, I am opposed to killing of any kind. There is already too much loss of life in the world. We should be doing much more to prevent loss of life, rather than encouraging further deaths.

2 Silvana's introduction
There is no straightforward answer to the question of whether euthanasia should be legalised or not. In this essay I will therefore first of all consider the arguments against legalisation, and then the reasons in favour. I shall conclude by arguing that euthanasia should be legal, but only under certain conditions.

3 Hiroko's introduction
For someone who is young or healthy, life is usually so enjoyable that it is difficult to understand why someone should want the right to die. It is as if such a person is insane. But the point of view of the person who is ill or old may be quite different. They may feel, for all sorts of reasons, that dying is better than living.

Task 1.2

In the body of the essay, it is important to signal clearly how the main ideas are connected together by using appropriate joining words.

✈ a) Linking expressions can be used to indicate cause and effect, comparison, contrast, addition, examples, conclusion, and time. Match the following expressions with their functions. List separately those expressions where you are unsure of either their use or meaning.

Functions	Expressions			
Cause/effect	as	on the contrary	in this case	consequently
Comparison	as soon as	since	in conclusion	finally
Contrast	at the same time	similarly	meanwhile	hence
Addition	at length	to sum up	on the other hand	in effect
Examples	but	although	otherwise	in particular
Conclusion	first of all	and	so	in addition
Time	for instance	as a result	thus	moreover
	in other words	and yet	therefore	on the whole
	in brief	besides	also	secondly
	in short	for example	accordingly	specifically
	likewise	however	as long as	too
	nevertheless	in contrast	because	while

✈ b) Compare your answers with another student's. Which expressions did you find difficult? Were there any you were unfamiliar with? Do you feel you know both what each expression means and how to use it?

✈ c) With another student, discuss when and how you might use the expressions you found difficult. You may also wish to write sentences using these expressions.

✈ d) Fill in the blanks in Sylvana's essay, using appropriate connecting words.

Sylvana's Essay

   Those who oppose the legalisation of euthanasia do so for three main reasons. —(1)—, they fear that it will increase the number of murders. They believe this is likely because it will be difficult to be sure in certain cases whether the cause of a person's death was their own wish or not. Someone wishing to murder an ill or elderly person will be able to make the death look like euthanasia. —(2)—, from this point of view, euthanasia is likely to endanger lives.

   The second main objection is medical. If euthanasia is permitted, some doctors argue that they would inevitably be the ones who were called on most often to carry it out. This would place an intolerable burden on them. It would —(3)— mean that the patient would be able to make decisions about whether to live or not regardless of the doctor's judgement. Doctors would —(4)— no longer be in a position to do whatever they thought was in the best interests of their patients.

   The third reason usually put forward for opposing euthanasia is that it is against

---

widely-held religious beliefs. According to this view, life is sacred, and no human being has the right to decide to take away life, even his or her own, or to help someone else to do so.

These objections are all seen as unreasonable by supporters of euthanasia, —(5)—. They say that even if euthanasia made it easier to commit murder, there is no proof that this would automatically increase the number of murders. The opportunity to commit a murder does not of itself cause murder to take place. As regards the medical objections, proponents of euthanasia say that doctors are already called upon to make life or death judgements, as when, —(6)—, the decision is made to turn off the life-support machine of a patient in a coma. They —(7)— argue that doctors do not have the right to make the ultimate decisions about a patient's care. —(8)—, those in favour of euthanasia argue that human beings are seen by many religions as responsible for their own actions. It is up to the individual in the end to decide what his or her behaviour will be, and to accept the consequences. —(9)—, from this point of view, deciding whether to end one's life or to help another to do so is a matter of individual responsibility.

Task 1.3

The conclusion should:
- say what your main topic/question/view in the writing has been and what main aspects of it you have covered (i.e. a brief summary);
- say what general point(s) can be drawn from the essay as a whole.
But it should *not*:
- include any further points of the kind mentioned in the body of the essay;
- introduce new information or ideas.

DECISION TIME.

a) Silvana has had some difficulty writing her conclusion. Here are the three attempts she has made so far. She thinks one of them is OK, but isn't sure. Help her make up her mind.

1 There are several main arguments against euthanasia. There are also a number of counter arguments in its favour. In this essay I have summarised both sets of arguments. Thus, it is clear that it is possible for one to be either in favour of or against the legalisation of euthanasia. It is difficult to decide which is correct.

2 In conclusion, I have outlined the main arguments for and against legalising euthanasia. A further argument in favour of legalisation sometimes put forward is that the practice already exists. According to this view, it would be better to legalise and thus control euthanasia, rather than simply continue to make it illegal.

3 To conclude, I believe it is necessary to take both sets of views into account. This could be done by making euthanasia legal, but only under strict conditions. Thus, the wish to die would have to be registered officially; more than one doctor would always have to be involved; no one need be involved who has religious objections.

b) With two or three other students, justify your choice.

2 GETTING THE PARAGRAPHS RIGHT

Good paragraph construction depends mainly on a) thinking through each idea so that you develop it logically and clearly, and b) then guiding

MAKING THE PIECES FIT

the reader through your thought processes by using appropriate joining expressions. This means making each of the parts of the paragraph – the sentences – fit together properly.

Task 2.1

The information contained within a paragraph is based on the topic sentence of a paragraph. The topic sentence is generally the first sentence and expresses the main idea to be developed within the paragraph.

a) Look at the topic sentences below and discuss what kinds of information you would expect to follow.
1 The government of the United States of America consists of three main branches.
2 The world-wide increase in road transport is a serious threat to the natural environment.
3 Deforestation has a direct effect on food supplies.
4 Although development in the Third World is intended to increase self-reliance, the actual result is often increased dependence on the West.
5 There is a mistaken idea that, because of pocket calculators, children no longer need to learn how to do basic arithmetic.

b) With two or three other students, discuss your answers.

c) The following are some basic paragraph structures.
1 reasons for a point of view
2 steps in a process
3 supporting details (first, second, third, etc.)
4 practical examples
5 a mixture of all the above
Which sentences from **a)** should be followed by each of them?

Task 2.2

Somchart and Alphonse have been writing essays on government subsidies (i.e. financial support by the government for the costs of food production, transport, etc.) for their Economics class. The paragraphs

that follow have been taken from a draft of their essays; each is concerned
with whether or not the arts (theatre, painting, etc.) should be subsidised.

1 Somchart's paragraph

When it comes to the arts, there is a clear case for subsidy. The arts have nothing to
do with making money. They exist in order to express certain essential truths about
human beings by means of new kinds of poetry, music, painting and so on. However,
these new kinds of art may not be popular, and thus there may be little support by
the general public for them, and so artists cannot rely on selling their work to provide
them with an income. In fact, history shows that many artists have not been properly
appreciated while they were alive. For example, Mozart, whose works are so popular
nowadays, lived close to poverty for most of his life.

2 Alphonse's paragraph

There are no grounds for subsidising the arts. The arts are not like food, education or
health, which are part of the basic necessities of life, and which should therefore be
subsidised if necessary. On the contrary, most of us live our lives quite happily without
paying any attention to the arts. They appeal only to a small minority and are a
luxury, rather than an essential. Furthermore, those who value the arts can usually
afford to pay the costs involved. The large corporations that buy the paintings of
artists such as Van Gogh for millions of dollars are a case in point.

a) The sentences within a paragraph need to be connected to each
other in such a way that they form a unified whole. This can be done
through a variety of ways.
  1 Joining words – *in fact, for example, first, …*
  2 Reference words – *a/the, it, these, …*
  3 Choice of vocabulary – repetition, word families, …
List the words and phrases Somchart and Alphonse each use to connect
their sentences together.

b) With two or three other students, compare your lists. How
successful do you feel each student was in 'knitting' their ideas together?

Task 2.3

Each paragraph usually ends with a sentence that paraphrases the main idea of the paragraph. This sentence also often leads the reader on to the next paragraph.

Look at the six sentences that follow. Which do you feel would best complete Somchart's and Alphonse's paragraphs?

1 In order to ensure their survival, thus, it is essential for the arts to be subsidised.
2 Companies which are capable of making such large payments should do much more to sponsor the arts.
3 If he had been subsidised, Mozart would not have been so poor.
4 In addition, if the arts are subsidised, then they are also likely to be controlled by the government.
5 Only essentials which cannot otherwise be paid for should be subsidised, and the arts should therefore be left to pay their own way.
6 When the arts have to make money, they are no longer fulfilling their true purpose, but instead become a branch of commerce.

Task 2.4

Maria is doing an essay for her Criminology class on drinking and driving. This is how she began one of the sections.

Why is driving when under the influence of alcohol so dangerous? Let us first of all look at how alcohol affects the body.

a) Complete this section of her essay by arranging the sentences below so that they form two clear consecutive paragraphs. Work on your own or with another student.

1 Coffee may wake the drinker up slightly – but that is all.
2 Three or four units make such drivers three times more likely to have an accident than those who have drunk no alcohol.
3 And although its action is rapid, the effects of alcohol wear off only slowly.
4 How does drinking affect driving?
5 Its effect is to lessen control over muscles, slow down reactions, make vision unclear and decrease awareness.
6 Thus psychologically as well as physically, and especially with young people, alcohol can have a serious effect on driving ability.
7 Alcohol is quick to act.
8 As a result, some drivers believe, wrongly, that they drive better after a few drinks.
9 It takes the body an hour to eliminate a single unit of alcohol (equivalent to half a pint of normal strength beer).
10 In fact, young and inexperienced drivers are unable to drive properly after drinking less than the legal limit of alcohol.
11 Nothing can remove alcohol from the blood, except time.
12 As well as its bodily effects, drinking gives drivers a strong (but false) sense of confidence, making it difficult for them to judge how fit they are to drive.

13   Even sleeping for eight hours only removes the alcohol from four
      pints of ordinary beer.
14   It takes just twenty minutes (less on an empty stomach) for it to pass
      into the bloodstream and all around the body, including the brain.

b) Just as it is important that the paragraphs are arranged in an
order that supports the main theme of your writing, so it is also
important that the ideas within a paragraph are arranged in a logical
order. With two or three other students, discuss any problems that you
had in completing a). How did you go about deciding the order? What
kinds of language helped you arrange the sentences in the order you
chose?

Task 2.5   The good paragraph

a) With two or three other students, construct a list of three or
four qualities of a good paragraph.

b) Take one of the sentences in 2.1 and write a paragraph which
conforms to the criteria for a good paragraph.

c) With another student, look critically at your writing and discuss
whether it conforms to your criteria, and how it might be improved.
You do not need to worry about grammar, spelling, punctuation, and so
on at this stage.

3   GETTING THE PROOF-READING RIGHT

Once you have got the overall structure of the essay and the paragraphs
right, the next task is to check the details of your written expression. This
includes checking the vocabulary, grammar, spelling, word order, sentence
order, and tone*, as well as re-checking for repetition, logical sequencing,
and so on.

Task 3.1 Proof-reading* for grammar, spelling, punctuation and similar problems

a) Eduardo has been writing an essay for his Philosophy class on
the topic of 'The two cultures: Myth or reality?'. The section that follows

has been edited using the commonly accepted symbols to indicate the problems. Read the passage below in order to

1 find the meaning of each symbol being used;

2 correct the passage.

It/commonly beliefed that scientists and artists has compleately different ways of watching at the world. What C P Snow call "the two Cultures" in his book with/same title. Accoarding/this view,/ scientist rely for his discoveries on "the scientific method"/ a carefully process of objectif experimentation and analysed. The Artist, on another hand/create his work/s of art as/result of "divine inspiration":/subjective leep to/imagination. I argue both of these view over-simplifies the picture, and similarities among the ways that Scientists and artists working/much greater/the differences are.

b) With two or three other students, compare the symbols that you use to indicate the same problem areas. Discuss which you prefer and why.

Task 3.2 Proof-reading for word and sentence order, signalling, logical ordering of ideas and addition and/or clarification of ideas

a) Here is the next part of Eduardo's essay. Work out what problems the symbols refer to.

However, many important scientific dicoveries have taken place, rather than because of the scientific method, by chance. Diesel/is said to have seen the structure/in the pattern of raindrops on a window. Next, the discovery of penicillin occurred when Fleming and his colleagues were actually working on a completely different problem. That he noticed the effect/on bacteria was purely good luck. Thus scientific discoveries cannot/only as a result of the scientific method be said to occur. There are many other examples of similar events.

b) Rewrite the section and then compare your answers with two or three other students.

Task 3.3 Proof-reading for repetition and redundancy

a) Look at the next section of Eduardo's essay. How could it be shortened by cutting out the parts where information is repeated or unnecessary?

Secondly, there is plenty of evidence that not all great works of art are the result of sudden inspiration. In whatever branch of the arts we look, things are similar. In painting and music there are certain basic rules of composition which are usually followed. The artist or the composer is not completely free. Poems which appear to have been written effortlessly are in fact often the result of many careful, conscious re-writings. Many poets constantly revise their poems. For example, in a famous essay, Edgar Allan Poe describes the procedure he followed in the process of composing the great poem 'The Raven'. This is one of his best-known poems. Each verse contains the word nevermore. In the essay, he talks about how he gradually thought out the smallest details of each part, working methodically from beginning to end, all the time attempting to produce the appearance of inspiration. The finished poem appears very natural, but was in fact very carefully constructed. The product was the result of a systematic working out of a plan. In other words, we should be careful not to mistake the appearance of the finished artistic product with the process that leads to it being produced in the first place. Whatever the nature of the former, the latter may be much closer to the methodical approach of the scientist than is usually realised.

b) Compare your answers with two or three other students.

Task 3.4 Proof-reading for tone

Language may be grammatically correct and clear in meaning and yet create a bad impression because the style or tone is wrong. It may be too informal for most academic writing because of, for example, contractions, overuse of *I*, colloquialisms*, etc., or too formal because of, for example, overuse of the passive voice, complicated words, etc. It is difficult to give precise guidelines about the correct tone to adopt, though probably in most cases one which is neither too formal nor too informal will be best.

a) Here is the remainder of Eduardo's essay. Use symbols to correct the tone as necessary.

As I've tried to show, it's just not right when people say that scientists and artists go about things in completely different ways. It is well known that chance can play a role in scientific discoveries. Similarly, a careful method of working can be an important part of producing a work of art. The real dividing line between scientists and artists may be not so much in their normal methods of operating, but in the materials they work with and the 'languages' they use to express their ideas. The scientist is mainly concerned with attempting to understand the natural world, the artist with the world of the imagination. The scientist conveys information by means of mathematics and facts, the artist's way of getting his message across is through colours, shapes, sounds and fiction. But, basically, what I'm saying is that both are concerned with trying to discover and express truths. The search for truth in any area involves both science and art. So it's quite clearly the case that the idea of the two cultures is therefore a myth.

KEEPING YOUR
WRITING IN TUNE.

b) Compare your corrections with two or three other students.

Task 3.5 General practice in proof-reading

 a) Proof-read the following paragraphs, which have been taken from Ali's essay for his Legal Studies class on the topic of patent law. In this part of his essay, he explains in the first paragraph how patent law originated and in the second he argues that patent law should be changed in order to encourage non-technological inventions. You will need to decide how the paragraphs could be improved, and then make your corrections by editing his essay.

Patent law, which protect an invention from being copied, was originally devised in Europe in the 15th century in order to encourage innovation. As a result before this time, an inventor had not legal way of stopping other people to copy his or her invention. This was because other people copied the inventions. This was difficult for inventors to make money from their ideas. However when patent law was began, a much greater number of inventions began to come into existence because the inventors were able to protect their ideas from being copied.

Most of these inventions have been of the same kind. Most of these inventions have been technological. This has been because inventors can usually make money more from technological inventions, as a result, Europe and other parts of the West have become highly technological societies. However, it has reduced the level of creativity and innovation in non-technological areas. This is because inventors are less interested in non-technological inventions because there is less money to be made from them. Such as better systems of education, new ways of looking after the sick and elderly, improvements in leisure-time opportunities, and so on. Patent law needs to be changed to encourage social as well as technological innovation. Unless this happens, there's a danger that technological inventions will lead to further industrialisation. And the need for social developments will be neglected.

 b) Now proof-read the paragraph you wrote in Task 9.2.5.

4 GETTING THE CONVENTIONS RIGHT

PUTTING ON THE FINISHING TOUCHES.

The last part of putting the finishing touches to a piece of academic writing involves making sure that special features such as paraphrasing, quotations, references, appendices, lay-out and so on, have all been done properly.

Note Other conventions are covered in other parts of *Study Tasks in English*, e.g. bibliographies can be found in 4.4.1–5; see the index for other conventions.

Task 4.1

If you use someone else's ideas or words, then you must do so properly. Failure to do this is plagiarism, and is regarded as a form of academic stealing!

a) This handout has been taken from the handbook for the course of study you are taking. Read it and then answer the questions which follow.

Plagiarism Coursework essays and the dissertation must constitute your own unaided work. Naturally in the course of presenting your own case you will refer to the ideas, findings and explanations of others, but when doing so you are expected to conform to the recognised standards of good academic practice: i.e. ideas, findings, phrases and sentences taken from the work of others must be acknowledged in the standard form.

There are broadly two ways of doing this. One is to paraphrase the views of another author, i.e. summarise them without direct quotation:

Dore (1976) claims that educational qualifications are valued as certificates of social acceptancy rather than as indicators that the possessors have learned something useful.

The second is direct quotation of short passages:

As Dore says, 'The paradox of the situation is that the worse the educated unemployment situation gets and the more useless educational certificates become, the stronger grows the pressure for an expansion of educational facilities' (Dore, 1976, p.4).

Then at the end of the essay:

Dore, R. (1976) The Diploma Disease, Unwin Educational Books.

If you do not acknowledge in this way the ideas of other writers, you run the risk of being regarded as a plagiarist. All cases of plagiarism will be heavily penalised.

Similarly, the Department encourages students to discuss their work with each other, but it is obviously inadmissible to copy work from another student's or to try to pass off someone else's work as your own. Any submission as your own work of essays or parts of essays originally written by someone else constitutes plagiarism.

---

1 What is plagiarism?
2 Are you allowed to use the ideas of other writers? Explain.
3 When do you not need to use quotation marks around others' ideas?
4 What does (1976) refer to?
5 What happens to students who do not follow the advice given in the handout?
6 Are students allowed to discuss their essays with each other? Explain.
7 What happens if you present your tutors' ideas as your own?
8 Why does the writer use the word *similarly* (final paragraph)?

b) Read this passage and then write two references using the writer's idea as you would in an essay.

The smart job-seeker needs to rid herself of several standard myths about interviewing before she starts pounding the pavement looking for a job. What follows is a list of some of these untruths and some tips to help you do your best at your next interview.

Dick Irish in *Glamour*
Cambridge University Press, 1982, p. 22.

Task 4.2

Lastly, it is important to take care over presenting the final version of your work in the proper way.

a) Listen to the discussion between two lecturers about the way some students present their written work. What faults in the students' essays do the teachers mention? What problems do the teachers say that the faults lead to? Make a table, like this:

	FAULTS	PROBLEMS
1		
2		
3		

b) In pairs, use your notes on the conversation you have just listened to and any other ideas you have about the use of conventions in writing to do one of the following activities.

1 Write a handout of the basic rules (conventions) suggested by the lecturers at the end of their conversation.
2 Make a poster illustrating how to set out your written work in the proper way. For this, you may wish to concentrate on one (or more) aspect(s) of the conventions in academic writing.

5 UNIT ASSESSMENT AND APPLICATION

One of the most common problems with most students' academic writing is that they do not do the extensive editing of their writing that is really necessary. As a result, the product is too often a one-sided dialogue, with the reader taken insufficiently into consideration. And yet the whole purpose of a piece of writing is for it to be read. Writing therefore involves constantly asking questions of yourself, so that you put yourself in the reader's shoes at all times.

Task 5.1 What makes something you read enjoyable and interesting?

a) Think about the different items you have read in connection with your studies (in any language).
1 Which of them do you prefer to read?
2 Which of them do you find difficult to read?
3 What is it about the writing in either case that affects your attitude?
Make a list of what you consider to be the most important characteristics of a good piece of academic writing.

b) Discuss your ideas with two or three other students, and reach a consensus about a short-list of such qualities.

Task 5.2 Evaluating your writing

a) Exchange a recent piece of your writing with another student. Evaluate each other's work in terms of the qualities of academic writing you identified in Task 5.1.

b) Discuss the results together. Work together to revise each other's writing to take into account your evaluations.

c) Look at the checklist you completed in Task 7.1.1.
1 Where do you feel you have improved in your writing skills?
2 Where do you think you still need practice?
3 How do you think you can further improve your writing skills?
Discuss your answers with another student.

THE MEASUREMENT OF GOOD WRITING:
HOW DOES YOUR WRITING WEIGH UP?

UNIT **10 Coping with research**

'Research' has two main meanings. It can refer to work done in a library, in which you look at books and articles written on a topic and then use the results to arrive at your own conclusions. It can also refer to empirical information collected 'in the field'. This second kind of research is relatively common in science and the social sciences, and may involve experiments, surveys, interviews, and so on.

In your studies, you will probably be expected to understand empirical research sufficiently to cope with it when you come across it in your library research. It is also possible that you will have to conduct your own empirical research, although it is likely that you will first of all be given further training in how to do this.

The aim of this unit, therefore, is to help you understand the basics of field-based research in order to make judgements about its validity and reliability in your own library-based research, as well as to provide a basis for beginning your own field research if necessary.

1 GOING TO THE SOURCE

In empirical research, it is helpful to look at not just the results but also the methods that were used to collect the information and the samples that were used, and to check if chance and various external factors are involved. This will help you decide to what extent you can rely on the validity of the findings.

Task 1.1 What is empirical research?

Empirical research is a way of solving some problem or uncovering information by means of observation and experimentation, as well as reading.

a) Listen to Kate and Jeffrey discuss the kinds of research they have done. What problem was each investigating? What difficulties do they mention?

b) With two or three other students, discuss the answers to these questions.
1 Have you ever done any empirical research?
2 If so, what did you do?
3 What methods did you use?
4 Did you encounter any problems?

Task 1.2 Are the methods appropriate?

There are many different ways to conduct research, and each method uncovers a slightly different kind of information. Some of the methods used are outlined below; you may be familiar with others. If you are aware of the different methods, it is easier to evaluate the degree to which you can rely on the findings.

Research Methods

a) **Observation (case study):** a kind of survey in which specific factors are observed and recorded without the observer becoming involved. Examples include watching a bee send messages to the hive or watching a child working out sums; often neither the bee or the child knows they are being observed. The purpose is to find out how something is done.

b) **Sampling:** a kind of survey in which representative* samples are collected for description and analysis; examples include collecting rock samples from a beach or asking people what kind of tea they drink – in both cases, a description of the population* is being gathered. A variety of techniques for obtaining information from subjects* can be used, including questionnaires, one-to-one interviews and group discussions.

c) **Examining records:** this method looks at information already collected in order to uncover new relationships or descriptions. This information may take the form of historical descriptions, developmental patterns, or forecasting trends. It may use, for example, past or present census findings, police records, past weather records, etc.

d) **Experiments:** experiments involve manipulating different factors, called variables, in order to see what happens. They usually involve at least two representative samples. The experiment is done to the first group (the 'experimental' group); nothing is done to the second group (the 'control' group). The two groups are then compared. Any change that has occurred is then attributed to* the experiment. This method is common in both science and the social sciences.

---

a) Match the various methods of obtaining information with the list of topics for study. Which method(s) could you use if you wanted to know more on the following topics? You do not have to use all the methods, and you may wish to suggest alternative methods.
1 Study habits of university postgraduate students
2 Problems of the unemployed
3 Using computers to improve writing
4 Voting patterns among the wealthy
5 Reasons for owning a car
6 The use of corporal punishment to promote learning

b) With two or three other students, compare your answers. Discuss what kind of information might be uncovered using the different methods. There is no one 'best' answer. Our *Research Methods* list is not comprehensive; you may wish to add methods of your own.

Task 1.3 Are the samples representative?

The *population* is the group being studied in a piece of research; the *sample* is the part of the population actually investigated. Usually the population is so large that it would be too difficult to describe all its members. It is also unnecessary. Instead, a sample is taken.

It is essential that the sample is representative, i.e. typical of the population as a whole. For example, if you wanted to describe the height of all the students in a school, you could measure twenty students and use their heights to indicate the range in height as well as the average height of all the students. This would only work, however, if the twenty students were representative of the school as a whole. If, for instance, an unrepresentative sample of twenty girls were measured, the average height would probably be lower than the average for a mixed-sex school.

Look at the samples given and discuss whether or not you feel they are representative. Give reasons for your decision. You may wish to suggest alternative samples.

1 A geographer is investigating shopping trends in the capital. She interviews 40 shoppers outside a major department store on Saturday morning.
2 A political party wants to find out if the voters support their policies. It sends out a questionnaire to all its members.
3 An environmental scientist is interested in the quality of water in a local district. He takes water samples from the river running through the town.
4 A medical student wants to find out how many children have colds in winter. In January, she decides to go to a local pre-school and see how many children have colds.
5 The government needs to know the rate people are moving from farms into the cities. They interview 200 people in the capital.
6 An economist wants to find out how earnings relate to qualifications within a large manufacturing company. He puts all the names of the employees in a hat and selects twenty to interview.

Task 1.4

One way of ensuring the samples are representative of the population is to make sure the sample is random. This means that each member of the population has an equal chance of being a member of the sample. In a random sample, individual members may not be typical, but the sample itself is typical in that the variety of members represents the variety in the population. Returning to the example of student height, if the twenty students measured had been selected randomly, e.g. by putting all their names in a hat, then some of the twenty would have been tall, some short, and the majority would be about average in comparison with the whole.

a) With two or three other students, select something that can be measured (i.e. counted). You may want to select the number of people wearing white shoes, the number of people with black hair, or the number of people who walk to class. Count the numbers and record them in a chart like the one that follows.

black shoes	total in class	% with black shoes

b) Now select a random sample of students in the class. You may vary the size of the sample, but make sure the sample you select is random (e.g. by drawing straws, choosing every third name on the register, etc.). Count the number of members of the sample in the same way you did for the class.

black shoes	total in sample	% with black shoes

c) Compare the results you got for the sample with the results for the class. How did the size of the sample affect your results?

d) If you have time, try to select a representative sample without using random techniques. Can you do it without knowing the description of the population? You may wish to try with a different characteristic.

2 CHECKING RELIABILITY AND VALIDITY

The findings of research need to be both reliable and valid. This means that they are not biased, do not rely on unclear definitions, and are not pre-determined by the researcher. In other words, if someone else wanted to check the information, they should be able to do the same thing and get the same result.

Reliability refers to whether or not the findings are constant and unchanging – and do not depend on what sample is chosen, who the researcher was, or how the questions are interpreted. In other words, you can rely on the results to describe the population accurately.

Validity refers to whether or not the results describe what they say they describe. In other words, do the methods used affect the results, and what populations can the results realistically be attributed to?

One important way of ensuring reliability and validity is to select a representative sample. There are several other factors to take into account as well.

Task 2.1 Check the language

Often interviews, questionnaires and records are subject to different interpretations which will bias the results.

A group of EFL students want to find out what a typical English family's eating habits are. They decide that the best way to determine this is to write a multiple-choice questionnaire.

English Eating Habits Questionnaire

1 What do you like to have for breakfast?
   a) bacon and eggs
   b) toast with jam
   c) coffee
   d) cornflakes
2 What do you usually eat for dinner?
   a) meat
   b) chicken
   c) fish
   d) eggs
3 How often do you eat potatoes for supper?
   a) every day
   b) frequently
   c) seldom
   d) never
4 Which food do you think is the best?
   a) Chinese
   b) Italian
   c) English
   d) French
5 Does your family sit down and eat together?
   a) yes
   b) no
   c) sometimes
   d) only on Sunday
6 Which of these statements do you agree with?
   a) British people do not like foreign food.
   b) British cooking is boring.
   c) British tea is old-fashioned.
   d) British people eat too much fried food.
   e) Convenience food is good for you.

With two or three other students, use their questionnaire to answer the following questions:
1 Are there any words that could have more than one meaning?
2 Are any of the questions open to more than one interpretation?
3 Will the answers on the questionnaire bias the responses given to the questions?
4 What assumptions do the writers of the questionnaire make about English eating habits?
5 How could this questionnaire be improved to make it more reliable?

Task 2.2 Making sure the language is reliable

a) With another student, select one of the topics that follow (or one of your own if you prefer). Write a short questionnaire to use to find out the needed information.
1 Attitudes to speaking English
2 Typical family life of the members of the class
3 How to make the best use of the weekend
4 Opinions on women–men equality
5 Attitudes to pets

b) Exchange questionnaires with another pair of students and answer the questions. With two or three other students, discuss any problems that occurred. Do you think the questionnaires would produce reliable and valid results if they were given to a representative sample? You may wish to use the check questions in Task 2.1 to help guide the discussion.

c) With two or three other students, discuss the advantages of testing the method before conducting the research.

Task 2.3 Check the background knowledge

Good research needs to do what it says it does. For example, if it is supposed to describe a typical house in England, it isn't much help if the description is based on Buckingham Palace. Similarly, if you want to describe what people eat, it isn't much help to devise a questionnaire that has already determined the answer before the questions have been asked. To help make sure that the research being conducted is doing what it claims, it is helpful to do a lot of background reading to find out what is already known.

a) With two or three other students, discuss what kinds of general background information would be useful before beginning a piece of research. Give examples.

b) For the questionnaire you wrote in Task 2.2, what kind of background information did you need? What additional information do you think would have been helpful?

Task 2.4 Are the results logical and clearly thought out?

Good research is based on clear, logical thinking. It is important that any research being conducted or read is based on the critical thinking skills outlined in Units 2 and 3.

 a) Read the summary of a research project that follows.

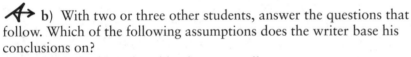

In conclusion, this research has shown that English people generally like their own pets, but cannot tolerate other people's pets. Of the twenty people who were asked if they had a pet, seventeen responded 'yes'. From this, we must conclude that the English are fond of pets. However, when the same twenty people were asked about controlling vicious dogs, all but one stated these dogs should either be put down or neutered. In addition, ten people also stated that they disliked cats digging up their gardens and thirteen people stated they disliked dogs barking at night. Fifteen people interviewed also believed that owners must take responsibility for their animals' behaviour. In other words, most people were not fond of other people's dogs or cats. This position is supported by the action of the government which now requires all vicious dogs to be registered with the police. Therefore, this research has disproved the saying that "England is a country of animal lovers".

 b) With two or three other students, answer the questions that follow. Which of the following assumptions does the writer base his conclusions on?

1 People who have dogs like dogs generally.
2 People do not differentiate between pets. If they like or dislike one kind of pet, they like or dislike all kinds of pets.
3 People who want vicious dogs controlled cannot tolerate other people's pets.
4 People who do not like cats spoiling their garden do not like pets.
5 People who do not like cats spoiling their garden do not have cats.
6 People who do not like dogs barking at night do not have dogs.
7 People who do not like dogs barking at night do not like pets.
8 People who believe that owners must take responsibility for their pets believe that other people do not control their pets at the moment.
9 People do not like cats and dogs that are not controlled.
10 Registration of dogs indicates that people do not control their pets.
11 People do not like pets that are not controlled.

 c) Which of the above assumptions do you think are logical, valid and reliable? Discuss.

 d) The writer draws two conclusions. What are they? Do you feel these are justified? Discuss.

 e) From the evidence given, what conclusion(s) can be drawn, if any?

Task 2.5 Recording results

Both validity and reliability depend on accurate record-keeping. It is not sufficient to rely on memory alone. It is usually helpful to develop a code or system for recording the results. If language is a problem, it is probably best to have questions for which the answers are written, or to use a tape-recorder.

a) Peter decided to use a tape-recorder to interview people about how much television they watched on Saturday, what they watched, and what they liked and disliked. Listen to the recording of several of his interviews. Develop a system to record the results.

b) Listen to the tape again and record the results. You will need to listen to the tape several times.

c) With two or three other students, discuss what you think are the most important points about recording results. What factors do you think are most important?

3 PRESENTING STATISTICS AND DIAGRAMS

Once information has been collected, it is usually analysed using a variety of statistical techniques and then presented in graphs, charts or tables. The aim of section 3 is to look at a few common techniques for presenting information in this way. The focus is on interpreting this kind of data, rather than calculating (though a certain amount of calculation cannot be avoided).

Task 3.1 Pie charts

Pie charts are often used to show the proportions of various parts of the findings in relation to each other and to the whole.

a) Look at the pie chart in Diagram 1.
 1 What does the circle represent?
 2 How many nationalities are in the Institute?
 3 What nationality is represented by the largest segment*?
 4 Which two segments are the same size?
 5 Are there more men or women from France?
 6 How many Italians are there?

b) Discuss what kinds of information can be represented in pie charts. What advantages do pie charts have over columns of numbers or a written description? What kinds of information must be omitted from pie charts?

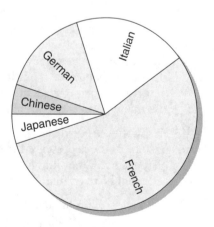

Diagram 1

Nationalities at the ABC English Language Institute

125

➤ c) The following information was collected in a survey of postgraduates. Construct a pie chart to illustrate the kinds of cars owned by postgraduate students. You may not need to include all the information given.

	Fiat	Honda	Ford	Renault	no car
men	6	5	5	3	8
women	2	5	8	2	6

Task 3.2 Histograms

Histograms (or bar graphs) are also used to describe findings, but the emphasis is usually comparing different parts to each other, rather than in relation to the whole.

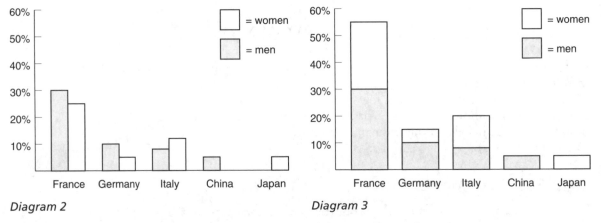

Diagram 2

Diagram 3

Nationalities at the ABC English Language Institute

➤ a) Look at the histograms in Diagrams 2 and 3. They show two ways to illustrate the same information.
 1 What percentage of women come from France?
 2 Which country has the fewest women?
 3 How many men come from Italy?
 4 What percentage of students come from Italy?
 5 How many people are in the Institute?

➤ b) With two or three other students, discuss what kinds of information can be represented in histograms. How do pie charts differ from histograms? What kinds of information can be included in or excluded from histograms? What are the advantages of using histograms?

➤ c) Construct a histogram that illustrates the car-owning patterns of postgraduate men and women, using the information in Task 3.1c. Remember, in most histograms, the horizontal axis* is used to indicate the different segments of the population and the vertical axis* indicates the number, percentage or amount of difference between groups.

Task 3.3 Line graphs

Often graphs are used to present experimental results which involve some kind of change. This usually involves two sets of measurements called variables.

a) You are measuring changes in the size of feet of pre-school children between the ages of two and five.
1 What are the two variables?
2 Which variable causes the change?
   (We call the variable that causes the change the *independent* variable and the other the *dependent* variable.)
Look at the first graph, in Diagram 4.

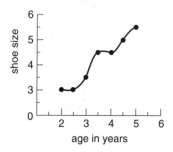

Diagram 4 Profile of Leanne's shoe size

3 Which variable is on the horizontal axis?
4 Which variable is on the vertical axis?
5 What size shoe does this child wear at three?
6 When does she wear a size 5 shoe?
7 Does she change shoe sizes every six months? Explain.

Look at the second graph, in Diagram 5.
 8 Which variable is the independent variable now?
 9 Which variable is the dependent variable?
10 Which shoe size is most common in pre-school?

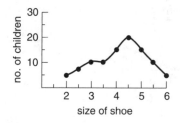

Diagram 5 Shoe size of children in Bo Beep Playschool

11 How many children wear size 4?
12 How old do you think the children in the play school are generally?
(You may wish to refer to Diagram 4.)

+> b) Line graphs can illustrate two sets of information on one graph, so long as the variables are the same. Construct a graph to compare Zubeda's Chemistry marks with those for Biology. Remember to decide which is the independent variable and place it on the horizontal axis.

	Chemistry	Biology
October	70%	45%
December	63%	50%
February	55%	53%
March	58%	58%
May	55%	60%
June	50%	65%

+> c) In which subject is Zubeda showing improvement? What are the advantages of presenting the results in a line graph rather than as statistics in a table? Are there any disadvantages? What is important to remember if you have to read or construct line graphs?

Task 3.4 Flow charts

Flow charts are diagrams used to describe processes involving decisions. They are also useful in showing alternative courses of action.

As part of their Business Studies course, Rabia and Fatmata visited several large firms to find out about the process of innovation in terms of adopting new products. They decided to present their findings in terms of a flow chart (Diagram 6, opposite).

+> a) Use the flow chart Rabia and Fatmata constructed to answer the following questions.
1 What kind of information is in the rectangles?
2 What kind of information is in the diamonds?
3 What do the arrows tell the reader to do?
4 If the product is cost-effective, what does the company do next?
5 If the company feels it needs new products, what does it do next?
6 What is the purpose of the small-scale trials?
7 What happens if the product proves unfeasible after it has been developed?
8 When will the companies stop the process of developing a new product?

+> b) What do you feel are some of the advantages of using a flow chart? Do you find them easy to follow? Have you ever had to construct one?

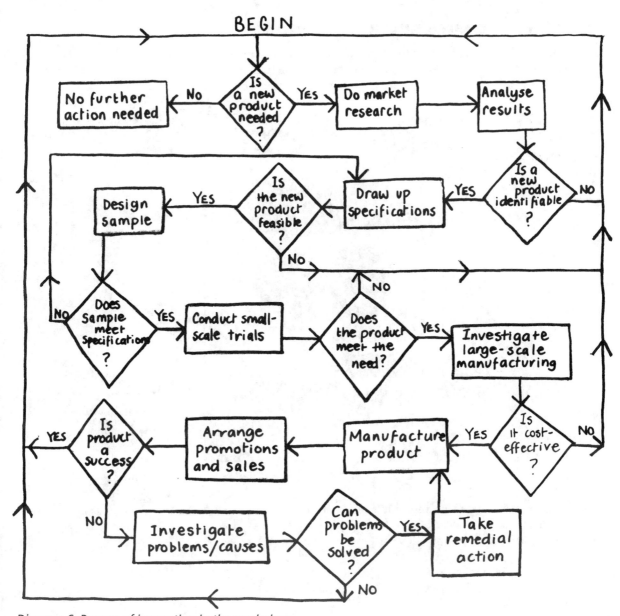

BEGIN

Diagram 6 Process of innovation in the workplace

c) Choose a process you are familiar with and construct a flow
chart showing the steps and the different decisions being made. You may
wish to describe some job or subject you are familiar with, or you may
wish to use one of the processes below.
1 washing the dinner dishes
2 finding a book in the library
3 buying a new pair of shoes
4 applying for a new job
5 mending a bicycle puncture

Task 3.5 Diagrams and illustrations

Diagrams and illustrations are commonly used to convey information or to clarify an idea. They are especially important in research where words may not sufficiently convey the meaning of what has been observed.

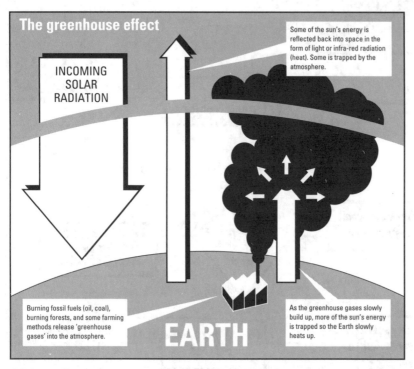

Diagram 7

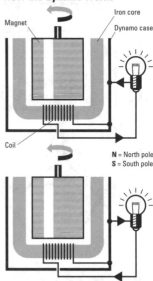

How the dynamo works

As the magnet rotates within the soft iron core, the constantly changing polarity (direction of magnetic attraction) creates an **alternating current (AC)**, which lights the lamps. The north and south poles refer to the opposite points on the magnet's surface at which magnetic forces are strongest.

Diagram 8

Look at the diagrams and illustrations above. With two or three other students, answer these questions.

1 What information is being conveyed in each illustration?
2 How are the parts labelled?
3 How has the information been simplified?
4 Write a set of guidelines for good diagrams and illustrations.

Task 3.6 Calculating the average

The average is a common statistic found in a wide variety of research, and it can be calculated in a variety of ways. It usually refers to what mathematicians call the *mean*. It is calculated by adding all the scores together and then dividing by the number of scores. For example, if five children wear the following size shoes: 5, 6, 6, 8, and 10, then the average shoe size (the mean) is 35 (the total) divided by 5 (number of children) = 7.0. It is interesting to note that none of the children wears a size 7 shoe.

Sometimes it is not possible to calculate the average in this way. For example, in describing a typical English breakfast, you cannot add up the kinds of food and divide by the number of possibilities. However, you can state which food was most frequently eaten. This kind of average, referring to the most frequent, is called the *mode*, and is also a very useful average.

a) A group of students wanted to compare the age of men and women reading* English at the local university, and a random sample of students produced the results that follow. Find the average age of men and women reading English. What conclusions can be reached?

student	sex	age	student	sex	age
A	F	25	G	F	19
B	M	21	H	F	27
C	F	29	I	M	20
D	M	21	J	M	26
E	M	26	K	F	29
F	F	20	L	M	18

Note A wide variety of statistics are available relating to correlation (see Unit 3) and reliability. Methods of calculating these have not been included here.

b) Represent the findings above using a bar graph, a pie chart, or a line graph. With two or three other students, compare your diagrams. Were there any differences? Discuss.

Task 3.7 The normal curve

Distribution (see Task 1.2) is often plotted on a graph. A graph shows at a glance the range of scores (from the lowest to the highest) as well as the frequency of each score. For example, if the scores of 20 students are plotted on a graph, it might look something like Diagram 9.

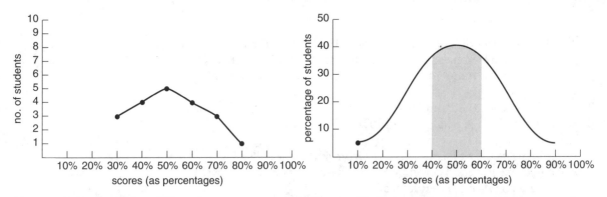

Diagram 9 *Exam results of 20 students*   Diagram 10 *University exam scores*

If the sample of twenty students was representative of the students at the university as a whole, then the most common score of university students would be 50%, and the majority of students would have scores around 50%, with a few students at either extreme (Diagram 10). Idealised

curves such as the one shown in Diagram 10 are called normal
distribution curves. The number of people on one side of the centre is the
same as on the other side, with about 50% of the students near the
centre.

Occasionally, distribution is not normal, due to outside factors. For
example, if the school was intended for basketball players, the curve
would hump* nearer the large end of the scale (Diagram 11).

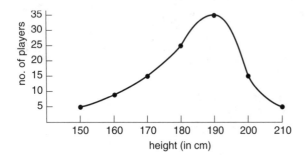

Diagram 11 Height of basketball school players

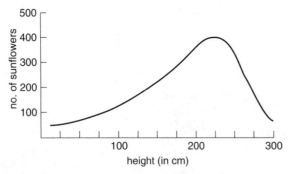

Diagram 12 Plant growth – fertile soil

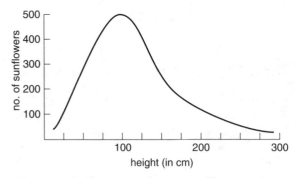

Diagram 13 Plant growth – poor soil

Use the curves in Diagrams 12 and 13 to answer the following
questions. Compare your answers with two or three other students.
1 What is the most frequent height of the sunflowers grown in fertile
   soil?
2 Which were the tallest sunflowers that grew in these experiments?
3 What is the average height of sunflowers grown in poor soil? What
   kind of average are you using?
4 What is the range of heights for the fertile and poor soils?
5 Are some sunflowers taller in poor soil than others grown in fertile
   soil? How could this be explained?
6 Is it better to grow plants in fertile or poor soil? Explain your answer
   in terms of the graphs.
7 If only two plants had been planted, one in fertile soil and one in poor
   soil, would it be possible to have shown that sunflowers grow better in
   poor soil? How?

4 PUTTING IT TOGETHER

The writing up of your research needs to be done in a way that conveys the information accurately and concisely*. The skills developed in Units 8 and 9 on writing apply equally to writing up research.

Research, however, has two additional parts: describing how the information was obtained and then describing the information itself. (If you are reading research, it is often helpful to look at these two sections in detail, rather than simply accepting the conclusions as outlined in the introduction or conclusion.)

Task 4.1 Parts of a research document

a) Below is a list of the parts of a research document and a list of what each part does. Match the description of each part with its name.

1 Introduction	a) summarises the research findings and analyses its conclusions and significance in respect to other research
2 Conclusion	b) presents the actual research findings – what was learnt; it may include graphs, statistics, tables, and so on
3 Summary/Implications	c) states what the research is about and what this paper will show; it may also indicate how the paper is organised
4 Description of research implementation	d) states what the research has shown and suggests ideas or limitations for future research; no new ideas presented
5 Description of related research and theory	e) describes precisely and in detail how the research was carried out, including details about the sample, where the research was conducted, and how it was carried out
6 Description of research findings	f) describes background information including details of previous research, as well as what is already known

b) The parts of a research paper listed above are not necessarily in the correct order. With two or three other students, decide what you feel is the best order of presentation. Are there any parts you feel have been omitted?

Task 4.2 Presenting a research document

With two or three other students, make a poster on writing a good research project. You may include points from this unit, or from Units 8 and 9, as well as using your own experiences in reading or writing research.

5 UNIT ASSESSMENT AND APPLICATION

Conducting reliable and valid research requires a wide variety of skills involving organisation, critical thinking, logic and presentation. Many of these skills are introduced elsewhere in this book. Research demands that these skills be used in a systematic way. When interpreting and analysing other writers' research, it is important to look at each step in the process and assess its organisation, methods, and conclusions for bias, logic, and relationship to background knowledge.

Task 5.1

With two or three other students, conduct and write up your own small-scale research project. You will need to make use of your library skills, reading skills and writing skills, as well as the information in this unit. If you have difficulty thinking of a project, there are some ideas for research projects scattered throughout this unit.

Task 5.2

Make a short presentation of the research you did in Task 5.1 to your classmates. You will need to summarise your work in order to present it in an interesting way.

Task 5.3

Discuss with two or three other students some of the problems involved in conducting small-scale research, and how these might be overcome.

UNIT 11 Getting to grips with assessment

Whether we like it or not, evaluation is an integral* part of education. Much of the assessment in higher and further education is based on projects, essays, reports, and other written assignments which you do on your own and then give in to be marked. However, most students are also required to take examinations. These tests usually include essays, short answer questions, and multiple-choice items.

1 WHAT IS EVALUATION?

Evaluation is the word used to describe the way your teacher or course assessor* determines whether or not your work meets the aims of the course, and to what standard. Another word for evaluation is assessment. It is helpful for you to know about the typical forms of assessment and what is generally being tested with each.

Task 1.1 Multiple-choice tests

Multiple-choice tests usually consist of an incomplete statement or a question that you have to complete by choosing the best response from a list of four or five possible answers.

a) You have five minutes to complete the test below. Write the correct answer to each question.

---

1 ? are lime-secreting marine polyps found living in colonies in tropical seas, whose skeletons build up to form a reef.
  A Coelacanths   B Gavil   C Coral
  D Symbiosis   E Deep sea clams
2 What were the characteristics of Neanderthal man found in palaeolithic Europe?
  A retreating forehead and massive brow-ridges
  B long limbs and dark hair
  C squat body and canine teeth
  D elementary speech and primitive paintings
  E none of these
3 Which of the following statements is false?
  A Puerto Ricans are United States citizens.
  B English is Puerto Rico's national language.
  C Most Puerto Ricans are of Spanish or African descent.
  D Most Puerto Ricans are Roman Catholics.
  E Puerto Rico is in the Caribbean.

---

b) The chances of you getting all the answers correct by guessing is 1 in 125. A student who only guesses in a multiple-choice test can expect to get around 20% correct. However, there are ways to raise your score – studying being the most obvious. Which of the methods below did you use to increase your chances of getting the correct answer?

1 eliminated* answers I knew were wrong
2 eliminated answers that contradicted common sense
3 used my own general knowledge
4 eliminated answers that I couldn't understand
5 looked for key words in the questions that indicated what kind of answer to expect
6 looked for patterns in the answers and avoided these
7 eliminated illogical answers
8 other – please specify

c) Discuss with two or three other students the different strategies you use to help you succeed in multiple-choice tests.

Task 1.2 Short-answer tests

Short-answer tests require you to supply the answer, rather than simply recognising the correct answer from a list provided. Usually these exams are testing your general knowledge of a subject and do not require you to apply your knowledge or develop theories. The important thing is to answer the question precisely and concisely.

a) Look at the test taken by John. You are the teacher. Correct his test.

~~bibliography~~   ~~bibligraphy~~   bibliography

a footnote is at the bottom and tells more information that's not important

This is probably an apple but it might not be.

How was this information obtained?
Why are these men bald?

To find information and to be able to know new ideas and to read quickly and to say it's

It is important to talk to your teacher and read lots of books and *(correct and* talk to your friends and to write clearly and neatly and to check *to find* your ideas and to write a bibliography and to make footnotes *details.)* and to underline important ideas.

---

b) What score did you give John? What mistakes did he make? How could he have received more marks? With two or three other students, compare how you marked John's test. Did you all agree? What advice would the group give John for his next short-answer test?

Task 1.3 Essay examinations

Essay examinations usually consist of a choice of questions. For example, you may be asked to answer two out of three questions or three out of five questions. It is unusual for the student to have to answer more than three questions in any one examination. Students are usually expected to provide more than just the facts in an essay exam – they may also be expected to give an opinion, explain a theory, develop an idea, or discuss a position.

a) Listen to Ian and Cecille discuss the essay exam they just took. With two or three other students, discuss how you think they did in their exam.

b) Write down the numbers of the items below that you feel are good advice for success in essay examinations. With two or three other students, compare your answers.
1 Read the test through before you begin.
2 Outline your ideas before you begin to write.
3 Make sure you answer one question completely before you begin the next.
4 Answer the questions in the order they are given.
5 Write everything you know about the topic.
6 Make your position clear at the beginning and end.
7 Use facts to support your opinions rather than the reverse.
8 Bring in past experience and related information if relevant.
9 Work out how long you have for each main question.

Task 1.4 Term* papers* and projects

Nowadays, students are often expected to write papers during the term as an alternative to final examinations. These papers require you to show your knowledge of the subject. However, the emphasis is not so much on how well you can remember or recall information, as is required in an examination. Rather, it is on how well you can use the information and present it in a logical, well-organised manner.

If English is a foreign language for you, being asked to write term papers, projects, or extended 'take-home' questions* has both advantages and disadvantages. With two or three other students, decide which of the points below are advantages and which are disadvantages of this form of assessment. How do you think some of the problems can be overcome?
1 Requires a lot of independent reading.
2 Allows you to work at your own pace.
3 Does not force you to learn a lot of new words.
4 Does not require you to think continuously in English.

5 Requires you to be organised.
6 Requires you to express yourself logically and clearly.
7 Allows you to refer to the dictionary and books as you write.
8 Other: please specify.

Task 1.5

You can expect to meet many different kinds of assessment techniques in
your studies in English. Some are more common in North America or
Australia and New Zealand, others in Britain. Some teachers prefer one
method of assessment to another, and some courses or subjects lend
themselves to one form of evaluation more than another. As a student,
therefore, you need to know about all the different possible forms of
assessment you might experience.

**HOW CAN I STUDY SUCCESSFULLY
FOR ALL OF THESE?**

a) John decided to list the different kinds of assessment he has
experienced, in order to help him know how to study best for each of
them. He made a table to help him. Here is what he produced.

Assessments	Purpose	Mark	What I studied	Comments/Suggestions
essay	explain causes of drug abuse in N.Y.	C+	books, classnotes, discussion with friends	didn't outline so paper tended to ramble; needed to know more facts.

Make a similar table to outline several ways you have been assessed.
Consider these questions:
– What was the purpose of the method of assessment in each case?
– Did you receive a mark? Did you think it showed your true ability?
– What did you have to do or learn for the mark?
– How do you think you might get a better mark next time?
– Which kind of evaluation do you prefer? Why?

b) With two or three other students, compare your answers.
Discuss the purpose of different kinds of evaluation. Which do you
prefer? Why?

2 GETTING READY

One of the most important steps in coping successfully with evaluation is preparation. If you don't study, you should not be surprised if you do not do very well! Looking at different kinds of examinations is an important step if you want to make the most of your preparation time. The next step is to prepare for your assessment constructively*.

Task 2.1 Put yourself in your teacher's shoes

It may be helpful to form the habit of asking yourself:
- What are the aims of the course?
- What am I expected to know or be able to do?
- What is the purpose of the test or piece of evaluation?
- What kind of things is the teacher looking for?
- Why did the teacher choose this type of evaluation?

The answers to these questions should help to provide a framework for your studies. For example, your teacher may give a short-answer test because she has 135 students and wants to find out if you know the basic facts. If you write a long essay, no matter how good it is, it will not impress her or get you higher marks. In fact, it is likely to reduce your mark because you will not have time to complete the exam and you may appear not to know the precise answer to the question asked.

With two or three other students, discuss ways of obtaining the answers to the questions at the beginning of this task. What other kinds of information might you want to find out about the examination before you begin studying?

Task 2.2 Aids to memory

Studying for an exam demands that you learn and remember facts and ideas. However, you may need to study differently for different types of exams. For example, if you are taking a multiple-choice exam, you will need to be able to recognise the answer, understand the content, and understand basic concepts. You will not need to be able to explain ideas in your own words or recall specific facts from memory.

On the other hand, if you are taking an essay test, you will need to be able to explain your ideas clearly and produce specific examples as illustrations – but you may not need to know as wide a range of topics. As a foreign speaker of English, you will also need to consider ways of remembering the basic vocabulary. Different people develop different techniques to help them remember facts.

a) Look at the list of memorisation techniques below. Write down the numbers and put a tick (✓) beside the ones you use most often. Put a * by those that you would like to try. Put a 0 by those that you know do not work for you.

1 Highlight (i.e. colour over or underline) the important details in colour – either in your book or in your notes. Different colours for different points.
2 Write out the important details in note form several times. The notes may be in any form you find convenient.
3 Recite the important ideas aloud several times, until you can repeat them from memory.
4 Skim read the book and notes over and over, underlining as you read.
5 Use rhymes and funny pictures to trigger ideas. For example, if you want to remember …
6 Associate the new ideas with something you have already learnt or experienced.
7 With a friend, quiz each other in test form – using possible questions.
8 Write out test answers in your own words for practice.
9 Other – please specify.

b) With two or three other students, compare and discuss your answers.

Task 2.3 Take control of your own study

You usually have no control over what kind of assessment the tutor will use, what will be assessed, or how it will be assessed. However, you can control your own study routine.

  a) Robert has an exam tomorrow. Listen as he tells Arthur about his problems. What do you feel is Robert's main difficulty?

b) The list that follows gives some advice that might help Robert. Put the items in order of priority, 1 being the most important. If you feel that several are equally important, give them the same number.
(a) Study a little bit every day, even if you think you already know the information – don't wait until the week before the exam.
(b) Study at the same time each day.
(c) Get a good night's sleep.
(d) Study in a quiet, relaxed atmosphere.
(e) Make sure you get enough exercise.
(f) Don't panic – practise relaxation techniques.

(g) Don't procrastinate and leave the most difficult topics or subjects to the last.
(h) Make sure you study in well-lit, comfortable areas.
(i) Make a timetable for your study.
(j) Take frequent breaks.
(k) Don't listen to other students moaning and panicking.
(l) Other (specify).

↗ c) With two or three other students, compare your answers. How does the advice you might give Robert differ from the advice you would give yourself?

Task 2.4 Relieving stress

Stress can be one of the biggest problems in taking exams – and the stress often starts long before the exam, thus interfering with effective study. Feeling in control of your own study (cf. Task 2.3) is essential as a way of lessening stress; there are a number of other techniques you can use as well.

↗ a) With two or three other students, discuss which of these techniques you find helps to relieve stress for you. Explain why. Are there any techniques you feel have been omitted?
1 yoga and meditation
2 jogging and walking
3 sports activities, including swimming, team games, ...
4 going to the pub
5 watching television
6 games, including board and card games
7 breathing exercises
8 other

↗ b) Better than developing techniques for relieving stress is to analyse its cause in order to minimise its occurrence in the first place. Stress can be induced* by a range of conditions, ranging from peer pressure* to unrealistic expectations of achievement to a lack of planning.
     With another student, discuss some of the conditions that can induce stress for you, and how these might be controlled.

Task 2.5 The day before

The day before an exam is usually the day that students begin to panic. If you have prepared properly, however, there will be no need to panic at this stage, though, of course, many students nevertheless do so!

↗ a) With two or three other students, answer these questions.
1 What are the most important things to remember the day before an examination?
2 What should you avoid the day before an examination?
3 Do you feel you usually follow the points you identified in 1 and 2? Why or why not?

b) Copy and complete this checklist of things to remember before
an exam.

> 1 Check to make sure you have several pens.
>
> 2 Check you know the correct time and place, and how to get there.
>
> 3 Make sure you have a clock or a watch.
>
> 4 ....
>
> 5 ....
>
> 6 ....
>
> 7 ....
>
> 8 ....

3 IN THE EXAMINATION ROOM

If you have prepared for your examination properly, you should have
little difficulty taking the exam. However, there are ways you can improve
your exam performance no matter how well you have studied.

Task 3.1 Presentation

Listen to Mr Jones and Ms Smith, two university lecturers,
discussing how they will assess their students, and then answer the
following questions.

1 What does Mr Jones consider to be most important when he marks
exams?

2 What does Ms Smith consider to be the biggest reason her students
have for losing marks?

3 Which lecturer do you feel has the better approach to assessment? If
you knew either Mr Jones or Ms Smith was to mark your paper, what
would you do to try to increase your marks?

Task 3.2

In a letter to his friend, Williem described his first examination in
England.

a) Read the letter opposite. What problems did Williem have?

b) Think of several examinations you have done well in and
several that you think you could have done better in. What did you do
during the examination in each situation? How did you feel?

c) With two or three other students, compare your answers.
Discuss the problems students sometimes face when they are taking an
examination.

Dear Sven

I just took my first English exam - in biology. I thought I was ready for it - a 2½ hour exam. The test had 20 multiple-choice, 10 short-answer, and a choice of 1 out of 3 essay questions.

The multiple-choice questions were first. There were so many words to read that I just panicked and my mind went blank. I must have just sat there for 10 or 15 minutes before I forced myself to take a look at the rest of the exam. Then I saw one essay question which I thoroughly knew (relief). I started writing and lost track of time. When I did look around, everyone else was on the essay so I didn't worry. I thought I had lots of time. With about 30 minutes left I started the multiple-choice, mostly guessing, but I felt lucky. Then I ran out of ink and lost 5 minutes getting a pen from the teacher. I never got to the short-answer questions, and they were worth 40% of the marks! I could have answered them all if I'd time!

➔ d) Williem decided that it would be helpful to make a list of tips for improving his performance during an exam.

TIPS FOR SUCCESS

1. TAKE A WATCH AND DIVIDE YOUR TIME BY THE NUMBER OF QUESTIONS / SECTIONS / MARKS.
2. TRY TO FINISH 10 MINUTES EARLY IN ORDER TO GO BACK AND CHECK.
3. DON'T WATCH OTHERS WORKING.
4. LOOK OVER THE EXAM BEFORE BEGINNING.
5. ANSWER THE EASY QUESTIONS FIRST.
6. PRACTISE RELAXATION TECHNIQUES DURING THE EXAM.

With two or three other students, discuss Williem's tips. You may wish to consider these questions:
1 Which are the most important ones for which different kinds of exams?
2 Which tips do you think are important?
3 Which do you already practise?
4 From your experience, are there any tips you feel should be added?

4 MAKING THE MOST OF EVALUATION

Task 4.1 When in doubt, ask!

When exams are over, most students give a big sigh of relief. However, you can learn a lot from your mistakes, so it is a good idea to get into the habit of taking a good look at your exam results and asking yourself how you could have done better.

If you cannot understand why you received a mark, if you feel that the mark is unfair, or if you don't understand the teacher's comments, it is important to ask for clarification. After all, the marks are subjective – they usually reflect what one person (the teacher or marker) feels is important, logical, relevant, and so on.

It is important that you understand the set of criteria you have been assessed by. You are then in a position to decide whether you have been fairly assessed, or whether you should request a second marker.

Musa did not understand why he received 65% in an essay exam and decided to ask his teacher, Mr Jackson, to explain why he received this mark. Listen to their conversation and then answer the questions. You may wish to work with two or three other students.

1 What suggestions did Mr Jackson give Musa?
2 Did Mr Jackson resent Musa asking these questions?
3 Do you think Musa is likely to do better in his next exam? Explain.
4 If Musa doesn't accept Mr Jackson's opinion, what can he do?

Task 4.2 The marking system

A common source of confusion for second language learners of English studying overseas is the difference in the system of marking. In many parts of Britain, a score of 70% is excellent – usually, no one gets 95% or 100%. In America, on the other hand, 70% is considered mediocre and 95% – 100% is excellent, but not unusual. The same applies to letter grades. In Britain, letter grades are less common than in other parts of the world. However, when they are used, an 'A' is difficult to achieve, being given to perhaps only 5% of the students, even at the postgraduate level. In America, an 'A' is likely to be given to more than 20% of a university population.

Musa was concerned because he felt that a score of 65% was low, whereas his teacher saw it as above average, if not outstanding.

With two or three other students, discuss the system of marking used in your own country.
– What kind of score represents excellent performance?
– What score represents failure?
– What percentage of the students tend to fail?
– Are students expected to answer all the questions in an exam correctly, or are the tests made difficult enough so that no one is likely to get everything correct?
– How can differences in marking lead to misunderstandings?
– What can you do to avoid these misunderstandings?

Task 4.3 Self-evaluation – making and adjusting goals

Students need to get in the habit of using exams as a means of making and adjusting their own educational goals. Every so often you need to take time out to assess what you have learnt and where you are going. A good time to do this is at the end of a term.

SELF - EVALUATION.

↯ a) Read the statements that follow. Write down the numbers. If you agree with the statement, put + in front of it. If you disagree, put –. If you don't know, put ?.

1 You need to re-assess your goals if you don't agree with the mark you received.
2 If you failed your exams, you are a failure and should change your educational goals.
3 The mark you receive doesn't matter if you feel you learnt what you set out to learn.
4 Examinations are a good way to determine how much a student has learnt.
5 The teacher is a better judge of how much you have learnt than you are.
6 Feedback after a test has little value at the end of a course as there will be no more exams.
7 Most evaluation criteria and standards are objective and can be spelt out.
8 Evaluation is an essential part of higher and further education.
9 A student who fails in attaining their educational goals is a personal failure.

↯ b) With two or three other students, compare your answers. Discuss those statements you feel are important, interesting, or ambiguous*. Add any others you feel should also be taken into account.

↯ c) How does self-evaluation relate to motivation, self-confidence and independent learning? With two or three other students, discuss how it may be seen as both a painful and a beneficial process. You may wish to refer to your work on Task 1.2.5.

MOTIVATION: A CARROT AND STICK PROCESS.

5 UNIT ASSESSMENT AND APPLICATION

Task 5.1 Writing an exam

Preparing a short exam is a good way to understand different kinds of assessment.

A→ You are a teacher. Working with a group of teachers, you want to make sure your classes know the passage opposite.
- Decide what kind of exam is best, how the test is to be marked, and how much time is allowed for your students to complete the test.
- Construct an exam to test the information.
- Make sure both the directions and questions are clearly presented.
- Write out the exam. Make three or four copies of the exam so that another group can take it.

Task 5.2 Marking an exam

For teachers, marking an exam can be more difficult than writing it, especially if it involves essays. If you understand the kinds of decisions a teacher must make, you will be better prepared as a student to attain the teacher's goals.

A→ a) Exchange exams with another group. Now, take their exam as if you were the students. When you have finished, return the exams to the group that wrote them.

A→ b) You should now mark the exams, but do not work as a group. Write your mark and comments on a separate piece of paper. When everyone in your group has independently marked all the exams, compare your marks. Were there any differences? Why?

Task 5.3 Evaluation: An on-going practice

Study Tasks in English began by asking you to assess your own study skills. There was no test to assess how well you study, though there is a profile at the end of the book to aid you in your assessment. There are no absolute answers about how to study, or what the best study skills are. You need to get into the habit of re-evaluating your study skills and needs and setting new study goals as old ones are met or change.

A→ Look back to the study goals you set in Unit 1.
- How have they changed?
- Do you feel your study skills have improved?
- Have you set new study goals? If so, what are they?

Is the Planet Earth Cracking Up?

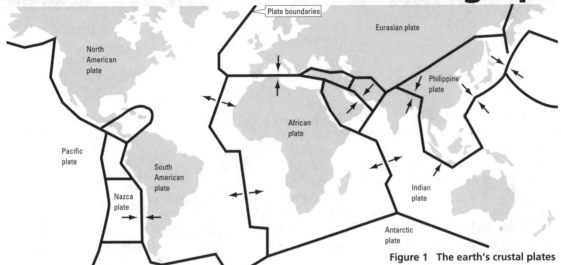

Figure 1   The earth's crustal plates

Earthquakes still occur without warning in spite of an enormous amount of detailed information available about those areas most at risk, such as San Francisco, Tokyo, Mexico and Armenia. The sheer complexity of events in the rocks at earthquake zones has made the task of predicting earthquakes a very difficult one.

Dr Peter Smith, of the Department of Earth Sciences at the Open University, said: 'There are hundreds of possible predictive phenomena such as tide levels, magnetic changes and stress patterns that could be useful, but none have so far proved a reliable signal.'

Earthquakes themselves are very different in their characteristics, making it difficult to make reliable predictions about them or future events. This is especially worrying for some of the world's major cities which lie within 100 miles of a potentially disastrous earthquake.

The earth's crust is a thin shell of solid rock which is divided into a number of pieces, called plates (Figure 1), rather like the scales on a fish. These plates are floating on a bed of molten rock – the mantle – and are moving slowly across the surface of the earth. It is thought that earthquakes and volcanic activities are linked to the movement of these plates.

Convection currents in the molten mantle drag the floating plates towards each other or away from each other at the rate of a few millimetres a year. As the plates move, so do the continents which sit on top of them.

Three types of plate movements can be identified (see figures 2 and 3):

(1) Where convection currents move upwards, plates are pushed apart so that material from the mantle is moved up to the surface to form a new crust, such as new volcanic islands.

(2) Where convection currents move downwards into the mantle, the plates are dragged towards each other and collide. Material from the crust is dragged down into the mantle and remelts. Often deep sea trenches are formed at these points where the plates break away from each other.

(3) Sometimes plates move sideways past each other and are a common cause of earthquakes.

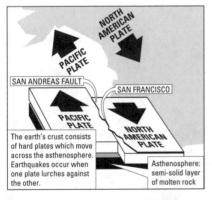

Figure 2   How the earthquake happened

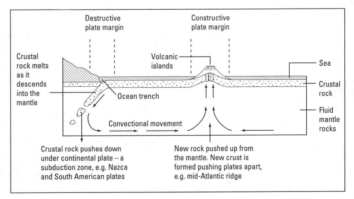

Figure 3   Types of plate boundaries

The next four units are intended to help you use and polish the study skills you have developed in the first eleven units of this book. Each unit in this part focuses on a different study topic, and gives you extensive opportunities to put your study skills into practice in a life-like way, through a series of typical academic tasks involving reading, note-taking, discussion, listening, oral presentation and writing. The subject matter of each of the topics is not specialised, and the tasks draw on a wide range of knowledge and interests. You should therefore be able to participate effectively in all the activities, whatever your academic specialism.

UNIT 12 Transportation in urban areas

You are studying aspects of transportation, specifically those associated with urban development. You may be interested in this subject from a scientific perspective, a sociological perspective or an engineering perspective. However, you are expected to complete all the course requirements. Variations in interest and perspective can be reflected in the topic for project work (see Task 1.2).

1 THE COURSE PROSPECTUS

Transportation in Urban Areas

Tutor: Dr Philip Mansfield
Time: Tuesdays, 1:30 to 4:00
Place: Beckerman Building, Room 205

Large concentrations of population involve problems of mass movement, almost by definition. Historically, transportation has been a problem in all large cities around the world. With the worldwide increase in population in the 20th century, much of it concentrated in large population centres, coupled with the invention of the internal combustion engine and the added mobility it has brought about, the problems of mass transportation have reached a crisis point.

In this course we will investigate many of the problems and suggested solutions associated with mass urban transportation. Such an investigation requires a knowledge of aspects of politics, health, engineering, science, management of change, sociology, and so on. This course will therefore build up a body of knowledge from different fields as relevant to transportation.

The course requirement consists of a three-hour examination at the end of the course and a project that critically investigates some aspect of the transportation issues presented in this course. A course outline and bibliography will be supplied at the beginning of the course.

Task 1.1

Do you live in, or have you ever visited, a large city? With a partner, list the different problems associated with transportation that you have encountered.
1 What do you feel is the most important problem, and why?
2 What kinds of solutions can you think of to some of the problems?
3 Do you think your solutions might work? Why or why not?

Task 1.2

With two or three other students or on your own, do a project on some aspect of a local transportation problem.
- Your project may be either a poster or a paper of not more than 1,000 words or ten pages.
- You will need to analyse the problem critically and then make a suggestion as to how the problem might be eliminated.
- You will need to use some of the information in this unit as well as your knowledge of local events.
- You may wish to interview people, make a survey of the number or kinds of vehicles using a road, or use local newspapers to gather data.

Here are some suggestions for topics:
1 Problems of heavy vehicles using the road in front of your institution
2 Speeding near sports fields
3 Fumes from vehicles causing health problems
4 Lack of safe cycle routes
5 Long traffic jams at rush hours
6 Motorists' lack of knowledge of the rules of the road

Task 1.3

Your teacher will tell you when your project is due. When you have finished it, you will be expected to present it to the rest of the class. Remember to present it in an interesting and informative manner. Here are some tips for doing this:
- Do not simply read it aloud – use notes.
- Use visuals.
- Speak to the whole of your audience.
- Speak clearly and loudly enough.
- Do not try to squeeze too much into the time available.
- Anticipate questions and allow time for discussion.

a) This list is not complete. With two or three other students, discuss what you feel are some other important features to bear in mind in order to make an oral presentation interesting.

b) Present your ideas to the rest of the class, and use the overall results to make a checklist of points to bear in mind for planning your presentation.

Task 1.4

Note Do this task after you have presented your project.
Which study skills were involved in your project? What kinds of problems did you have (if any)? How do you think you would improve your project if you had to do it again?

2 TRANSPORTATION ALTERNATIVES IN THE 21ST CENTURY

Dr Mansfield has had three seminars so far on questions related to his lectures about some of the problems of transport in large urban areas. Today's lecture and follow-up seminar concern the alternatives we must face in the next century.

'PROGRESS'

Task 2.1

Listen to the talk given by Dr Mansfield on transportation alternatives in the 21st century. You will need to take notes in order to participate fully in the seminar which it relates to.

Task 2.2

Your teacher will lead a seminar discussion with you on the following questions arising from Dr Mansfield's talk.
1 What do you think will be the major transportation problems facing the world in the year 2010?
2 What kinds of solutions do you think are the most viable?
3 What are the major factors that might prevent these problems from being solved?
4 Ideally, how would you solve the transportation problems in your country in the next few decades?

a) On your own, prepare your answers to the questions.

b) Take part in the seminar.

Task 2.3

With a partner, look back at how well you were able to listen to the lecture and participate in the seminar. You may wish to consider these questions:
1 Was I able to follow the flow of the lecture and anticipate what was coming next?
2 Were my notes useful in helping me participate in the seminar?
3 Were there any words I didn't know? Was I able to deal with these satisfactorily?
4 Did I develop my ideas satisfactorily in the seminar?
5 Was I able to follow the other speakers?
6 Were my arguments logical and well thought out?
7 Was I able to recognise oversimplifications, faulty logic or unsupportable conclusions if and when they occurred?
8 Did I consider cause, effect, consequences, hidden factors, definitions, and other factors affecting the arguments?

3 SAFETY ISSUES IN URBAN AREAS

Task 3.1

Dr Mansfield gave the class the following excerpts from a report on the traffic situation at a British university, as background reading for another of his seminars, on the topic of 'Traffic safety issues in urban areas'. With two or three other students, answer the following questions:

1 What is the major problem?
2 What is the suggested solution?
3 Do you think the solution will solve the problem? Why or why not?

A

Introduction
There is considerable traffic movement on the campus at all times of the day due to a substantial number of residents, non-resident staff and students, and visitors to the University. Bus services and trade vehicles also enter in considerable numbers. The great majority of traffic enters and leaves the site via the main gate.

A traffic count survey during a sample week in May 1993 showed 16,000 vehicles entering the site through the main gate in a seven-day period.

Whilst a majority of pedestrian movements occur within the confines of an area protected from vehicles, there is nevertheless some conflict between pedestrians and traffic, mainly in the car-parking areas which are situated on the periphery of the buildings. The principal problems however appear to be associated with traffic movements on the surrounding roads system.

Following discussions with staff, and a subsequent tour of the roads network, it was apparent there were specific causes for concern:
  (i) Excessive speed
  (ii) Adverse driver behaviour
 (iii) Speed and lighting on the underpass
  (iv) Reversing out of parking spaces into traffic flow
   (v) Driving across roundabouts
  (vi) Pick-up point for hitch-hikers
(vii) Joggers

(i)   *Speed*
      There is genuine concern about excessive traffic speed on site, substantiated by a survey carried out in co-operation with local police which confirmed average speed on some sections of road well above the imposed limit of 20mph. Indeed the 85 percentile speed in an easterly direction on the main feeder road was measured at 36mph, whilst that in the underpass was 37mph. Additionally, 16 vehicles exceeded 50mph during one week on the main feeder road, whilst 42 vehicles exceeded 50mph on the underpass. This is clearly perceived as being dangerous. The question must be asked however if it is dangerous in reality.

After all there have been no accidents on the feeder road or underpass. Perhaps one of the most difficult concepts to impart in accident prevention work is that speed in itself is not dangerous — only excessive speed for the prevailing conditions.

On the public highway, an 'appropriate' speed for a stretch of road is obtained by measuring 100 vehicles in free-flow situations, ranking them in ascending order, then taking the speed of the 85th highest. This is determined as the 85 percentile speed on the basis that this number of drivers will contain their speed within a level appropriate for the conditions. It must be accepted that 15% of drivers will drive too fast for the conditions, some excessively so.

Should accidents occur on this stretch of road due to excessive speed then further measures should be taken such as strict enforcement, warning signs or lines, and as a last resort, physical obstruction to reduce speed. However, it would be totally ineffective in this situation to install a reduced speed limit sign without continuous presence of police enforcement.

Statistics show that only 400 of 16,000 drivers on the main feeder road of the campus drove at a speed less than the imposed 20mph, whilst 15,600 perceived the appropriate speed to be somewhere between 20–50mph. A similar situation exists on the underpass with but 260 vehicles within the limit and 9,500 above it. Clearly the blanket limit of 20mph for the whole site is unrealistic — on the south-east leg for instance — and some compromise should be reached.

It is therefore recommended that the speed limit on site be raised to 30mph.

Having perhaps alarmed the reader with this recommendation, the particular circumstances of hazardous locations are now examined.

It is undoubtedly true there are certain locations on the campus where excessive speed is potentially dangerous. Particularly at roundabouts, acute bends, the underpass, and in the vicinity of car-parking areas. Speed here will have to be reduced by enforcement, signs and lines, or physical obstruction.

B

Shortest stopping distances – in feet

mph	Thinking distance	Braking distance	Overall stopping distance	
				On a dry road, a good car with good brakes and tyres and an alert driver, will stop in the distances shown. Remember these are shortest stopping distances. Stopping distances increase greatly with wet and slippery roads, poor brakes and tyres, and tired drivers.
20	20	20	40	
30	30	45	75	
40	40	80	120	
50	50	125	175	
60	60	180	240	
70	70	245	315	

Task 3.2

Dr Mansfield has also asked students to read the following items, concerning another case study of safety issues affecting transport in urban areas. The seminar will critically assess the issues arising from them.

You need to decide whether or not you agree with the positions taken in each of the items, and then critically assess how each writer arrived at his or her conclusion. You may find it helpful to note down not only the important facts in each item but also areas which are unclear or seem illogical or inaccurate.

This is a letter to the Safety Officer at the Office of Town Planning:

A

Dear Sir,

<u>Re: Speed Bumps</u>

1. I am once again writing to ask whether speed bumps can be installed at strategic locations on Marsh Road near the children's playing fields and local shops.

2. Recent press coverage of work done by the Road Improvement Laboratories has highlighted the effectiveness of speed bumps in reducing accidents to pedestrians. I am certain that without measures of this kind, the huge increase in traffic along Marsh Road over the last 10 years will inevitably exert its toll in terms of injuries or worse.

3. I do hope renewed consideration can be given to this issue, as a matter of urgency.

Yours sincerely,

John Davidson

Mr. Davidson

This is the Safety Officer's reply:

SAFETY OFFICE
OFFICE OF TOWN PLANNING

Dear Mr. Davidson,

SPEED BUMPS

Thank you for your recent letter requesting the installation of speed bumps on Marsh Road. As I informed you in March last year, a technical officer from our office has made a detailed report on the control of vehicle speed in built-up residential areas. His comment concerning speed bumps was that they are not very effective in comparison to rumble strips. I have enclosed a copy of his report for your information.

The report was submitted to the City Council. However, there was only qualified support for the rumble strips. When £5,000 was requested for general safety improvements in the area, the request was denied. This may have been because the £5,000 requested was mostly for signposting, and this was seen as an excessive amount merely for signposting.

I regret we plan no further action at this time.

Yours sincerely,

R. Jameson

Miss R. Jameson

B

This is an excerpt from the Technical Officer's report:

C

Speed Control Bumps (sleeping policemen) are disliked by drivers. This leads to driver frustration that increases with the number of bumps installed. In addition, it has been found that drivers tend to speed up between the bumps or as soon as they leave the controlled area. Bumps can also cause a great inconvenience to milk lorries, delivery vans and long wheel based vehicles.

It is therefore felt that speed bumps placed along Marsh Road near the shops and children's playing field would increase the drivers' frustration, cause them to drive recklessly, and cause drivers to speed in nearby areas.

As a result, **the installation of speed bumps is not recommended.**

If speed barriers must be installed, rumble strips would be far more effective. These consist of 15 c.m. rough-hewn granite strips which protrude 1 c.m. above the road surface. They give a slightly uncomfortable ride if crossed at a high speed, and thus encourage drivers to slow down.

Far more effective would be to consider slowing down the traffic by other means. There is a need for more signs warning drivers to watch out for children and pedestrians. There is also a need for traffic officers to go into the nearby schools and warn the children about the dangers of the road.

I feel the dangers have been exaggerated in this area as no one has been killed.

Task 3.3

With your teacher, take part in a seminar discussion of the issues raised by the two case studies. What conclusions, if any, can you reach about traffic safety in urban areas?

Task 3.4

In pairs, look back over how well you were able to prepare for and participate in the seminar. What problems arose, if any? Do you feel this seminar was more successful than the one in Section 2? Why or why not? (You may wish to consider the questions in Task 2.3.)

4 TRANSPORTATION, EFFICIENCY AND GREEN ISSUES

Dr Mansfield has suggested the following items might be of use in preparing your project and in studying for the end of term examination.

A1

DEMAND MANAGEMENT ALTERNATIVES

An appealing alternative to providing costly supply alternatives is to attempt to achieve higher levels of performance from existing urban transportation infrastructure by decreasing demand during peak periods or re-orienting demand so that the road and public transport networks are used more effectively. A variety of quick, dirty, and clever responses to the seeming failure to come to grips with overall urban transportation policy issues have evolved. Whereas no one claims that any one of the policy alternatives to be discussed in this section will ultimately solve our current dilemma about urban transportation, recent experience indicates an array of smaller-scale actions that policy makers can take to alleviate the worst aspects of existing problems. These alternatives now in vogue are good examples of Berry's "ameliorative problem-solving" type of planning. If properly packaged, however, and instituted in association with an integrated approach to urban planning in general, *traffic system management options* may, in fact, end up playing a central role in designating satisfactory paths for the gradual evolution of U.S. metropolitan area structure.

A2

NONTRANSPORTATION TRANSPORTATION ALTERNATIVES

Types of alternative work schedules

1. **Flexible work hours ("Flex-time").** Employee chooses his or her own schedule, within some constraints. Employee may be free to vary the schedule daily, vary the lunch break, or "bank" hours from one day to the next or one pay period to the next. Typically all employees are required to be at work five days per week during designated "core" periods (usually 9:30 a.m. to 3:30 p.m.).
2. **Staggered work hours.** Employee works a five-day week, but starting and ending times are spread over a wider time period than usual. Individual employee schedules are assigned by management; employees do not choose them.
3. **Four-day (or compressed) work week.** Employee works the same total number of hours as in a typical five-day work week, but reports to work only four times per week. The four days may be the same each week, or the extra day off may rotate from week to week.
4. **Job-sharing/part-time work.** Employee works less than the standard 40-hour work week, either by working fewer than five 8-hour days, or by working less than 8 hours per day. Job-sharing means that two or more people share the same office space and work responsibilities.

A3

SOCIAL IMPACTS OF THE AUTOMOBILE

Urban transportation systems are both a cause and a consequence of the separation of land uses in the American city. Transportation improvements have especially encouraged the separation of home and work. The widespread use of the electric streetcar in the first half of this century, which led to real estate developments at the periphery, gave way after World War II to the automobile. Automobiles, combined with a plentiful and inexpensive supply of mortgage funds, sustained massive suburbanization. Given that resident suburbanization was primarily composed of middle- and upper-income whites who required urban highways to connect their residences with their white- and blue-collar jobs concentrated in the central city, it follows that major benefits have gone to them while the negative impacts of highway construction and use have fallen most heavily on lower-income, and often minority, inner-city neighborhoods, which were politically powerless to prevent such impacts.

A4

Air and Noise Pollution

The ongoing problems of air and noise pollution associated with urban highways are perhaps the most important, and socially inequitable, legacies of urban transportation and land use changes from the 1950s and 1960s. In spite of more recent improvements in many cities, high levels of air and noise pollution persist in most cities. Although it is difficult to isolate the effect of automobile use from other sources of urban pollution, there is general agreement that transportation is the major source of most types of urban pollution. Once again we find that low-income and minority populations, whose residences are concentrated in the central city where pollution levels are typically highest, are most at risk. An example of the socially unequal burden of air pollution is portrayed graphically in Figure 13-1. In most of the cities identified, lower-income households have greater exposure to total suspended particulates while the differences for blacks are even more dramatic. This pattern is also true for elderly households, who are typically concentrated in inner-city neighborhoods where pollution levels are highest (Greenland & Yorty, 1985).

It is difficult to assess the full long-term effects of these higher levels of exposure to air and noise pollution. Increasing numbers of studies are finding evidence linking noise and air pollution to an even wider set of physical and mental problems as well as learning disabilities that may be systematically reducing achievement levels in affected youth. While the debate over the total effect continues, the unequal impact of air and noise pollution associated with the automobile continues to discriminate against low-income and minority social groups.

A5

SOCIAL IMPACT OF MASS TRANSIT

The major social and equity issues associated with mass transit differ significantly from those associated with the automobile. In part this is due to a difference in goals, in part to a difference in physical impact on the city, and in part to a difference in funding. Although both highways and mass transit operations can be thought of broadly as public goods, that is, they are both financed by governments, their underlying motives and support differ sharply. They both have a general goal of helping individuals move from place to place, but there the similarity ends. Highways are funded largely by user taxes on gasoline and annual vehicle license taxes and simply provide the opportunity for private transportation. Mass transit is funded largely by nonuser taxes. Community support of mass transit is generally considered appropriate, since, in addition to moving people, mass transit is designed to reduce the negative impacts of the automobile on urban life as well as to provide services to those unable to use autos.

A6

Rather than developing new technology and searching for new modes, recent trends have pointed toward reemphasizing older forms of public transportation. Interest now centers on designing public transportation options that involve a variety of modes and on allowing involvement by the private sector (Schofer, 1983). Under the Carter administration renewed attention was given to buses. Buses are, in fact, by far the predominant mode of publicly financed urban transportation, accounting for almost three-quarters of all public transportation trips in the U.S. As we have seen, however, buses have earned a negative image in the minds of U.S. urban residents. Curiously, in Hungary, where buses have only recently been provided as an alternative to the traditional tram (streetcar) routes, just the opposite impression is in vogue.

B

PRIVATISED TRANSPORT INFRASTRUCTURE AND INCENTIVES TO INVEST

It has often been asserted that public ownership in the UK resulted in over-investment in capacity. Rees (1989) considers that this is "perhaps the greatest single failure of the system of government control of public enterprise, at least up to the early 1980s".

Conversely it has also been asserted that privatised utilities face few incentives to invest efficiently. This would hardly be a surprising result if the firms were allowed to follow profit maximising policies after privatisation. Monopolies (and especially natural monopolies) maximise profits by tightening capacity margins. In practice, however, the consequences of changes of ownership have been more complex. Privatisation has, in the main, replaced regulation through state ownership by regulation through licences. Each newly privatised utility has been granted a licence which entitles it to supply monopoly services in return for undertakings related explicitly to pricing, and, in some cases, service quality. These are in effect contracts between the firm and the community, monitored and arbitrated upon by a regulator. Whether privatisation results in efficient levels of investment thus depends upon the interaction between the firm's strategies and these regulatory constraints.

There has been considerable debate about the static efficiency consequences of privatisation, but little attention has yet been paid to the longer term effects on investment decisions and the resulting levels of capacity and service quality. This is somewhat surprising, given the preceding agreement that privatised suppliers may face inadequate incentive to invest efficiently. If this belief is correct, the dynamic effects of inadequate road provision, crumbling railways and congested airports and ports are likely to be just as relevant as static gains or losses in efficiency.

C

Dear Sir,

I am again writing to express my concern over the city's plans to build a northern by-pass around the city centre and to widen the five feeder roads from neighbouring towns.

As I have explained before, more and larger roads do not solve traffic and congestion problems; instead, they encourage more cars and greater congestion in the end – and bring more noise, pollution, accidents, ...

The only reasonable solution must be the development of a mass transport system, embracing trolley cars, trains, trams, and park-and-ride schemes. Such a scheme would reduce pollution, car accidents, noise, congestion and so on.

This solution must be funded by the government, as it is relatively expensive and could not generate a reasonable profit in the short term. However, low fares would encourage wide-spread use, resulting in fewer cars on the road and all the benefits the accompanying benefits for the community at large.

Building more roads is an expensive, short-term solution. I beg the government to put the money into a innovative, long-term solution.

Dr. M. Kelly, Transport engineer

Task 4.1

✈ a) Quickly skim-read the items above.
- What is the gist of each item?
- Are any of these items helpful for the project you are doing?

✈ b) Your next seminar will be on some of the issues arising from these articles. What do you feel are some of the better solutions to present-day urban transport problems?

Task 4.2

Quickly scan articles A1–C on the previous pages in order to find the answers to the questions that follow. Compare your answers with a classmate.
1 What is 'flex-time'?
2 What kind of transport resulted in the first American suburbs?
3 Who typically lives in the inner-city areas?
4 Who typically funds mass transport?
5 What impression do Hungarians have of buses?
6 Does privatisation ensure competition?

Task 4.3

In pairs, discuss how you found the answers to Tasks 4.1 and 4.2. Did you look for key words? If so, which ones? What other strategies did you use? Do you feel you need more practice in skimming and scanning?

Task 4.4

With your teacher, take part in a seminar discussion about the solutions you prefer to present-day transport problems where you live.

5 UNIT ASSESSMENT

Task 5.1

Did you enjoy completing the tasks in this unit? Why or why not? Were the ideas challenging? Did you find the tasks too difficult or too easy? Were the problems mainly language (i.e. the kind of English used) or content (the ideas being presented)?

Task 5.2

Look at the Study Skills Profile at the end of this book. Use it to assess how well you were able to complete the tasks assigned. What study skills were needed to complete the tasks successfully? What study skills do you need to concentrate on to become a more successful student?

UNIT **13 Crime in the modern world**

You have just enrolled in the course 'Crime in the Modern World'. It is an introductory course for students who may eventually wish to train as probation officers, social workers or police officers. You are concerned about the recent increase in crime and feel it would be helpful to gain a better understanding about what is happening.

1 WHO (AND WHAT) IS A CRIMINAL?

Dr Maria Hudson, your lecturer, is giving the introductory lecture for her course on crime in the modern world.

Task 1.1

Listen to Dr Hudson's lecture and take notes of the main ideas.

Task 1.2

Your teacher will lead a seminar discussion on the definition of a criminal and ways of categorising law-breakers.

➤ a) In groups of three or four, prepare for the seminar by first of all discussing your answers to these questions:
1 How does Dr Hudson define a criminal?
2 Do you think that most people who break the law are criminals?
3 Law-breakers can be divided into smaller categories of 'kind of law-breaker', e.g. thieves, murderers, shop-lifters, and so on. Make a list of the groups you would use to categorise all law-breakers.
4 What criteria did your group use to categorise law-breakers? Were there some who were hard to categorise? Why?

➤ b) Take part in the seminar.

Task 1.3

In pairs, discuss how successful you were at following the lecture and taking part in the seminar. You may wish to refer to the Study Skills Profile at the end of the book for a list of the skills you need to have mastered to complete this part successfully.

2 THE CAUSES OF CRIME

Dr Hudson has requested her students to read as widely as possible on the causes of crime. She has suggested that you might find the following items helpful.

A

Church and state try to ease friction over riots

By Richard Ford and Ruth Gledhill

THE prime minister yesterday sought to prevent a full-scale controversy erupting between church and state over who was to blame for inner city riots.

As the Archbishop of Canterbury defended his claim that the recent disturbances on Tyneside were rooted in social deprivation, John Major insisted that many of the incidents had been pre-planned and that not all the rioters were from deprived backgrounds. Senior cabinet ministers joined in with rebuttals of the archbishop's views while opinion within the church rallied behind George Carey.

In the current phase of speculation about a possible general election, both sides appeared anxious to prevent a revival of tensions between church and state and a rift between Downing Street and Lambeth Palace.

The government's tactics in countering Dr Carey's claim that the riots were linked to poverty and poor housing and his criticism of its education policy switched during the day with Downing Street taking a relaxed view of his comments. Initially ministers robustly attacked Dr Carey with Kenneth Clarke, the education secretary, describing him as old fashioned and Kenneth Baker, the home secretary, demanding that the church give young people a lead.

Dr Carey said he did not condone violent criminal behaviour and added that he agreed with Conservative charges that the church itself had a role to play in tackling the spiritual malaise in society. "My reference to Newcastle must be set in the actual context of the address itself, in which I was making the point that we cannot simply label things spiritual and sinful. We have to see it as a whole matrix of illiteracy, delinquency and other aspects of human wrong-doing. I want people to judge me on what I actually said".

B

'Wrongdoing is linked to poverty'

This is a partial text of the speech Dr Carey gave on Thursday to the Anglican Secondary School Heads, meeting in Chester.

THE Church of England, not the state, took the initiative in building schools and providing an education for the generality of young people.

That involvement did not begin because the church simply wanted to create and nurture good Anglicans. The primary aim was to improve the possibility that ordinary young people might aspire to a life which was more satisfying – morally, spiritually and physically. We worry today, and rightly, about the alienation of some of our young people, such as those who were involved in the riots in Newcastle last week. But 200 years ago similar problems were endemic.

The children were generally employed in the factories, the mines, and the mills six days a week, but, as the Bishop of Chester wrote in 1785, "on Sundays they are too apt to be idle, mischievous and vicious". The bishop was right to recognise the presence of our sinfulness, but he no doubt ignored the fact that human wrongdoing is inextricably linked to social deprivation, poverty, poor housing and illiteracy.

We cannot ask of education a means of solving problems which wider society chooses to ignore. What schools can do is make a most significant contribution in preparing pupils for their future citizenship.

We are told that this is a "climate of unbelief" and that materialism rules.

C

Soft hearts breed crime

Dear Sir,

I am fed up hearing soft-hearted liberals moaning that the cause of street terror, car theft, gangs bullying whole communities and the yearly increase in crime is SIMPLY a matter of social injustice and economic and social inequalities.

There have always been, and there always will be, inequalities; the question must be why are things getting worse. The obvious answer to this question is the 'understanding' of those soft-hearted liberals which makes certain that crime does pay.

Soft policies promote:

1. a prison life which is often better and easier than life outside prison;

2. rehabilitation programmes for criminals when the honest poor can't obtain training;

3. a police force more concerned with community relations and human rights than catching criminals; and

4. a justice system committed to short sentences, community work, and other light sentences intended to reduce the numbers in prison (but not, I might add, the number of criminals outside prison).

It is about time we faced facts and recognized that the real roots of crime are a lack of moral fibre and an inherited criminal intelligence, combined with a soft society and a lack of tough policing practices. A firm and certain policy dedicated to making sure that crime NEVER pays is desperately needed.

(name and address supplied)

D

Classless society causes crime

Dear Sir,

Your recent coverage of crime in the community has been very thorough. We all know that community approaches do work, and that investment in prevention is preferable to the high economic and social cost of the cure – prison.

I would like to add, however, that the real root of crime on our streets is low self-esteem.

Youth (and unemployed adults) today are continually bombarded with images of people owning and controlling wealth, and as the class boundaries break down, these youths are increasingly led to believe that wealth is within the reach of everyone – and they adopt this image as their ideal self.

Reality, on the other hand, blocks the possibility of reaching this ideal. This discrepancy between reality and ideals, and the futility in reaching these ideals creates the crime on the street.

Prevention is a matter of either providing the means through education and training, or changing the images and returning to a class/caste society.

Dr. Raymond Alter
Institute of Prison Relations

E

For the drug barons, Third World countries like Nigeria are a rich source of couriers, many of them women who are unaware of the severe penalties the crime carries.

Joanna Reid reports

Prisoners of the poverty trap

WHEN DIDI Godsama discovered that her three-year-old daughter was suffering from a serious blood disease, she had several options to rise the money for her treatment: prostitution, theft or drug smuggling. Her husband was unemployed, the family had no money and in Nigeria there is no NHS or social security.

In 1989 Godsama was paid £1,000 to bring 900gm of cocaine to Britain, arrested at Heathrow Airport and sentenced to six years' imprisonment here. Her daughter died earlier this year; Godsama continues to serve her sentence.

To John Sussex, senior probation officer at Cookham Wood prison in Kent, Godsama's story is not unusual. Twenty per cent of women in prison are drug couriers, but at Cookham Wood the proportion is even higher: around half its 120 inmates are drug smugglers from Third World countries, with Nigerians making up approximately a third of them. For the drug barons, a country like Nigeria – with no state medical care or schooling, and widespread poverty – means easy pickings when it comes to finding willing couriers.

Two recent research reports showed that although some of the women in British prisons are professional traffickers, the majority are not. They are not drug users, they don't understand the value of the drugs they carry and the worst penalty they expect is deportation. "You know the familiar story," says John Sussex. "They go off, leaving their children with the local landlord for a few days, and end up being away for eight or nine years. People don't do that if they know the true situation."

The courts here make no distinction between professional couriers and impoverished women like Didi Godsama. Unlike those of UK residents, their trials do not include a Social Inquiry Report, describing home background and likely motivation, and sentences are rigidly meted out according to the amount and type of drug imported. The average sentence is six years.

Once in prison, very few see the children they have left behind. In Cookham Wood, Funke Showunmi, serving a 10-year sentence, has four children in Nigeria, but has heard nothing of them since March when her husband's letters abruptly stopped during an illness. "I brought my children into this world to look after them," she says. "Here I eat, I sleep, I can survive. What I cannot stand is that they are going through the worst period of their lives."

She shows the same mental deterioration as a Jamaican woman featured in tonight's Channel 4 programme, Mules; both rely on tranquillisers and sleeping pills. Long lock-up times and poor facilities exacerbate Showunmi's problems; she sees British drug traffickers transferred to open prisons, while she is refused permission to transfer to Holloway, where she could develop a saleable skill. "If I was white," she says, "they would provide for me."

These women, already disadvantaged by a far smaller chance of early release on parole than British drug couriers, now face a new horror in the form of Decree 33, a Nigerian law sentencing all drug traffickers to a further five years in prison in Nigeria after serving sentences here.

To try to help them, John Sussex and Olga Heaven, of the Female Prisoners Welfare Project, have set up Hibiscus, a voluntary organisation with offices and trained social workers in Lagos. The group can provide home circumstances reports, send inmates news of their families and trace abandoned children. Unfortunately, although well-funded in Nigeria, Hibiscus may well collapse through lack of funding here.

The new Criminal Justice Act, to be implemented next October, could also shift the balance, ensuring mandatory Social Inquiry Reports for foreign nationals and a provision for release at the discretion of the Home Secretary. How the new measures are put into practice, however, will still depend on the attitudes of judges and politicians.

The argument for long sentences is, of course, deterrence. But, as Olga Heaven says, "Wherever people are poor, drug barons will find couriers – if Nigeria gets difficult, they'll move somewhere else."

So what are we achieving by locking up Third World men and women for years? According to John Hedge, co-author of A Study of Foreign Offenders (Inner London Probation Service) and a worker with drug users, "It reassures the public that something is being done – that if we can catch the 'foreign devils' who bring the stuff in, then we'll be all right. In fact, our drug-takers are society's problem and because of the threat of Aids, we're now being less punitive towards them here. Why, then, adopt such a primitive stance towards these women, who are very small fish in the drugs trade, when it won't really affect the problem either way?"

Task 2.1

Read the items given. What is the gist of each of them?

Task 2.2

Use the items to answer these questions as quickly as possible:
1 Where did the riots occur that were referred to by Dr Carey?
2 When did children work in the mines and mills six days a week?
3 Where did Dr Carey give his speech?
4 Who are the 'soft hearts' that are referred to?
5 What does Dr Alter say is the normal 'cure' for criminals?
6 What is the average prison sentence for smuggling in England?
7 Where are the women often imprisoned if they are caught smuggling drugs in England?
8 What Nigerian law requires people imprisoned in England for smuggling to be imprisoned in Nigeria after serving their English prison sentence?

Task 2.3

Look in your local newspapers and your library to find some information about local crime. See if you can find some articles that attempt to identify the cause of the crime taking place.

Task 2.4

With your teacher, take part in a seminar discussion on the causes of crime. You may wish to choose one kind of crime, or you may wish to consider crime more generally. Use the information you gathered in Tasks 2.1, 2.2 and 2.3 to support your arguments.

Task 2.5

With a partner, discuss how successfully you feel you were able to complete Section 2. You may wish to use the Study Skills Profile at the end of this book to help you isolate any areas of difficulty.

3 CRIME PREVENTION

The second half of the course on 'Crime in the Modern World' turns from its causes and looks more closely at methods that are often used to help prevent crime. Methods of crime prevention can be based on the certainty or unpleasantness of punishment, as well as community and police efforts to make crime itself more difficult or less likely, or to increase the likelihood of the criminal being caught.

You have been given the following items to start you thinking about the question of crime prevention.

A

The Effectiveness of Intervention: Recent Trends and Current Issues

Ted Palmer

From the 1960s to the early 1970s, there was a broad surge of confidence in intervention's ability to change and control offenders on both a short- and long-term basis. This high optimism was largely replaced by widespread pessimism during 1975–1981. Since the mid-1980s intervention regained considerable strength in terms of focus, direction, and "legitimacy." This partly resulted from several major meta-analyses and literature reviews that showed its frequent effectiveness. Intervention's relegitimization is a major development in American corrections, one with sizable program and policy implications. As the 1990s begin, intervention has an increasingly recognized and accepted role, especially, but not only, with serious and multiple offenders.

B

Crimewatch 'inspired raids'

CRIMEWATCH, the BBC TV programme, inspired two masked raiders to hold up 11 banks and building societies with a water pistol, Cambridge crown court heard yesterday.

Colin Hannaford, aged 26, and David Youngman, aged 28, used a broken and painted water-pistol belonging to Mr Youngman's son to steal more than £30,000, it was alleged.

The raids across Cambridgeshire, Essex, Norfolk and Kent, ended when Mr Youngman reported Mr Hannaford to police.

Mr Youngman, of Ely, Cambridgeshire, is awaiting sentence after admitting 12 robberies. Mr Hannaford, also of Ely, denies 11 charges of robbery and one of handling £1,000.

The trial continues.

C

How to make life difficult for the criminal

How to make your personal property more secure

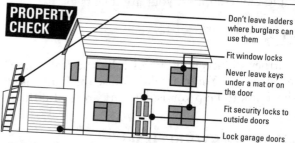

PROPERTY CHECK

Don't leave ladders where burglars can use them

Fit window locks

Never leave keys under a mat or on the door

Fit security locks to outside doors

Lock garage doors

Property-coding

Valuable property, especially TVs, videos, stereos, cameras, etc. – often the burglar's favourite targets – should be marked with your postcode followed by the house number or the first two letters of the house name. Property can be marked by etching, die-stamping, branding, engraving, identification paint or by a security marker pen which uses invisible ink that can only be read under an ultra-violet lamp.

Cycles should also be postcoded by die-stamping the bottom bracket. The police will be able to advise owners where this can be done. Cycles should also always be locked when not in use.

D

Police pledge on building deaths

Scotland Yard yesterday agreed to instruct its officers to investigate allegations of criminal negligence in building site deaths, writes Seumas Milne. Building workers' unions have been campaigning for construction firms to be prosecuted for manslaughter in such cases.

Peter Lenehan, of the Union of Construction, Allied Trades and Technicians, said the police commitment was a breakthrough. Last year more than 150 building workers died on sites.

E

What is Neighbourhood Watch?

Neighbourhood Watch began in the United States in the mid 1970's. It came about because of a massive escalation in the incidence of crime, where whole neighbourhoods were being affected. The idea of the Neighbourhood Watch Scheme proved to be a popular one, enjoying overwhelming support from the public. Regular meetings were organised and property marking encouraged – in some areas, an overall reduction in crime of over 50% was achieved.

Neighbourhood Watch rests on the concept of good neighbourliness. The basic idea is simple; neighbours join together to keep watch on each other's homes and their immediate surroundings.

e.g. – they might remove newspapers and milk bottles from the door step where these are accumulating,

– they might hold a key for a neighbour who is on holiday, in order to 'pop-in' to remove post, open and close curtains, etc.

Neighbours are also encouraged to report suspicious persons and unusual events to the police.

Essentially, the Neighbourhood Watch Scheme concerns crime prevention in the sense of individuals acting together in an attempt to protect themselves and their property from criminal activity.

It is widely accepted that within every community, there is the potential for crime prevention. Neighbourhood Watch is a way of tapping this and of drawing a community together. It is a way in which a community can achieve

F

Police visit schools

Today police constable John Winters visited Valley County Primary School. He used puppets and slides to show pupils how to avoid being abducted.

This is part of a local campaign to encourage positive attitudes in the youth towards the police and the law. It is also intended to develop closer links with the community as well as reducing the chances of children being attacked or abducted.

Everyone at the school enjoyed the visit, and learnt a great deal.

G

Crime Statistics   Differences in the legal systems, police recording practices and statistical classifications in the countries of the United Kingdom make it impracticable to analyse in detail trends in crime for the country as a whole. Nevertheless, it is clear that, as in Western Europe generally, there has been a substantial increase in crime since the early 1950s. However, official statistics cover only crime recorded by the police and can be affected by changes in the proportion of crimes which are undiscovered or unreported.

Table 5.1: Notifiable Crimes Recorded by the Police in England and Wales 1989

Offence group	Crimes Recorded	Crimes Cleared up
Violence against the person	176,959	136,066
Sexual offences	29,733	22,215
Burglary	827,354	226,604
Robbery	33,163	8,772
Theft and handling stolen goods	2,012,760	630,522
Fraud and forgery	134,490	89,429
Criminal damage	630,084	111,581
Other	26,202	25,222
Total	3,870,745	1,250,411

Source: Home Office.

Table 5.1 shows the number of offences recorded by the police in England and Wales in 1989 and their clear up rates. There were 3.9 million crimes in 1989, of which 32.3 per cent were cleared up. Violence against the person accounted for only 4.6 per cent of recorded crimes. The Scottish police recorded 493,000 crimes, of which 33 per cent were cleared up.

Crime tends to be concentrated in inner cities and deprived areas; the risk of burglary can be as high as one in ten houses a year in inner city areas, compared with one in 100 in rural areas. Rising affluence has provided more opportunities for casual property crime. In 1957, for example, car crime was only 10 per cent of total crime but 30 years later this had risen to over 25 per cent.

Most crime is committed by young males; it is opportunist and is not planned by hardened professional criminals although these do exist. Only a small proportion of young male offenders go on to become serious repeat offenders.

Crime Prevention   The national crime prevention programme is overseen by the Ministerial Group on Crime Prevention. National publicity campaigns, such as the Crack Crime campaign launched in 1988, are a regular feature of the Government's programmes. The Home Office's Crime Prevention Unit helps local agencies to design and implement preventive measures and to assess the results. In Scotland national publicity is administered through the Crime Prevention Committee.

Other government departments are brought together with the Home Office in the Ministerial Group to deal with crime prevention strategies. The Department of the Environment's Priority Estates Project and Estate Action Programme are designed to encourage improvements in the design, layout and management of housing estates. The gas and electricity suppliers have speeded up their programme of replacing domestic prepayment meters by cashless or 'token' meters, so removing a prime target for burglaries.

Local crime prevention panels – each one assisted by the police crime prevention department – identify crime problems and try to tackle them through publicity, marking goods and equipment and fund raising to buy security devices. The panels have been closely involved in setting up some 74,000 neighbourhood watch schemes in England and Wales. There are some 1,100 watch schemes in Scotland.

In 1988 an independent national crime prevention organisation, Crime Concern, was launched to encourage local initiatives such as crime prevention panels and neighbourhood watch schemes, and to stimulate business participation in crime prevention. Crime Concern in Scotland was established in 1989.

In 1986 five local projects were set up with government support to see how crime and the fear of crime could be reduced through action by local government, private businesses, the police and voluntary agencies. As part of the Government's Safer Cities projects, this model is being adapted for use in 20 inner city areas in England and Wales. Each project is led by a local committee, drawn from local agencies and supported by a co-ordinator funded by the Home Office. Four projects are also being established in Scotland. The aim is to encourage local communities to devise their own crime prevention activities. Similar projects are being funded by the Government in Northern Ireland.

Strengthening the Law

A number of measures to strengthen the criminal justice system have been taken. The Drug Trafficking Offences Act 1986 and the Criminal Justice (Scotland) Act 1987 provide powers to trace, freeze and confiscate the proceeds of trafficking. Under the Acts a court can issue an order requiring the offender to pay an amount equal to the full value of the proceeds arising from the trafficking. The laundering of illegal money associated with trafficking is unlawful. Because of the international nature of the problem, the legislation also provides for restraint and confiscation orders made by courts to be enforced against assets held overseas, and vice versa. These arrangements apply to countries with which mutual enforcement agreements have been concluded.

Under the Criminal Justice Act 1988 a court may also make a confiscation order against the proceeds arising from offences such as robbery, fraud, blackmail and insider dealing in shares. A Serious Fraud Office with wide powers to investigate and prosecute serious or complex fraud in England, Wales and Northern Ireland was established in 1988 under the Criminal Justice Act 1987.

Legislation has been passed to increase controls on firearms and the carrying of knives. In 1988 the Firearms (Amendment) Act 1988 prohibited the private ownership of certain highly dangerous types of weapon such as high-powered self-loading rifles and burst-fire weapons. It also tightened police regulation of the possession, safekeeping and movement of shotguns. Similar legislation applies in Northern Ireland. Under the Criminal Justice Act 1988 it is unlawful to manufacture, sell or import certain weapons such as knuckledusters or, in England and Wales, to carry a knife in a public place without good reason.

The Public Order Act 1986 and similar legislation in Northern Ireland strengthened the law against incitement to racial hatred and created a new offence of possessing inflammatory material. It also introduced in England and Wales a new order for convicted football hooligans to prevent them attending certain matches and created a new offence of disorderly conduct to enable police to deal with hooligan behaviour. The Act gave the police powers to impose conditions on assemblies in public places.

Task 3.1

You have a seminar tomorrow on methods of crime prevention. You have read all the items you were assigned and have given a lot of thought to crime prevention. Now decide which methods of crime prevention you feel are most effective, and prepare your notes accordingly.

Task 3.2

With your teacher, take part in a seminar discussion about what methods of crime prevention are likely to be effective, and why.

Task 3.3

In pairs, discuss how successfully you used your study skills to complete section 3.

4 CRIME WHERE I LIVE

A course requirement is that students do a project on a local aspect of crime, attitudes to crime, or crime prevention.

Task 4.1

You are required to write a project of not more than 1,000 words on any local aspect of crime.
- You may choose to do it as a paper or in the form of a poster presentation.
- You may work with two or three other students, or on your own.
- Here are some suggestions for projects:
1 A collection and analysis of different kinds of crime reported in the local press, and the sentences that were given for each. (Does the punishment fit the crime?)
2 Attitudes to crime (or punishment) of students, the elderly, etc.
3 Crimes against certain sections of society.
4 A local crime prevention project.
5 A visit to the court or probation office.

Task 4.2

Present your project to the class, and answer their questions about what you found out. Try to make your presentation interesting by not reading it out word for word and by making any illustrations large and easy to see (see Unit 12, Task 1.3).

Task 4.3

In pairs, discuss how you went about completing your project. Did you have any difficulties? How did you get around these? Do you feel you have mastered the skills needed for writing papers and doing projects?

5 UNIT ASSESSMENT

Task 5.1

Did you enjoy completing the tasks in this unit? Why or why not? Were the ideas challenging? Did you find any of the tasks too difficult or too easy? Were the problems mainly language (e.g. the kind of English used) or content (the ideas being presented)?

Task 5.2

Look at the Study Skills Profile at the end of the book. Use it to assess how well you were able to complete the tasks assigned. What study skills were needed to complete the tasks successfully? What study skills do you need to concentrate on to become a more successful student?

UNIT **14 Communication and the media**

You have enrolled on a course entitled 'Communication and the Media'. Sections of this course are presented in which you are expected to participate as a student of the subject. As well as learning about the relationship between communication and the media, you will be expected to step back and evaluate how well you are applying the study skills you have learnt to the tasks in hand.

1 DEFINING *COMMUNICATION* AND *MEDIA*

 Dr White is your lecturer in charge of the 'Communication and the Media' course. You have just arrived in class, and you have your pencil ready to take notes. She is about to speak.

DOES THE MEDIUM CHANGE THE MESSAGE?

Task 1.1

Did you take notes of the aims of this course? Do you feel it is important to write down the aims of a course? Discuss this with a partner.

Task 1.2

What did Dr White say the aims of this course were? (If you did not take notes, try to remember what she said.)

With a partner, compare your answers. How did they differ? Are the aims clear? If not, what questions might you wish to ask Dr White?

Task 1.3

How does Dr White define the terms *media* and *communication*? Are these the definitions you usually use for these terms? Your teacher will lead a seminar discussion on these issues.

a) With two or three other students, discuss different kinds of media and methods of communication you are familiar with. Which kinds would you include in your definition of *media* and *communication*? See if your group can agree on clear definitions for both terms.

b) Take part in the seminar.

Task 1.4

With a partner, discuss how well you feel you were able to understand the

lecture and participate in the small-group and seminar discussions in Task
1.3. You may wish to consider the following questions.

1 Was I able to follow the main ideas of the lecture?
2 Did I take notes of the main ideas?
3 Was I able to understand the important vocabulary?
4 Did I get lost in the details?
5 Did I listen to and evaluate the logic and underlying messages in
   addition to surface meanings and words?
6 In the discussion, did I stick to the point?
7 Did I summarise ideas and present my own ideas clearly?
8 Did I listen to other speakers and use their ideas to modify or
   substantiate my own thinking?
9 Did I use my critical thinking skills, or did I simply accept what was
   said?

2 THE MEDIUM IS THE MESSAGE

You have been asked to read several articles on the impact of the choice
of language and media on the message conveyed.

Task 2.1

Read the following articles to help you develop your position to the
question:
   Does the choice of language or media significantly affect
communication? Give reasons and examples to justify your position.

A

In our time, political speech and writing are largely the defence of the indefensible.
Things like the continuance of British rule in India, the Russian purges and deportations,
the dropping of the atom bombs on Japan, can indeed be defended, but only by
arguments which are too brutal for most people to face, and which do not square with
the professed aims of political parties. Thus political language has to consist largely of
euphemism, question-begging and sheer cloudy vagueness. Defenceless villages are
bombarded from the air, the inhabitants driven out into the countryside, the cattle
machine-gunned, the huts set on fire with incendiary bullets: this is called *pacification*.
Millions of peasants are robbed of their farms and sent trudging along the roads with no
more than they can carry: this is called *transfer of population* or *rectification of frontiers*.
People are imprisoned for years without trial, or shot in the back of the neck or sent to
die of scurvy in Arctic lumber camps: this is called *elimination of unreliable elements*. Such
phraseology is needed if one wants to name things without calling up mental pictures of
them. Consider for instance some comfortable English professor defending Russian
totalitarianism. He cannot say outright, 'I believe in killing off your opponents when you
can get good results by doing so'. Probably, therefore, he will say something like this:

While freely conceding that the Soviet régime exhibits certain features which the humanitarian may
be inclined to deplore, we must, I think, agree that a certain curtailment of the right to political
opposition is an unavoidable concomitant of transitional periods, and that the rigours which the
Russian people have been called upon to undergo have been amply justified in the sphere of
concrete achievement.

B

There is, however, a further grammatical change which has an important ideological component. Between the onset of the use of the term**, with or without qualifiers, and about the beginning of the postwar period (it is not possible to date this precisely) the dominant metaphorical usage is essentially of a passive object. The economy is something which has things done to it or is shaped by other forces. Thus:

The British national economy has been converted from one based on competitive free enterprise into one whose strategic centres are controlled. (*Economist*, 3 Aug. 1940)

It is increasingly clear that our economy is taking its shape from the war. (*Economist*, 27 July 1940)

In the postwar period, however, there begins to appear a further change in metaphor. The change is not abrupt, nor is it total, but it certainly is there and it is one which has clearly accelerated in recent years. It consists in a move from a passive conception – the economy which has things done to it – to an active conception – an economy which has the capacity to act by itself, has needs of its own and which ultimately acquires an almost anthropomorphic status. Thus:

If the British economy is to be given the room to manoeuvre on which its efficiency depends ...

and:

... to the needs of the economy as a whole ... (both in *The Economist*, 5 Jan. 1952)

An important part of this new conception of the economy is the wholesale adoption of mechanical and biological metaphors to depict economic activity:

The economy was working at such high pressure that any additional burdens ... were bound to blow price valves. (*Time* magazine, 10 Jan. 1944)

Since the U.S. economy came through the first quarter full of vigour expressions of doubt about its health for the rest of 1957 all but disappeared last week. (*Time* magazine, 15 Apr. 1957)

... what the economy can produce going full out. (*London Times*, 11 Apr. 1967)

During this period, but increasingly since 1970, similar metaphors to those noted by Goldway have been applied to other items in economic discourse. Thus we are said to be fighting a war against 'the disease of inflation'. Units of currency too are endowed with health or sickness – 'the dollar is ailing', 'the yen is strong', 'the pound had a bad day' and so on. But it is in references to the economy that this process is best seen. The following remarks made recently by Australian politicians are revealing:

We were too optimistic about what we or the economy, working in partnership could perform. (Prime Minister Fraser, *National Times* 25 Aug. 1979)

The economy can employ more people. (Minister for Employment and Youth Affairs, Mr Viner, ABC radio, 20 Nov. 1979)

The economy urgently needs tax reductions. (Queensland Premier, J. Bjelke-Petersen, ABC radio, 4 Jan. 1980)

Here the economy has become a business partner, an employer and a taxpayer. Its anthropomorphization could hardly be more complete.

** "*the* economy" (previously there was no article)

C

'McLuhanism'

Looking back through history, says McLuhan, we can see that, until the advent of printing, the predominant medium of expression and communication was speech. By its nature, speech is largely conversational, random and 'discontinuous'. The pattern of conversation is not typically very organised (witness the saloon bar on a Saturday night!). Conversation allows nearly everyone to express his opinion. If he wants he can change his position in the midst of an argument. All the time a speaker is assessing, re-expressing his ideas as he puts them to the group around him.

The invention of printing, and its rise as a predominant means of communication – and especially of education – tended to bring in a different set of standards. Printed matter is necessarily heavily organised . The ideas are presented in an 'orderly' and 'logical' way. The characteristic form is 'linear', i.e. starting with an introduction to the subject, developing it and finally coming to a conclusion. The typical essay plan is a good example.

Reading and writing are essentially individual rather than group tasks, and are also 'selective', in the sense that not everyone is able to practise them successfully. Print, therefore, tends to create both the 'insider', who is at home in the medium, and the 'outsider', whose background and abilities do not allow him easily to participate. The most able 'insiders' also tend to be 'inner-directed', because reading and writing are solitary occupations, which tend to cut people off from the community. In some ways, too, print has tended to concentrate power in the hands of those able to use it most effectively. Thus print is socially and culturally divisive in a way that (at any rate as far as the United States is concerned) conversation is not.

Such has been the situation for hundreds of years, with education and government constantly reinforcing the dominance of the printed word. In the present century, however, and especially since the Second World War, we have seen the development of broadcasting on an ever increasing scale. Radio and, to an even greater extent, television have become more and more significant in people's lives. These 'electric media' have their own kind of grammar, which in some ways resembles that of speech. From the point of view of the listener and viewer there is often little apparent order and logical development. Instead, ideas tend to be presented with no logical pattern, in a somewhat random way (consider especially the popular disc-jockey type of programme, the commercial break or the morning 'magazine'). Anyone, educated or not, can enjoy, listen and to some extent participate in the performance. As time goes on, McLuhan feels, printed books may well degenerate into 'simple works of reference', while radio and television take over the area of spontaneous living discussion and interpretation of the world in which we live.

The importance of all this, it is argued, is that the medium of communication, be it radio, television or the printed book or newspaper, determines to a large extent the kind of information it can purvey. At the very least it affects the way such information is perceived. We should, in fact, reconsider what we mean by the information (or message) anyway. Perhaps the real activity is not what we read, but that we read. We buy a newspaper, for example, because we enjoy the kind of experience that reading it provides, with no prior knowledge of its contents. Similarly with television. All this can be summed up as a kind of slogan: 'The medium is the message.'

Task 2.2

With a partner, discuss the position you have taken. How did you use the articles to support your position? What other information influenced your position? What kinds of additional information would have been helpful?

Task 2.3

With two or three other students, discuss the topic. You may wish to choose a discussion leader to report the conclusions of the group to the whole class in the next task.

Task 2.4

As a class, take part in a seminar discussion of the topic with your teacher. Present and discuss the conclusions different groups reached.

Task 2.5

How well do you feel your group was able to discuss the question?

a) On your own, consider the following questions.
1 Did everyone listen to each other's point of view?
2 Were your notes adequate?
3 Were you able to summarise other points of view?
4 Do you agree with the conclusion your group reached? If not, why not?
5 Do you feel the discussion could have been improved? If so, how?

b) With a partner, compare your answers.

3 ADVERTISING AND THE MEDIA

You have now been asked to read the following articles on the topic of advertising and the media. You expect to have an examination on this topic at the end of term, and therefore wish to make sure you understand and remember the information.

A

General Motors' fondness for multiple comparatives extends to its 1979 *More Pontiac to the Gallon* campaign (Sports Illustrated, 5/28/79). This is a multiple comparative, for two models of the Pontiac are compared – the 1979 and 1976 Catalinas – with respect to both size and gas mileage (see Photograph 4.5).

The sense in which the 1979 Catalina was said to be more Pontiac than the 1976 Catalina was that the former had more headroom, more legroom and more overall passenger and luggage volume. Moreover, the 1979 Catalina was said to get better mileage than the 1976 Catalina did. Consider

(45)   *What's more, the estimated MPG figure is 38% better than just a few years ago. (Percentage increase less in California). That's comparing '76 and '79 Catalinas equipped with standard engines. Rather impressive.*

The key phrase in this passage is *standard engine*, a phrase that has a constant meaning ('the engine that comes with an automobile at no extra charge'), but can vary in reference from year to year. In fact, General Motors achieved its better gas mileage in 1979 in part by radically decreasing the size of its "standard engine" from 400 cu. in. in 1976 to 231 cu. in. in 1979. Thus, while the 1979 Catalina may have gotten 38% better mileage over the 1976 Catalina, it did so, in part, by reducing the engine size by 42% and the horsepower of the engine by 20% (from 170/4000 rpm to 135/4000 rpm).

Nowhere in the General Motors advertisement for the 1979 Catalina does General Motors reveal that the reference of the phrase *standard engine* changed from 1976 to 1979. As a result, the unwary reader might not realize that while the 1979 Catalina might be "more car" along one dimension (passenger and luggage volume) it is clearly "less car" along another (engine size).

One might go one step further and raise the question: How much can a car model (or any other product) change before it ought to be given a different name? This question involves both meaning and reference distinction. General Motors would very probably take the position that the "meaning" of any particular General Motors car model name is defined relative to the other models General Motors makes. According to this view, Pontiac cars remain in the same position relative to Cadillacs, Buicks, Oldsmobiles, and Chevrolets, for all have changed in essentially the same ways in recent years. I have no real quarrel with this line of reasoning, but consumers should be aware that while the "meaning" of *Pontiac Catalina* may not have changed in recent years, the reference has changed a good deal.

6

The Ideology of Advertising

INTRODUCTION

Consider an advertisement for a hair conditioner. This advert starts off by canonizing a type of behaviour – blow-drying – which is admittedly harmful to your hair – but desirable because useful. It then goes on to present its solution to the problem: the commodity, which is supported by references to its reliance on another well-known victim of overheating, the cactus, extracts of which are among the ingredients of this product.

In other words, while the advert chooses to ignore the basic causes of the problem of overheated hair and its possible damaging longterm effects, using heated hair appliances is presented as the only normal thing to do. And any reader who might have got worried after reading the horror story about weak and brittle hair is rapidly and authoritatively brought back to the herd of blow-dryer loyalists: she is reminded that, obviously, she won't want to give up using a blow-dryer.

Adverts which state their desired behavioural norms as openly as the one mentioned are relatively infrequent. It is much more usual for adverts to take a certain *behavioural normalcy* for granted as if incontestable. An advert for foot deodorants (*Cosmopolitan*, July 1977) labours to establish as necessary and normal the use of foot deodorants. The method is to draw a historical parallel to underarm deodorants, which are thus taken as an unquestionable necessity: 'There was a time when no one used an underarm deodorant either.' The advert is therefore trying to evoke and to exploit people's disgust at the mere thought of the days when people smelled like people under the arms, in order to make them equally disgusted with the natural smell of their feet, thus alienating them from their own body sensations.

Admittedly, sweaty feet can be quite nasty, and the advert actually mentions the causes of the problem: 'Shoes made of synthetic materials, so your feet can't breathe. And tights and tight boots, which don't help either.' It therefore requires a considerable amount of impudence to continue with a sentence which suggests that the solution lies not in the abolition of the causes but in the use of yet another commodity: '*So* not surprisingly, a good few people have already discovered the solution. [X] Foot-Deodorant.' (our italics).

In addition to illustrating the phenomenon of implied behavioural normalcy, this advert thus provides a clear example of *problem reduction*: Instead of solving the problem of smelly feet through non-suffocating alternatives to your present foot and leg wear, the advert offers a product which helps you to offset the undesirable side-effects of following unhealthy fashions, while increasing your dependence on bought products.

C

Chapter 10

Conclusion

Although television is primarily viewed as being a visual communications medium, there can be no doubt that what is said in television advertising is of decisive importance to its effectiveness. The reason for this is simply that there are very few products that have sufficient visual appeal to be sold on that ground alone. The attractiveness of an automobile can better be shown than described, and some aspects of its performance are better shown than described. But it would be very difficult to establish that some car is "more car for less money" nonverbally.

Automobiles have been sold on the basis of how they look for years. In certain other cases, though a product has little or no intrinsic visual appeal, it can be promoted visually through a live action or animated visual product demonstration. In most such cases, however, the demonstration would be meaningless were a verbal interpretation of what is going on on screen not provided. Moreover, the lesson to be learned from a product demonstration is normally better stated than shown.

The majority of products promoted on television have too little intrinsic visual appeal to be promoted on this basis, cannot be demonstrated visually, or differ too little from competing products at a visual level to be promoted visually. In such cases what is said during a commercial is of great importance to the effectiveness of the commercial and this is true whether or not claims are being made about a product, a consumer's opinion about a product is being solicited by an interviewer, or people are shown using and enjoying, and, in the process, talking about a product.

Television advertising occurs in real time and employs both the auditory and visual communications channels. This fact coupled with a perceptual uncertainty principle (namely, that although we can absorb information simultaneously on both the visual and auditory channels, we cannot consciously focus on both channels simultaneously) presents something of a problem to television viewers. Advertisers have exploited this in several ways:

- by presenting long, small print disclaimers in competition with the auditory message as well as other visual material;
- by presenting differing printed and oral verbal messages, one relatively weak and one quite strong;
- by presenting conflicting oral claims, e.g., a relatively weak claim early on in a commercial and a quite strong claim toward the end;
- by using misleading discourse nonsequiturs, i.e., claims that pre-suppose the prior establishment of the truth of some proposition which, in fact, has not been established as true;
- by saying things that sound good but that in fact don't say anything at all; and
- by implying, rather than overtly asserting, claims.

Given that television occurs in real time and thus cannot be studied carefully, and that it uses both the auditory and visual communications channels, it would be surprising if viewers were very often able to see through such techniques. The fact that viewers tend not to examine television advertising carefully renders this even less likely.

The fact that advertisers very commonly imply rather than overtly assert claims raises the question of what advertisers should be held responsible for. Clearly advertisers like everyone else should be held responsible for what they assert and for what their assertions entail and conventionally implicate. According to what I have called the "literalist" theory of truth in advertising this is all advertisers should be held responsible for. However, according to what I have called the "pragmatist" theory, advertisers should also be held responsible for conversational implicatures of what they say.

What an advertisement asserts, entails, or conventionally implicates follows directly from the meanings of the sentences that make up the advertisement. On the other hand, what an advertisement conversationally implicates, though dependent in part on the meaning of what is said, depends crucially on consumer reasoning. Moreover, different viewers can and sometimes will draw different conversational implicatures from the same advertisement. A literalist might argue that advertisers should not be held responsible for the results of consumer reasoning for they have no control over this reasoning. It might also be argued that the procedure for "calculating" conversational implicatures is too indeterminate to give incontrovertible results.

The central difficulty with the literalist theory of truth in advertising is that it presumes a cognitive-cum-semantic ability that logically untutored speakers do not have, namely the ability to distinguish valid from invalid inferences. To a logically untutored speaker, the distinction between an entailment or conventional implicature and an invalid, but compelling, conversational implicature is a distinction without a difference.

A realistic theory of truth in advertising must, I think, be based on actual, rather than ideal, human cognitive-cum-semantic abilities, that is, on how people will actually interpret the language of an advertisement rather than on how a logician might say they should interpret this language. If this principle is accepted then advertisers should be held responsible for what their advertisements conversationally implicate, which is the thesis of the pragmatist position.

That differing people can draw different conversational implicatures from the same advertisement is, in my view, a pseudoproblem. Generally this happens whenever the Maxim of Strength and the Maxim of Relevance are opposed. We noted that a claim like (1) will implicate (2) to anyone who uses the Maxim of Relevance and (3) to anyone who uses the Maxim of Strength.

(1)   Wartsoff contains vivaline and vivaline removes warts instantly.
(2)   Wartsoff removes warts instantly.
(3)   Wartsoff probably does not remove warts instantly.

Sentence (1) is relevant to the consumer who has warts if and only if Wartsoff does what vivaline does. To a reflective and critical consumer, the fact that the advertiser does not actually assert (2), but merely implies it, would implicate, given the Maxim of Strength, that (2) either isn't true (Maxim of Truth) or can't be defended (Maxim of Evidence), and, thus, that (3) is true. In my view, when a conflict like this exists, any but the most critical of consumers will opt for inferences based on the Maxim of Relevance, which is to say that the Maxim of Relevance is perceptually more salient than the Maxim of Strength in such a case.

A use of the Maxim of Strength in a case like (1) depends crucially on recall of precisely what was said, but the fact that television advertising occurs in real time makes such recall rather difficult. Moreover, it has been established experimentally that people tend to recall pragmatic inferences of sentences with as much or more frequency than they recall what was directly asserted. It would be surprising if television viewers were not to do the same in the case of what is asserted and what is implied in television advertisements.

Task 3.1

a) What was the gist of each article? With a partner, compare your answers.

b) Were you able to state the main idea clearly? Did you need to read and understand every word? Did you read the article more than once? What kinds of problems do you feel you had completing this task?

Task 3.2

a) You are taking an 'open book' test*. Find the answers to the questions that follow as quickly as possible. You may answer in note form.

1 How can 'meaning' stay constant but reference change? (Passage A)
2 Why is using heated hair appliances presented as a normal thing to do, despite its damaging effects? (Passage B)
3 What use can be made of 'behavioural normalcy' in advertisements? (Passage B)
4 What is 'problem reduction'? (Passage B)
5 Why is verbal language important in television advertising? (Passage C)
6 What happens when we receive information on both visual and auditory channels? (Passage C)
7 Why do viewers usually not realise how advertisers exploit a perceptual uncertainty principle? (Passage C)
8 What is the difference between what an advertisement asserts and what it 'conversationally implicates'? (Passage C)
9 Why is it argued that a theory of truth in advertising should be based on how people actually interpret the language of advertisements? (Passage C)
10 Do people remember inferences better than assertions? (Passage C)

b) Compare your answers with a partner. Do your answers agree? If not, go back to the articles and check to find the best answer.

c) How quickly were you able to find the correct answer? How could you have improved your speed and accuracy?

4 THE IMPACT OF THE MEDIA ON COMMUNICATION

Task 4.1

You have been requested by Dr White to complete a project on some aspect of communication and the media.

The project should not be more than 1,000 words and needs to include some outside reading or research. Your research may be either in English or in your own language.

You may wish to include pictures, graphs, drawings, examples, and any other information that supports your position. You may present your project as either an essay or a poster.

You may work in groups of two or three, or on your own.

You may choose a topic of your own, or you may wish to develop one of the following topics.

1 Look at several newspapers in your country and compare the way they cover various news items. How does the language and presentation vary? What underlying messages are being conveyed? Do you consider the coverage reasonable and fair? Discuss.

2 Do a survey of what kinds of media people use to find out the news. What are their attitudes to the various news media? What conclusion could be drawn?

3 Look at the different kinds of advertising found in different magazines and newspapers. What does the kind of advertising indicate about the advertisers' attitudes to the readership? What sort of picture of the world do the advertisements present? You may wish to interview someone at a newspaper or in an advertising agency.

4 How do different kinds of media handle one of the following issues: sexism, ageism, racism, political bias? What examples can you find of the issue you select? What kinds of rules govern how media handle this issue?

5 Should freedom of the press and the public's 'right to know' have precedence over the individual's 'right to privacy'? You may wish to read about this, interview various people, or give some examples to support your position.

Task 4.2

Present your project to the class. Try to make your presentation as interesting as possible. Don't try to read it all aloud or present all the details.

Task 4.3

Which study skills were involved in your project? What kinds of problems did you have, if any? How do you think you would improve your project if you had to do it again?

5 UNIT ASSESSMENT

Task 5.1

Did you enjoy completing the tasks in this unit? Why or why not? Were the ideas challenging? Did you find the tasks too difficult or too easy? Were the problems mainly language (i.e. the kind of English used) or content (the ideas being presented)?

Task 5.2

Look at the Study Skills Profile at the end of the book. Use it to assess how well you were able to complete the tasks assigned. What study skills were needed to complete the tasks successfully? What study skills do you need to concentrate on to become a more successful student?

UNIT **15** **Study in an academic context**

You have just begun your study in the medium of English. The introductory programme for all new students consists of an interview with their adviser, followed by a series of seminars on successful study and a project on an aspect of studying. If you find you still have problems after this, you have been advised either to talk to your adviser again, or to your course tutor, or to attend English language classes at the EFL Centre.

1 AN INITIAL INTERVIEW WITH YOUR ADVISER

Students in higher education in English-speaking countries are usually assigned a lecturer who acts as their personal adviser. Some colleges and universities may also have a counselling centre which acts in a similar fashion. You will need to find out what kind of initial study advice is available where you study.

WHY NOT BEGIN AS YOU
WISH TO CONTINUE?
AFTER ALL, THE ROAD
TO HELL IS PAVED
WITH GOOD INTENTIONS.

Task 1.1

Your friend Ali has just been assigned to Dr Margaret Jones. She has made an appointment to talk to him about his course of study. Listen to his interview. You may wish to take notes on the advice he is given.

Task 1.2

In groups, use your notes from the interview Ali had with Dr Jones to answer the questions that follow.
1 What advice does Dr Jones give Ali about his course of study?
2 What advice is given about getting behind in his studies?
3 Whose responsibility is it to identify when Ali may need extra help?
4 What kinds of help are available if Ali gets into difficulty?
5 What problems does Ali expect to have? Why?
6 If you were Ali, what kinds of questions or problems would you want to talk to an adviser about initially?
7 Do you think having a personal tutor adviser is helpful? Discuss.
8 If you don't have a personal tutor adviser, who could you turn to if you needed help?

Task 1.3

You have an appointment to see your adviser. Assume it is either an initial interview, or one you made at a later date because you have had a problem you wish to talk about. Write a dialogue between yourself and your adviser.

Task 1.4

With a partner, compare the dialogues you have written. Discuss the advice you gave yourselves. What other advice could have been given? If you have not yet begun to study in English, what kinds of problems do you feel you are still likely to have when you do? What do you intend to do about them?

2   SELF-ASSESSMENT

Self-assessment has been a theme throughout *Study Tasks in English*. There is no *one* right way to study, any more than there is only one kind of student. Your adviser has given you the following passages to read on the importance of self-assessment for successful study.

A

My plea here is simple. Look at yourself long enough to know you are there ... and then go as you choose.

Bob Samples

This book begins with you. It begins with you because asking questions and thinking about yourself and your lifestyle can give you insights into your individual learning style. With these insights, you can make your learning and study more satisfying and effective.

Your body, your emotions and your beliefs, who you live with and where you study – all these affect your learning. Your physical state and your emotions influence your ability to learn, and too little sleep or exercise may affect your enthusiasm for study. A belief in the value of hard work may make you a conscientious student. An argument with the people in your household can create difficulties when you try to concentrate on study, and moving house or changing jobs can leave little time and energy for formal learning.

As people and as students we're all different. If you're slow and ambling, a study task may take you longer. This may leave you feeling inadequate, or you can enjoy the leisurely savouring of new ideas. At the other extreme, if you've a high energy level and live at a fast pace, you might wish you could occasionally slow down enough to integrate in more depth what you learn, or you might enjoy the speed with which new insights come to you. There's no one way of learning and studying that suits everyone. And because you change daily, weekly and monthly, there's no one way of studying which always suits you. So you need to get to know who you are and examine how you live.

B

Get to know your study strengths and weaknesses and you may be able to work more effectively, says **Pennie Hedge**

CONGRATULATIONS! You've made it to the fellowship of students. And a wonderfully diverse group it is – from the inside. From the outside, students are often seen as an unpleasant, homogeneous mass made up of people rather worse than school children. Unfortunately advice for students sometimes also seems to assume that there is only one type of student and only one way of studying.

The fact is that as you have been accepted on to a course you have the ability to succeed at it. What often makes the difference in getting a good class of degree is doing that little bit more than other students, or working more effectively. And here we return to the different ways of studying and who they suit.

Students are people and therefore unique. But they follow certain patterns of studying. The trick is to understand your natural approach to study. Once you know your strengths and weaknesses, you can be selective about the advice you take and make it work for you.

Let me introduce some of my favourite students: Neo, Bingo, Ricky-Tic and Cherry. Everyone knows Neo, always the first to the library in pursuit of a new subject. He ignores all catalogues and bibliographies, makes straight for the shelf and the book with the brightest cover. Three interesting facts and two names later, he drops it on the desk and heads for the coffee bar to impress his friends. Then he skips a lecture to buy some new trainers, starts reading ahead for next week's tutorial, but is called to the Union to set-up the new disco equipment.

At exam time, Neo disappears, but his light blazes all night. He re-emerges in the exam room with manic eyes, where he fills several books with fascinating facts, some relevant, others not, and finishes none of the questions.

Ricky-Tic feels smug while Neo stammers out another excuse for not finishing an essay. She has a large timetable on her wall, filled with targets for the whole term. Each time she ticks off one of these goals she feels closer to being a qualified lawyer. She has at least three goals to tick off each week. Her essays are always on time, although the marks aren't brilliant. She can't understand why other students with perfectly good brains waste so much time; college is just the boring slog on the way to a good job.

At exam time, her concise and indexed notes are a breeze to revise. But one year she caught a virus a month before the exam. It laid her up for a week putting an unfillable hole in her timetable, so she refused to sit the paper.

You won't ever find poor Bingo in the bar much before closing because he's always behind with his work. It isn't that he doesn't put in the hours, so he thinks it must be because he's thick. But as he really wants a good Civil Service career he's got to aim for an upper second at least. And that means reading through the entire book list, and more, to lift his essays above average. Bingo gets very dispirited if he gets lower than A– for a piece of work, so after all his revisions he's often late handing work in. You can always spot Bingo at the exam room door: he's the one still reading his notes.

Cherry, of course, is everybody's darling. She doesn't believe that she deserves to be at college, so is determined to enjoy it before she is slung out. She belongs to several clubs, but always makes sure that her work is on time. She doesn't use the library much, preferring to rely on her lecture notes, but does read recommendations from the lecturer. Her essays aim for a rounded view.

Cherry conscientiously learns her notes for the exams, but it doesn't take very long. She has no trouble finishing the right number of questions within the set time, but then worries that she hasn't used much paper.

THEY'RE all very different and they can all get their degrees. But they might achieve more, with less angst if they learnt a bit from each other. Imagine Neo with Bingo's set periods of work and a book list. He could still exploit his flair and serendipity, but within a framework. And if Bingo would only lift his eyes from the page, he would see that it is realism not cleverness that gives other students more time. With Ricky-Tic's goals and more of Cherry's limitation of research and reading added to his conscientiousness, he could really succeed.

Ricky-Tic herself doesn't need any more study skills, but her world is fragile and built on future enjoyment. With some of Neo's flexibility and less tunnel-vision she might enjoy college and improve her marks.

Finally, Cherry would not be any less likeable if she adopted some of Ricky-Tic's ambition, looking forward instead of over her shoulder. And she would find essays more interesting if she added Neo's approach of taking a vigorous line of argument to her good understanding of the various views.

C

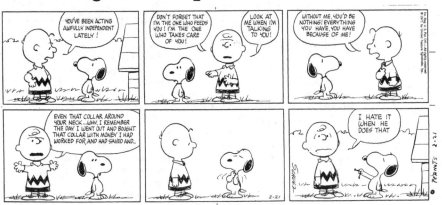

Becoming an Independent Student

Starting university or college can be bewildering as well as stimulating. Whether your study is full-time or part-time, internal or external, the adjustments you have to make are considerable and you'll be faced with the challenge of learning independently. You're likely to spend the first couple of weeks mostly in organising your timetable and in finding your way round campus and through administrative requirements. Hopefully you can do most of these things during an orientation period before classes start. You'll also begin to recognise faces among staff and students, and may discover some of the social activities that can be part of a tertiary student's life.

* * *

D

Allow yourself time to discover what university or college is like for you. Expect to feel both confused and excited in the first six to twelve months while you settle in, while you begin to understand what's expected of you and to define some of your own objectives. During this time, as well as trying to pass courses, put some energy into learning how to learn and into making contact with staff and students. Remember that outside school you have learned many things on your own, and that you do know how to learn when you want to.

Think about what you want from university or college, and how you can reach your objectives. After a while it may make sense for you to defer your study for a short period or to leave university or college because of other interests, because your studies aren't sufficiently stimulating, or for pragmatic reasons. (If you are thinking of withdrawing from study, find out what you need to do in case you later want to return.) If you continue to study, your objectives in your formal learning will probably change. Any serious attempt to come to grips with new ideas, especially those which raise questions about yourself, your world and your beliefs about learning always engenders confusion and suggests new directions to consider. Learning that is important to you changes you, often in unexpected ways. Universities or colleges can offer you real learning if you explore what's offered and if you are able to make your own independent decisions about learning.

Task 2.1

Use your notes on the passages as well as your general knowledge about successful study to answer the questions that follow.
1 What is the main problem with much of the advice for students?
2 What is the gist of the article by Pennie Hedge?
3 What advice would you give Neo, Bingo, Ricky-Tic, and Cherry?
4 Do you feel you resemble any of these students? If so, which one?
5 What is the most important contribution a student can make to independent study?
6 How can non-academic factors influence how successful a student you are?
7 Do you think ability and academic skills contribute more to success or failure in higher education than other, non-academic and affective influences?

Task 2.2

You have been asked to do a short essay or project on one aspect of study that you find interesting.
- You may present this as a series of posters or as a paper of not more than 1,000 words. You may work on your own, or in small groups.
- You may use the readings in *Study Tasks in English* as well as other references on study that you may have access to. These references may be either in English or in your own language.
- You may wish to do some original research on your own, either in English or in your own language. However, the project itself must be in English.
- You may wish to do your project on one of the following topics.
  1 How study skills are taught in my own language, for study in my own language.
  2 How do the students in this class prepare for their lessons?
  3 How much time do students at my school spend doing homework?
  4 How many students really do plan their study time in advance?
  5 What do mathematics students (or students of any other appropriate subject) feel is the most important study skill they need?
  6 How do teachers in my institution assess essays?
  7 What do teachers in my institution think are the most important study skills?
  8 When (or how) do students in my institution (or class) prepare for exams?

3 TIME MANAGEMENT

'Time management' really means making sure you do the planning and thinking ahead that will enable you to be on top of your studies. You are probably used to your teachers telling you what to read, and when. However, as you progress in further and higher education, you are increasingly expected to make these decisions yourself. Lecturers give assignments and set the dates for exams; you then have to decide when and how you will attain these targets.

Task 3.1

Your adviser has given you the two articles that follow to read in preparation for a seminar on Time Management. Read them in order to discuss this question:

> *Managing your study time is the most vital skill to learn in higher education.*

To what extent do you agree with this statement?

A

All work and no play . . .

As a student you're likely to be involved in campus or community activities, socialising, sport, hobbies, personal relationships, domestic chores, childcare or a paid job. These involvements may enhance your learning, for example, if you're a keen athlete taking physical education courses; or they may conflict with your study, for example, if your drinking mates scorn your study. What part does study play in your life?

Learning can be one of the most creative and satisfying pleasures you experience. However, there are inevitably times in your formal learning when you have to make yourself work – when you're not interested in a topic, when you have difficulty with an assignment, or when you have other things on your mind. It is at these times that planning can be useful.

Planning how to spend your time can give you the opportunity to explore the pleasures of using your mind and can help you cope with times when it's difficult to study. If you're happy working to a plan, don't make it too ambitious, and don't let it rule your life so that you rarely do anything spontaneously. Any schedule needs to be flexible.

Whether or not you like to plan your time, examining your objectives and workload for a year is important.

Your objectives. Planning a year's study involves formulating your objectives for the courses you'll take, and drawing up a schedule of work to be done. For each course think about:
- where it fits into the overall objectives of your formal education
- how it's connected with your other courses
- your knowledge of the course content
- your interests or questions concerning the subject
- skills you want to acquire, and
- grades you hope to achieve.

B

Schedule for passing the test of time

Andrew Northedge on the most vital skill to learn at college – managing your study time

I WAS in a student coffee bar during my first week at university soaking in the atmosphere when a lad from Oldham, of conspicuously cool and languid manner, announced calmly that he intended to get a first in classics. He would work 25 hours a week, study five hours a day on weekdays and leave the weekends free. That would be sufficient.

I was vaguely committed to endless hours of work. I imagined that at some point I would spend weeks of intensive study. The vice-chancellor had told us in his address to freshers to look at the person on either side and note that in all probability one of us would not be around the following year. The message struck home: I would turn myself into a paragon of academic virtue. I could see that the classicist in the coffee bar had got it all wrong, or was bluffing.

Three years later he sailed to his first whilst other friends struggled to very modest achievements. As I discovered when sharing his lodgings, he worked more or less the plan he had outlined. He slept late in the mornings, only stirring himself if there was a lecture to attend. He played cards with the rest of us after lunch. Then he moved to his desk and stayed there till around seven. The evenings he spent more wildly than most – hence the late mornings.

Nevertheless, when I came to look back I realised he had studied more than anyone else I knew. Through sticking assiduously to a modest but well-defined, realistic plan, he had achieved a great deal. He had enjoyed work much more, too.

He argued that it was not possible to work productively at intensive intellectual tasks for more than a few hours at a time. I aimed to do much more. But I was easily distracted. By the time it was apparent that stretches of a day had slipped away, I felt so guilty that I blotted studies out of my mind, comforting myself with the thought of all the days which lay ahead.

I was too inexperienced at looking after my own affairs to realise I was already failing one of the major tests of studenthood, the organisation of time. I thought that success in studying was to do with how brilliantly clever and original you were; I had yet to discover that one of the central challenges of adult life is time management.

At school the work timetable was defined for us and teachers made sure we fitted all that was required into the school year. At university I was at sea. Time came in great undifferentiated swathes. What to do with it all? With 168 hours in a week – or 105, allowing nine a day for sleeping and eating – how many was it reasonable to spend on study? Individuals vary and different subjects make different demands. Nevertheless with a target you can plan your studies, not just stumble ahead in hope. The sketchiest of weekly timetables, setting aside 40 hours to cover all study, is an invaluable aid in defining time. Then you can divide it into segments and use it strategically, rather than let it dribble away.

Sticking to a modest but well-defined plan, he achieved a great deal

Defining what to do is harder. Take the booklists. How many books are students expected to read? How long should a book take? It took me so long to read just a few pages that I felt defeated when I looked ahead. Should I take notes? How many? What would I need them for?

I would sit in the library for a whole day, dipping into one book after another, often with glazed-over eyes. What was my purpose? How would I know when I had achieved it? By comparison I went to lectures gratefully – at least I knew when they started and finished. Although my lecture notes weren't up to much, I could tell myself I had accomplished something, which would bring down my anxiety level.

Much later I discovered I could learn a great deal from close reading of selected sections; that taking notes could sometimes be very satisfying and at other times was not necessary. The trick was to take control; to decide what I wanted to find out – something specific – and then work at it until I had taken in enough to think about for the time being.

Dividing big jobs into smaller sub-tasks helps to bring work under control, allows you to set targets and check your progress. There is so much pressure to be ambitious – to go for the long dissertation, to read the huge tomes. Yet achievement arises out of quite modest activities undertaken on a small scale. The trouble with the big tasks is that you keep putting them off. Their scope and shape is unclear and we all flee from uncertainty. The more you can define your work as small, discrete, concrete tasks, the more control you have over it.

Organising tasks into the time available can itself be divided into strategy and application. It is useful to think of yourself as "investing" time. Some tasks require intense concentration and need to be done at a prime time of day, when you are at your best and have time to spare. Others can be fitted in when you are tired, or as "warm-up" activities at the start of a session. Some, such as essay writing, may best be spread over several days. Some need to be done straight away.

There are few reliable guidelines. Essentially you have to keep circling round a self-monitoring loop: plan an approach to a task, try it out, reflect afterwards on your success in achieving what you intended and then revise your strategy.

Once you start to think strategically, you begin to take control of your studies rather than letting them swamp you.

Andrew Northedge is author of The Good Study Guide (Open University, £5.95)

Task 3.2

Your teacher will lead a seminar discussion on the importance of time management for successful study.

✦ a) Use your notes and any other knowledge and experience you have in order to prepare for the discussion.

✦ b) Take part in the seminar.

Task 3.3

How well do you feel you and the other members of your class were able to discuss the question?

a) On your own, consider the following questions.
1 Did everyone listen to each other's point of view?
2 Were your notes adequate?
3 Were you able to summarise other points of view?
4 Do you agree with the conclusion the seminar group reached? If not, why not?
5 Do you feel the discussion could have been improved? If so, how?

b) With a partner, compare your answers.

4 COPING WITH EXAMS

To many, exams are synonymous with learning, especially at university and college. However, anxiety can interfere with your memory and general performance in an exam.

Task 4.1

Your tutor has decided that your final seminar should be looking at how to cope with exams. She knows that you have been told before how to prepare for exams, but she feels a final reminder might help relieve some remaining anxiety. She has therefore given you these two final readings on coping with exams. Read them and take notes as necessary.

A

Revision skills help to reinforce memorised material, and help you to relate new information to facts that you have learned already. They strengthen your understanding of the subject and increase the likelihood of your continuing to take useful notes.

Revision should be an integral part of your studying timetable. One suggested plan is as follows:

- Start each study session by reviewing the last session.
- Review each week's work at the end of the week.
- Review each month's work at the end of the month.
- Review each term's work at the end of the term.
- End the year with a review of the course.

If you work like this you will review each topic five times. This will mean that you forget less between each session, so by the end of the course, most of the work is done!

Methods of revising

We have already stressed the importance of active rather than passive learning in order to make memorising interesting and effective, for example:

- Summarise your notes.
- Test yourself regularly.
- Write outlines for possible essays.
- Recite or dictate your notes into a tape recorder.
- Attempt problems you haven't tried before.
- Discuss your subject area with another student.

Avoid passively sitting and reading through copious notes. Don't attempt to memorise an essay in order to reproduce it in an exam; summarise it. Read your past assignments and essays critically to find out where you went wrong.

B

With students preparing for exams, **Liz Hodgkinson** offers some tips for handling the stress

Learning to cope with exams

EVER more, it seems, the future hangs on examination results and hardly anybody can now escape being judged on what can be remembered and reproduced in a few hours of writing and writhing.

The run-up to important exams, from GCSE to degree finals, is, for many, punctuated by periods of intense anxiety and stress, panic that not enough work has been done, fears that results may not be good enough to take one to the next stage – and possibly yet more exams.

But although a certain amount of keyed-upness may be necessary to bring out the best, stress and anxiety are counter-productive, and actually prevent concentration and clear thinking.

Dr David Lewis, a clinical psychologist from Sussex University, who holds regular de-stressing workshops for examination candidates, says: "A great fear of examinations seems to be built into us from an early age. You have to bear in mind that there is nothing you cannot achieve, that you need only ordinary intelligence levels to pass most exams, and that if you build up confidence through adequate preparation, there is simply nothing to fear."

It is even possible to avoid exam stress and enjoy the challenge, buzz and sense of achievement that exams can bring, by bearing in mind these essential examination dos and don'ts:

● Remember that you can actually decide to succeed – and that everything follows from that.

● Bear in mind that stress can be catching, and can be worked up deliberately, so don't moan constantly to friends about how much work you haven't done, or listen to people who tell you they can't sleep, are going mad with worry, chain-smoking or taking tranquillisers. Avoid highly stressed friends during this time, and seek to reassure each other. This is most important with people taking university exams, who may not be able to avail themselves of home comforts during this time.

● Realise that we all have a limited concentration span, and that even the world's greatest geniuses will start flagging after an hour and a half, at most. Take short breaks every hour or so for 10 minutes, then you'll start revising with renewed energy. A run or walk round the block several times a day clears the head and induces concentration.

● Don't drink lots of strong coffee. Caffeine encourages adrenaline production, which in turn increases anxiety. One or two cups a day is enough. Otherwise drink herb teas, fruit juice or mineral water.

● Don't shun absolutely all delights to live laborious days. The occasional party, night in the pub or social evening does no harm (so long as it's not the night before an important exam) and can even contribute to concentration the next day. Reward yourself with leisure activities and interests, particularly after a hard bout of revising.

● Relax and unwind before going to bed by listening to a relaxation tape, soothing music or watching a relaxation video. Do not attempt to relax by watching a horror movie late at night – this will increase stress the next morning and may prevent sleep.

● When revising, put a few drops of a favourite fragrance on your wrist, and use it again during the actual exam. Scent is a powerful memory enhancer. But make sure you don't annoy the other candidates by drenching yourself in patchouli or lavender.

● If you have difficulty sleeping, practise simple yoga techniques, or place a soothing herb pillow under your usual one. A good night's sleep wards off anxiety and reduces stress next morning.

● Although intense revising the night before the exam is a bad idea, glancing through notes just before you go to bed helps to imprint the subject on the memory.

● Do not attempt, at this late stage, to learn any facts you don't understand. You'll never be able to recall them properly.

● When sitting an exam, don't worry if time runs out during essay papers. Writing notes, rather than fully rounded sentences, can clock up a surprising amount of marks. Also, remember that thoughts often flow during the writing of exams – it's not always necessary to plan every single thing before writing.

● Whatever you do, never indulge in detailed post-mortems after each exam. It's over – forget it. Post-mortems are infinitely anxiety inducing and achieve nothing.

● Most important of all, believe in yourself. Believe that you can do well in these exams. Don't fall prey to negative self-fulfilling prophecies or tell yourself that you are no good at exams. Everybody can be good at exams. They're not a test of your worth as a human being, just an indication of your current level of expertise in a particular subject.

● Even if you do fail, all is not lost. Most exams can be retaken these days, and the will to succeed is always more important than any perceived ability or inability in any subject. Do retake exams where possible – it's unlikely that they are "too hard" for you. Remember that most exam failures are caused by lack of self-confidence rather than lack of intelligence or learning ability.

Task 4.2

Do you agree or disagree with the following statement?

'Students who fail examinations study far fewer hours than students who pass.'

There is some evidence to show that this statement may be, in fact, incorrect. Malleson (1961; quoted in Allen, 1966) shows that medical students at University College, London who failed their second Bachelor of Medicine examinations studied just as long on average as those who passed. How can this be so?

With two or three other students, discuss how this could be so. Then, use the two articles on coping with memory and exams to write down a list of strategies that could be helpful to increase the likelihood of you being in the group of successful students. Try to put these hints in order of priority.

5 COURSE ASSESSMENT AND EVALUATION

Task 5.1

Look back at the study targets you set in Unit 1 and the Study Skills Profile at the end of this book, and compare them with the comments you have made throughout this unit. What study skills do you feel you have made the most progress in? Which skills do you feel are the most difficult to master?

Task 5.2

Present your study project (Task 1.3) to the class. Are you surprised at any of the outcomes? Explain.

Task 5.3

Go back through *Study Tasks in English* and then answer these questions:
1 What parts of the book did you find the most interesting? The most boring? The most helpful? The least helpful?
2 Which methods did you prefer and why: small group work? Pair work? Discussion? Projects? Individual written assignments? Class summaries?
3 If you were a writer of this book, what changes would you make and why?
Compare your answers with those of other students.

PART **D**   Study Information

This part contains information to facilitate the work in Parts A–C. It includes a Study Profile to help you assess your progress, a glossary of study words to help you understand the vocabulary of learning to study, a list of common abbreviations and Latin terms that you may need to understand or use, and a list of editing symbols.

Study Skills Profile

This Profile contains a list of all the Study Skills covered in Units 1 to 11 of *Study Tasks in English,* with columns where you can check how well you can use each of the skills.

We strongly recommend that you use the Profile regularly to assess your progress. The first time you use the Profile, decide how well you have mastered each skill. Write the date in the appropriate column. The next time you assess yourself, write the date in the columns for those skills where you feel you have shown improvement. This should show you both your progress and the areas where you need more work.

The right-hand column shows where you can obtain information in *Study Tasks in English* about each of the skills. Only Units 1 to 11 are mentioned in this column, since Units 12 to 15 provide integrated practice in all the skills.

Skill	I can do this well.	OK, but I need more practice.	I can't do this.	I don't need this skill.	Reference **Unit:** section. task.
1 Organisational and self-awareness skills					
a) I can keep an accurate record of new words.					1:1.2
b) I can keep an accurate record of assignments.					1:1.2
c) I am an independent learner.					1:2 (all)
d) I am aware of my learning style.					1:2.1–3; 8:1.2
e) I am a confident learner.					1:2.4; 8:1.3
f) I am aware of my study needs.					1:2.5; 1:4.1–3; 8.1.1
g) I follow a healthy life-style.					1:3.1
h) I have a good working environment.					1:3.2
i) I have a study plan.					1:3.3–4
j) I follow study plans.					1:3.3–6

2 Thinking skills					
a) I have a clear purpose for **studying.**					1:2.5
b) I ask factual questions.					2:1 (all); 2:2 (all)
c) I ask probing questions.					2:1 (all); 2:2 (all)
d) I ask questions as I work.					2:1.2–3

194

Skill	I can do this well.	OK, but I need more practice.	I can't do this.	I don't need this skill.	Reference **Unit:** section. task.
e) I draw conclusions based on evidence.					2:1.1–4
f) I infer logical conclusions.					2:1.1–4; 3:4 (all)
g) I recognise illogical conclusions.					2:1.1–4; 3:4 (all)
h) I understand issues behind facts.					2:2 (all)
i) I define words precisely.					2:3 (all)
j) I differentiate fact from opinion.					2:4 (all)
k) I am aware of bias by omission.					2:4.1; 2:4.3–4
l) I can account for different points of view.					2:4.2
m) I can analyse why something happened.					3:1 (all); 3:2 (all)
n) I consider a variety of consequences.					3:2 (all)
o) I can consider the likelihood of an event happening.					3:2 (all); 3:3 (all)
p) I can assess the validity of cause-effect relationships.					3: 2.3; 3:3 (all)
q) I can establish a set of problem-solving criteria.					3:3 (all)
r) I can determine possible alternatives.					3:3 (all)

3 Information-locating skills					
a) I know where to find specific information in a book or journal.					1:1.1; 4:4.1–4
b) I know all the facilities available in my library.					4:1.1–3
c) I can locate a book or journal in the library.					4:1.4–6; 4:3.3
d) I can determine the relevant parts of a book.					4:2 (all)
e) I can find the journal I need.					4:3 (all)
f) I can find a reference for a topic.					4:3.2

Skill	I can do this well.	OK, but I need more practice.	I can't do this.	I don't need this skill.	Reference **Unit: section. task.**
g) I can keep a record of where I find information.					4:3.4; 5:1.7; 5:4.1–2
h) I can read for the gist of an article (skimming).					6:2.2–3; 6:3.4
i) I can read for specific details in an article (scanning).					6:2.2–3; 6:3.5

4 Skills for coping with extended use of English					
a) I know the criteria for good note-taking					5:1.2
b) I know when to use various methods of note-taking.					5:1.3–4
c) I can make linear notes.					5:1.3–4
d) I can make pattern notes, including flow charts.					5:1.3–4
e) I can take effective notes while reading.					5:1.5; 5:2 (all)
f) I can take effective notes while listening.					5:1.5; 5:3 (all); 6:4.3
g) I can use abbreviations in note-taking.					5:1.6
h) I can record the source of a piece of extended English.					5:4.1–2
i) I can make notes from a variety of information sources.					5:4.3–4
j) I can state my own reading strategies.					6:1.1
k) I can state my own listening strategies.					6:1.2
l) I can take an active approach to reading.					6:2 (all)
m) I can take an active approach to listening.					6:2 (all)
n) I set goals when I read or listen.					6:2.2
o) I predict what information I will read next.					6:2.3
p) I predict what information I will hear next.					6:2.3
q) I use organisational cues to aid understanding.					6:2.4

Skill	I can do this well.	OK, but I need more practice.	I can't do this.	I don't need this skill.	Reference **Unit:** section. task.
r) I infer meanings and read 'between the lines'.					6:2.5
s) I infer hidden meanings when listening.					6:2.5
t) I read or listen for specific details (scanning).					6:3.2–3; 6:3.5
u) I read or listen for the gist (skimming).					6:3.2–3; 6:3.4
v) I cope with unfamiliar words in context.					6:4.1–2
w) I cope with unfamiliar grammar in context.					6:4.4

5 Discussion skills					
a) I can prepare my position in advance.					7:1.1–2
b) I can consider all other positions in advance.					7:1.2
c) I take readings into consideration.					7:1.3
d) I critically evaluate all positions.					7:1.3–4
e) I can get my own ideas across.					7:2.1
f) I can organise my own ideas.					7:2.1
g) I can illustrate my ideas.					7:2.1
h) I can use 'signposts' when speaking.					7:2.1
i) I can build on what others have said.					7:2.2
j) I can understand and use phrases that request clarification.					7:3.1–2
k) I can understand and use phrases that express agreement.					7:3.1–2
l) I can understand and use phrases that express disagreement.					7:3.1–2
m) I can paraphrase what a previous speaker has said.					7:3.3–4
n) I can take an active and responsible part in discussions.					7:4 (all)

Skill	I can do this well.	OK, but I need more practice.	I can't do this.	I don't need this skill.	Reference **Unit:** section. task.
6 Academic writing skills					
a) I can construct a bibliography.					4:4.5–6
b) I have a positive attitude towards writing.					8:1.3–4
c) I can determine the constraints on the writing.					8:2.1–4
d) I can narrow (focus) the topic.					8:2 (all)
e) I can read and question to focus and expand my ideas.					8:2.3
f) I can organise my ideas to develop the topic.					8:3.1–3
g) I consider the audience.					8:3.3
h) I can integrate readings into the writing.					8:4.2
i) I can make an outline.					8:2.3: 8:3 (all)
j) I can select relevant ideas.					8:3.2; 8:4 (all)
k) I can order ideas logically.					8:3.1; 8:3.4; 8:4 (all)
l) I can organise paragraphs.					8:4 (all)
m) I can re-draft.					8:4 (all)
n) I can write an introduction.					9:1.1
o) I can use appropriate expressions to link main ideas.					9:1.2
p) I can write a conclusion.					9:1.3
q) I can construct well-organised paragraphs.					9:2.1–5
r) I can use expressions to knit paragraphs together.					9:2.2
s) I can punctuate correctly.					9:3.1
t) I can spell correctly.					9:3.1
u) I can proof-read.					9:3.1–5
v) I can use correct grammar.					9:3.1–2
w) I can stick to the point.					9:3.3
x) I can be precise and clear.					9:3.3
y) I can get the tone right.					9:3.4
z) I can quote correctly – both directly and indirectly.					9:4.1

Skill	I can do this well.	OK, but I need more practice.	I can't do this.	I don't need this skill.	Reference **Unit:** section. task.
aa) I can make headings and sub-headings.					9:4.2
bb) I avoid plagiarism.					9:4.1
cc) I can use appropriate presentation conventions.					9:4.2
dd) I can describe tables, charts and diagrams.					10:3 (all)

7 Research skills					
a) I can recognise empirical research.					10:1 (all)
b) I can recognise representative samples.					10:1 (all)
c) I can select simple random samples.					10:1 (all)
d) I can identify biased language in research.					10:2 (all)
e) I can associate research within a context.					10:2 (all)
f) I can discuss reliability in research.					10:2 (all)
g) I can record simple research findings.					10:2 (all)
h) I can read pie charts and histograms (bar graphs).					10:3.1–2
i) I can read information on a line graph.					10:3.3
j) I can read information in a flow chart.					10:3.4
k) I can calculate averages.					10:3.6
l) I can recognise normal distribution curves.					10:3.7
m) I can write an introduction to research.					10:4 (all)
n) I can write a description of the research.					10:4 (all)
o) I can write an analysis of the research.					10:4 (all)
p) I can discuss the conclusions and implications of specific research.					10:4 (all)

Skill	I can do this well.	OK, but I need more practice.	I can't do this.	I don't need this skill.	Reference **Unit:** section. task.
8 Examination skills					
a) I can use strategies appropriate to the kind of assessment.					**11**:1 (all)
b) I can manage study time effectively.					**11**:2 (all)
c) I can analyse what I need to know and do.					**11**:2.1
d) I can use a variety of memory aids.					**11**:2.2
e) I have a positive study routine.					**11**:2.3
f) I can cope with pre-exam stress.					**11**:2.4
g) I can manage exam time effectively.					**11**:3 (all)
h) I can cope with exam stress.					**11**:3 (all)
i) I can learn from exam mistakes.					**11**:4 (all)
j) I can understand the marking system used.					**11**:4 (all)
k) I can use exams for self-evaluation.					**11**:4 (all)

Glossary of study terms

alternatives	other possibilities (p. 22)
ambiguous	having more than one meaning (p. 145)
analyse (analysis)	look at carefully to find out what something is made of (p. 22)
appendices	sections added at the end of an essay or book, containing further information (*appendix* is singular) (p. 2)
assessor	person who assesses, i.e. tests, decides on the value of a piece of work, etc. (p. 135)
assignments	essays and other pieces of academic work you are expected to complete (p. 20)
associate	to think of as belonging together (p. 15)
attribute (to)	regard as being the cause (of) (p. 119)
authorities	important sources of ideas (p. 16)
axe to grind	a point of view involving personal *bias* (p. 16)
axis	horizontal or vertical line on a graph going to or through the point of origin (p. 126)
bias	point of view supported by (your) feelings (p. 16)
causal	that which causes (p. 22)
chronological	arranged in order of time (p. 72)
chunks	pieces (p. 93)
coincidence	two or more events happening together by chance (p. 23)
colloquialism	everyday expression (p. 113)
comprehensive	complete, covering all areas (p. 46)
concentrate	pay careful attention to something (p. 6)
concisely	in as few words as possible (p. 133)
consensus	agreement (p. 71)
consequence(s)	result(s) of an action (p. 22)
constructively	positively, in a helpful way (p. 139)
conventions	methods of quoting, doing bibliographies, referencing, etc., in academic writing (p. 104)
co-operative endeavour	an activity in which everyone tries to work well together (p. 89)
criteria	the standards used to judge the value of, e.g. a piece of writing (*criterion* is singular) (p. 14)
cues	helpful hints (p. 75)
data	information (often in the form of *statistics*) (p. 48)
determine	decide, identify (p. 24)
distorted	made untrue (p. 23)
draft	the form of a piece of writing before it is revised for the last time (p. 100)
eliminate	remove (p. 136)

evaluate	decide the value of something (p. 22)
excerpt	small section of writing taken from a longer piece (p. 20)
feedback	comments on your work from, e.g. your tutor (p. 92)
field	area of study (p. 53)
forecast	say what you think will happen in the future (p. 22)
format	the way information is presented, e.g. on a page (p. 52)
gist	the essential point in a mass of information (p. 74)
hierarchy	arranged in order of highest to lowest, most important to least important, etc. (p. 72)
highlight	to mark words or sections of text to make them clearer (p. 60)
hump	the part of a curve that looks like the top of a hill (also a verb) (p. 132)
hypothesis	possible explanation (p. 72)
implication	something connected with an idea but which has not been directly expressed (to *imply*) (p. 22)
in a vacuum	without connection with other information (p. 24)
indentation	space left at the beginning of a line of writing (to *indent*) (p. 54)
induce	to make happen (p. 141)
infer (inference)	reach a conclusion from facts or by reasoning (p. 22)
integral	joined to closely (p. 135)
ISBN	International Standard Book Number – a unique identifying number for a book (p. 41)
linking words	words which join together parts of writing or speaking (p. 103)
misrepresentation	presenting information in a false way (p. 16)
modify	change or adjust (p. 83)
non-verbal clues	ways in which meanings are expressed without words, e.g. by the look on the face, the way of standing or sitting, etc. (p. 63)
OHP	overhead projector – a method of projecting information onto a screen from acetate (clear plastic) slides; mainly used for notes, diagrams and graphs (p. 63)
open-book test	a test in which textbooks and reference books are used (p. 181)

pamphlet	small book (p. 38)
papers	essays and other pieces of academic work (p. 137)
paraphrase	someone else's ideas expressed in words of your own (p. 16)
peer pressure	views of others like yourself which you are expected to agree with (p. 141)
perspectives	ways of thinking about information, different points of view (p. 18)
population	a group of people (or animals, etc.) used for research purposes, and from which the sample is selected (p. 119)
prejudice	a view based on insufficient information or knowledge (p. 16)
preliminary	at the beginning, the first, what you start with (p. 95)
premise	a statement on which an argument is based (p. 33)
prioritise (priority)	put in order of importance (p. 30)
project work	an investigation of a topic in which information from a variety of different *sources* (written, spoken, etc.) is used (p. 12)
proof-reading	checking writing for mistakes (p. 111)
qualify	state the conditions necessary for something to be true (p. 13)
reading	doing a degree in a subject, e.g. *reading Chemistry* means studying for a degree in Chemistry (p. 131)
references	i) abbreviation for reference books and materials (p. 48) · ii) information about books, etc. that you have mentioned in your writing or consulted during your research (p. 49)
representative	a member of a group which resembles the group as a whole (p. 119)
ring binder	a hard folder with two or three rings on the inside to hold paper with holes on one side. It is possible to get dividers to divide the notes into topics (p. 3)
scanning	finding a particular piece of information when reading or listening (p. 74)
segment	a part of the whole (p. 125)
seminar	in British education, an academic discussion in a group of about twelve students with a tutor (p. 36)
skimming	finding the *gist* when listening or reading (p. 74)
source	the place where information is obtained (p. 47)
statistics (statistical)	information in the form of numbers (p. 31)
strategies	methods for trying to solve a problem (p. 69)
subjects	people (or animals, etc.) in an experiment (p. 119)

take-home questions	a form of examination in which students answer the questions outside the examination room (p. 137)
tentative	not certain (p. 95)
term	one of (usually three) periods the academic year is divided into (p. 137)
tone	the general style of a piece of writing, e.g. academic, informal, etc. (p. 111)
variable(s)	thing(s) that can vary or change in an experiment (p. 33)
wordbook	a record of new words and their meanings, uses, etc. (p. 2)
word processor	computer program used for writing (p. 6)

Appendix 1

Questions for Unit 2, Task 2.2

— Where is the school? (town? country?)
— Who attends the school? (handicapped children? infants?)
— When will the play area be used? (daytime only? nights?)
— What facilities are available at the moment?
— Why do they need a new play area?
— What kind of materials are suitable?
— What materials are available?
— Where is the entrance being built? (new location? view?)
— How much money is available?
— Who will do the actual building work? (volunteers? professionals?)
— What are the local planning regulations?
— Who will decide on the plans?
— What kind of play areas have been developed at other schools?
— How large is the play area?
— When does the design have to be completed?
— Why have I been asked to do the design?
— How will the play area be used? (supervised? open?)

Appendix 2

The school plan for Unit 2, Task 2.3a

Key: | | doors

paved areas

trees

fence

shrubs

5m = 1cm

nursery = under 5 years old

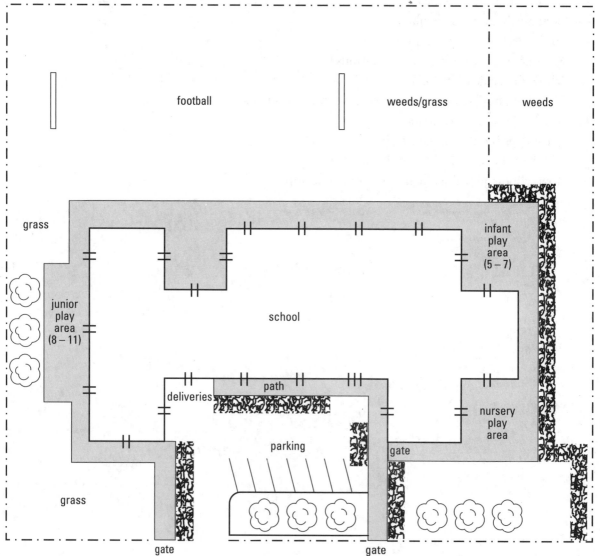

Appendix 3

Criteria for good notes for Unit 5, Task 1.2b

1 They are accurate.
2 They contain the essential information only: they are not too detailed, nor too brief.
3 They show the overall organisation of ideas clearly.
4 They are concise, i.e. they use abbreviations and other techniques for shortening information whenever possible.
5 They help you listen or read more successfully.
6 You can use them effectively later on, e.g. for exam revision.
7 They include follow-up points, i.e. your own comments on or reactions to ideas.

Appendix 4

List of words for Unit 6, Task 4.2c

phenomenon
Peter Principle
mismatch
demands
psychologically disturbed
self-conversations
dysfunctional
self-induced
invest
comprehensive health investment procedure
criteria
job trialling
articulated
pragmatically

Appendix 5

STUDY ABBREVIATIONS AND LATIN TERMS

AD: since the beginning of the Christian era
a posteriori: reasoning from effect to cause
a priori: reasoning from cause to effect
ad hoc: not arranged beforehand
approx: approximately
BC: before the beginning of the Christian era
c.: approximately
cf.: compare
ed.: editor
edn.: edition
e.g.: for example
et al.: and others (used when a work has several authors)
f., ff: and the following pages, e.g. 10 ff. refers to page 10 and following pages
fig.: figure, i.e. drawing, table, chart, etc.
ibid.: in the same place/work previously referred to
i.e.: that is
MS, MSS: manuscript(s)
NB: this is important
no.: number
op. cit.: in the work already quoted
p.: page
pp.: pages
re: concerning
ref.: with reference to
stet: as it was originally
sic: exactly as it is (used when the original has a mistake)
viz.: namely
vol.: volume (of a journal, etc.)

Appendix 6

EDITING SYMBOLS

$\wedge$	something missing
$\bigcirc$	spelling mistake
——	grammar mistake
～～	vocabulary mistake
/	omit
⬚↗	move words in box to place indicated by arrow
T	tense
NP	new paragraph
P	punctuation
?	unclear
→←	join together
↰↱	reverse the position of the two items

Bibliography of study skills books

Buzan, T. (1973) *Use Your Head*. BBC Publications.

Cohen, L. and L. Manion (1980) *Research Methods in Education* (2nd Edn.). Croom Helm.

Gibbs, G. (1981) *Teaching Students to Learn: A Student-Centred Approach*. Open University Press.

Marshall, L. and F. Rowland (1981) *A Guide to Learning Independently*. Open University Press.

Parsons, C. (1976) *How to Study Effectively*. Arrow Books.

Smith, R.M. (1983) *Learning How to Learn: Applied Theory for Adults*. Open University Press.

Wallace, M.J. (1980) *Study Skills in English*. Cambridge University Press.

Index

Acknowledgements

The authors and publishers are grateful to the authors, publishers and others who have given permission for the use of copyright material. It has not been possible to trace the sources of all the material used, and in such cases the publishers would welcome information from copyright holders.

The extract on p. 17 from Sir Peter Medawar: *The Limits of Science* (1985), © 1984 by Peter B. Medawar, by permission of Oxford University Press and HarperCollins Publishers Inc.; the PEANUTS cartoons on pp. 21 and 186 are reproduced by permission of United Features Syndicate, Inc.; notes on p. 55 from David Crystal: *Cambridge Encyclopedia of Language* (1987) by permission of the author and Cambridge University Press; notes on p. 56 reproduced from INTRODUCTION TO PHYSICS by permission of Usborne Publishing Ltd, London. Copyright © 1990, 1983 Usborne Publishing Ltd; notes on p. 56 from P Brown: 'Arguments to the death' and notes on causes of the collapse of Communism in Eastern Europe and the Soviet Union both on p. 57 © The *Guardian* 1993; extract on p. 61 from T Radford: 'Climate' and extract on p. 62 from David Lawson: 'Open and shut case' both © The *Guardian* 1990; extract on pp. 66–7 from article on UN Forces © The *Guardian* 1993; extract on pp. 71 and 79 from V Chaudhary and Dr M Weller: 'A history of war's killing code' © The *Guardian* 1991; extract on p. 98 from 'Rote learning was a winner' by Greg Hadfield from The Sunday Times of 11 September 1988 © Times Newspapers Ltd. 1988; extracts on pp. 100–2 from E Pilkington: 'Zoos' © The *Guardian* 1991; diagram by P Allen: 'The greenhouse effect' and diagram of bicycle dynamo by Medridian Design both on p. 130 © The *Guardian* 1990 and 1991 respectively; extract on p. 147 from 'Is the Planet Earth cracking up?' by Jeff Battersby in *Worldwide* Vol 1(3) © Philip Allan Publishers 1990; extract from Lancaster University Traffic Safety Report on pp. 152–3 reproduced by kind permission of the Royal Society for the Prevention of Accidents; table on p. 153 'Shortest stopping distances' from p. 15 of *The Highway Code* reproduced with the permission of the Controller of Her Majesty's Stationery Office; extracts on pp. 156–8 from S Hanson (Ed.) *The Geography of Urban Transportation* by permission of The Guilford Press; extract on pp. 158–9 from 'Privatised infrastructure and incentives to invest' by D Helm and D Thompson © 1991 *Journal of Transport Economics and Policy*; extract on p. 162 from 'Church and state try to ease friction over riots' by Richard Ford and Ruth Gledhill from The Times of 21 September 1991 © Times Newspapers Ltd. 1991; extract on p. 163 taken from *Sharing a Vision* by George Carey published and copyright 1993 by Darton, Longman and Todd Ltd and used by permission of the publishers, copyright © 1993 by George Carey reprinted by permission of (DLT info.) and Morehouse Publishing (US edition); extract on p. 164 from Joanna Reid: 'Prisoners of the poverty trap' © The *Guardian* 1991; extract on p. 166 from Ted Palmer: 'The Effectiveness of Intervention: Recent Trends and Current Issues,' CRIME & DELINQUENCY, Vol 37, No 3, July 1991, 330–46 © 1991 Sage Publications, Inc. Reprinted by permission of Sage Publications, Inc.; extracts on p. 166 from 'Crimewatch "inspired raids"' and from 'Police pledge on building deaths' both © The *Guardian* 1991; extract on p. 166 from 'How to make life difficult for the criminal' in *Neighbourhood Watch* published by Central Office of Information and Her Majesty's Stationery Office, Crown Copyright 1985; extract on p. 167 from Lancashire Constabulary: *Neighbourhood Watch: A Guide to Community Action Against Crime*; extract on pp. 168–9 from *Britain 1991: An Official Handbook* published by Her Majesty's Stationery Office and the Central Office of Information, Crown Copyright 1991; extract on p. 173 from THE COLLECTED ESSAYS, JOURNALISM AND LETTERS OF GEORGE ORWELL, Volume IV, IN FRONT OF YOUR NOSE 1945–1950 copyright © 1968 by Sonia Brownell Orwell, reprinted by permission of Harcourt Brace & Company and of the estate of the late Sonia Brownell Orwell and Martin Secker & Warburg Ltd; extract on p. 174 from H Davis and P Walton: *Language, Image and Media* published by Basil Blackwell Publishers 1983; extract on pp. 176–7 from Michael L Geis: *The Language of Television Advertising* Copyright © 1982 by Academic Press, Inc.; advertisement on p. 177 for a 1979 Pontiac Catalina advertisement reproduced by permission of Pontiac Division, DMB&B; extracts on pp. 178–80 from T Vestergaard and K Schroder: *The Language of Advertising* published by Basil Blackwell Publishers 1989; extracts on pp. 184, 186, 188 from L A Marshall and R Rowland: *A Guide to Learning Independently* (1st Edn.) 1983 Open University Press; extract on p. 185 from Penny Hedge article on study skills © The *Guardian* 1990; extract on p. 189 from Andrew Northedge: 'Schedule for passing the test of time © The *Guardian* 1991; extract on p. 190 from ILEA: *Access Study Skills* published by Academic Press; extract on p. 191 from Liz Hodgkinson: 'Learning to cope with exams' © The *Guardian* 1991; extract on p. 192 from Michael J. Wallace: *Study Skills in English* by permission of the author and Cambridge University Press.